The Bounty of Texas

THE
BOUNTY
OF
TEXAS

TEXAS FOLKLORE SOCIETY PUBLICATION X · L · I · X

Edited by
Francis Edward Abernethy

CORRER DEL PAISANO

UNIVERSITY OF NORTH TEXAS PRESS

First edition 1990
Requests for permission to reproduce material from this work should be sent to:
University of North Texas Press
P. O. Box 13856
Denton, Texas 76203-3856

Photographs not credited are by Francis Edward Abernethy

Library of Congress Cataloging-in-Publication Data

The Bounty of Texas / edited by Francis Edward Abernethy.
    p. cm. — (Publications of the Texas Folklore Society ; no. 49)
    Includes bibliographical references and index.
    ISBN 0-929398-14-9 : $19.95
    1. Folklore—Texas. 2. Texas—Social life and customs.
I. Abernethy, Francis Edward. II. Series.
GR1.T4 no. 49
[GR110.T5]
398' .09764—dc20
                                             90-12417
                                              CIP

CONTENTS

The Bounty of Texas

PREFACE:

In which the editor discusses the personal
legend as part of folklore and
sneaks in one of his own

YEARS AGO George Lyman Kittredge said that
Texas was a happy hunting ground for folklorists.
It still is. The bounty of Texas consists of a state full
of rich living and traditions, stretching centuries back to the Indians,
through the Spanish, Mexicans, and Anglos, to all the many nation-
alities that moved in and then spread out through Texas and the
Southwest. It was and is a land of plenty, and one can go down any
road, say the Camino Real, and glean a wealth of folklore at every
crossroad and filling station and barbecue stand. A folklorist can live
off the bounty of Texas easy enough—and get fat.

The idea of living off the bounty of the land is where this book got
its title, more particularly from R. A. Hill's "The Bounty of the
Woods." I do not know when I have received a paper that I enjoyed
as much as Rusty Hill's reminiscences of living off the land and
trapping in the Big Bend and West Texas during the late Twenties.
Rusty's double first cousin, Roland Broaddus of Dallas, had a copy of
Rusty's hand-written memoirs which he was kind enough to send me
in typed form. And I thank Florene Hill, Rusty's wife, for letting the
Society publish them. Mr. Hill lived a long and interesting life, but
when it came to putting something down for posterity, that which
was most vivid in his memory was two trapping seasons he spent with
his buddies when he was nineteen years old. During this rich time in
Rusty Hill's life he did truly live off the bounty of the woods.

I have long recognized this phenomenon but have never put it
down, that man—yea and woman too—defines his life through
particular times or episodes that have little to do with his workaday
world. I have known those whose bright defining times were their

< 1 >

high school football days—or their experiences in World War II— or working in the oil patch—or playing in a country band. What were really small parts of their lives chronologically became the episodes that defined for them their personalities—or what they romantically wished their personalities to be. This can best be exemplified, I think, at stand-around-and-talk gatherings of all sorts as each person will work the conversation around to one of his own fields of personal illustration. He might not dwell on it, but he will get it into the conversation—because that is what he wants his listeners to remember him by.

And lest you think that I have drifted far from the field of folklore and its investigation thereof, let me say that there is as yet an area for study but dimly classified and only barely explored. This is personal folklore, and Rusty Hill's tales are an example of one sort, the personal legend. There are other kinds of personal folklore—customs and beliefs, for example. An individual evolves customs just as a culture does, and these customs serve the same purpose for the person as they do for the culture. They give order and regularity and familiarity to life. Customs are life's personal patterns, and the individual eats salmon croquettes on Friday, sleeps late and has waffles on Saturday, dresses up on Sunday, plays golf on Tuesday, and watches St. Elsewhere on Wednesday. To violate this order, these personal customs, causes anxiety. Equally so, each person develops his own personal belief system, consisting of superstitions and religious attitudes that are peculiar to himself and are not a part of his culture's traditions and beliefs. I, myself, consider it the worst of luck to mention the contents of a story before I have written the first draft—and I once touched God in a pine tree.

Then, there is the personal legend, of which we previously spoke. These distinct essences of an individual's life which he tells and retells—the defining times, mentioned above—are his personal legends. These oral narratives are to an individual's history what the family legend is to a family's history—or the legend of Davy Crockett is to Texas history—or the Arthurian legends are to English history— and Troy is to the world. Paul Patterson's account in this book of his hoboing summer is one of his own personal legends. He has told these tales so many times that he has created a pattern. He remembers what he wants to remember; he tells what he wants to tell.

< 2 >

Personal legends might have strayed from the absolute verifiable facts considerably, but they still tell more about the keeper and the teller than any academic vita or factual biography ever can. They tell the listener what the teller wants to be, what his ideals and dreams are, what he considers to be the best in maybe a very good life. A country idealizes its heroes in its legends; a person idealizes himself. He tells the tale to represent the best of his values. When his values change, he either changes the tale or quits telling it. And often he has told the tale for so long that he can no longer distinguish between actual facts and fictional restructuring. You can draw some pretty good conclusions about a person by noticing what personal legends he regularly trots out. The folklorist becomes the psychiatrist, which is nothing new.

Our lives' stories are saffroned full of personal legends, and as is always the case, drawing the line between factual history and personal legend becomes quite difficult. I have several in which I happily define myself as a woodsman, a hunter and gatherer and a fisherman, who like Rusty Hill and his bunch of trapping buddies can thriftily and skillfully live off the bounty of the woods. It is, of course, an outrageously romantic illusion but one that I have confidently lived with as long as I have been going into the woods.

So if you and I are in a casual conversation some day and you accidentally say the word "water" or "boat" or "river"—or anything tangential to—you very well might hear me chime in, "Well, that's like that six-day float trip down the Neches me and old Mott took back in '47." And while you are pondering how it could possibly be "like" anything involved in the ongoing conversation, I am off and running with one of my own personal legends.

Really, the float trip was not all that dramatic. Nothing life threatening occurred. We saw no big game nor caught any big fish. And it lasted just six days. And that was forty-some-odd years ago! But I can still feel the long and steady flow of the river and see the deepness and the beautiful isolation of the river bottomland. I can still remember the softness of the rain that fell and the fragile greening of the woods in that gentle spring . . . and all the life scampering through the treetops and scurrying along the banks and

< 3 >

Hubert Mott during Easter of 1947.

gliding in the brown water of the river . . . and the huge white splashes of dogwood in the blooming forest . . . and that Christ was hung from that same dogwood tree whose blossom still bears the prints of the cruel nails and whose berries hang like drops of His precious blood. The time was Easter and the resurrection of life on the Neches.

We put the home-made, scrap lumber boat in the river on Highway 59, south of Diboll. Hubert Mott's dad and his wife Evelyn

< 4 >

and my Hazel had hauled us down there, and they stood on the bank looking doubtful at best as their voyageurs pushed off in the Neches at flood stage with a fine rain falling. We waved cheerily and then began paddling frantically trying to get around the bend and out of sight before we and the boat and all our gear sank from the water spewing in through all the cracks and old nail holes. Everything we had was floating by the time we made land.

We unloaded and dumped the boat and then heated and caulked the cracks with canned pitch that became part of our clothes and skin for the rest of the trip. Barely seaworthy, we reembarked and drifted and bailed water till dusk, when we lucked in to somebody's camphouse, where we stayed, and in to a young coon, which we ate.

The rain stopped during the night, and the morning bloomed clear and clean and freshly washed, with Good-Gods yammering around a towering pine stump and cat squirrels scampering through the pin-oak tops. Our plan was to float all the way to Beaumont where Hubert had an uncle who would bring us back to Nacogdoches. This in itself was a sign of our naiveté, in spite of the fact that we were veterans a year home from the Big War and college students on the GI Bill. I never have figured out how far it was from Diboll to Beaumont by way of the Neches River (I believe our miscalculation was 125 miles.), but we learned that first day that covering a lot of water was not what we were going to do during these Easter holidays.

As it was, we moved down the river at the same turgid pace as the flow of the water. We went through periods of paddling, but in one splashing chase after a wounded squirrel Hubert broke one of the two paddles. The most we did thereafter was paddle just enough to keep us in the midstream current. The boat was still sticky with pitch, but the cracks had swelled and sealed during the night so our gear stayed fairly dry.

We didn't have much gear: a change of clothes, a .22 and a .30 carbine, a hatchet, and a kerosene lantern. Because we were going to live off the bounty of the woods we had very little food: a loaf of bread, a couple of cans of beans, sweet potatoes, an onion, and peanut butter and jelly. We had coffee, sugar, some lard, and a few eggs packed in the cornmeal. We had a skillet and a can to boil coffee in. We each had a quilt wrapped in a GI poncho, and we had a GI cot-size mosquito bar under which we both slept. We were not trying to be

< 5 >

Spartan; the boat wouldn't hold any more and still leave us space to sit in.

We made the second day quite well. Most of the time we were between cut banks and in the middle of the channel. We stopped when we got bored or tired of sitting and hunted and explored the woods along the bottom. We met a commercial fisherman running his nets, and he was the only person we saw during the whole trip. We learned early not to shoot a squirrel over the water because it sank like a stone. We trailed lines baited with squirrel and bird innards and picked up a catfish now and then. We had a good camp on a clean bank that second night. We ate fried squirrel and catfish, fried hot-water cornbread, and sweet potatoes dipped in sugar and fried. Hubert did the cooking, and I remember that supper as one of the great meals in my life.

The river crested during that night. It was flowing clean of trash the next morning when we shoved off. And it got wider as we flowed along with it. Sometime during that morning we took target practice at a huge water moccasin lying on a very distinctive looking log. We were shooting a .30 carbine I had brought home from the service, and we couldn't hit the side of a barn with it—nor a monstrous water moccasin who soon tired of the sport and slid off the log to explore more exciting fields. After six hours of floating and as evening drew nigh, we again came alongside the very recognizable snake log. We couldn't believe it! We speculated on coincidental similarities among logs and whether or not logs could get out on the bank and run down the river to get ahead of us. In the end we realized that we had spent a good part of the day going in a circle in an oxbow or a backwater current and that we were lost in an ocean of water and the sun was setting. We did not panic but we became terribly concerned.

We paddled and tree-pushed around until we came to what we hoped was the channel and very seriously began looking for land of any description—which was what we found. Right at dusk we located an island of mud which had obviously been under water for many days. It was about the size of a good Mexican rug. It was six inches out of the water at its highest, topped with squishy, ankle-deep gumbo, and harboring a prosperous snake population that reluctantly and with many a backward glance gave up their territory at our insistence.

< 6 >

That was an intense night, very valuable as one of life's memorable experiences, and very bad. We had no firewood so we couldn't cook sweet potatoes or make coffee or keep off the night's spring chill or provide a bright comfort against the darkness. Mankind is definitely better off having discovered fire. We did have a kerosene lamp as our touch of civilization's light. And we had a can of pork and beans.

Hubert's sophisticated palate precluded his eating plain-old cold beans, so he cut up part of our one onion on his supper. The result was that he got indigestion and moaned and groaned and thrashed about much of the night. It was a long night because we went to bed early rather than sit around in the mud. I guess we thought it was better to lie around in the mud. However, we were plagued by subliminal snakes. Everytime we drifted off to sleep the thought of the snakes crept in on us, and one of us would have to get up and make a snake check of the island. Going to sleep was dangerous also because if one of us happened to touch the other it conveyed the certain and deadly knowledge that the moccasin monster of the log was bed-friending us in reptilian revenge for using him in our target practice.

We were off that mud bank and in the river by the first gray light of dawn. We eventually found the channel and by good sunrise began to find pieces of the river bank. Before long we were again among high dry banks where we beached the boat, cooked breakfast, washed off mud, and basked in the sun. We ate all of our eggs that morning.

The weather had turned East Texas springtime warm, and that day was a good day to float on the river. It was one of those test times when you ask yourself, "Where would you be if you could be anywhere in the world?" If the answer is, "Right here," you are truly blessed. We were truly blessed. Life was everywhere. We were wary of drifting into the bank brush because snakes were abundantly draped along the limbs—probably because somebody had shwooshed them off their mud bank. Wood ducks and mallards were just getting their young off the nests, and old mamas trailing strings of biddies would paddle off to hide when we showed up around a bend. Hubert caught two mallard chicks that got separated from their siblings. He fed them on cornmeal and kept them through the trip, mostly in the bib of his overalls, to take home to raise. One huge alligator slid off the bank close enough to give us a start once when we were poking

< 7 >

The editor preparing to live off the land.

around in a slough, and we saw the eyes and snouts of several more. We did not see a deer the whole trip; that is how scarce they were in East Texas in the Forties.

We came around one bend and saw a terrible thrashing about in the debris of a big eddy. We armed ourselves and moved with one-paddle speed to the scene, thinking we had caught a 'gator in the midst of a kill. When we pulled alongside we saw that it was a very large, three- to four- foot long-nosed gar. We shot it and then crashed

< 8 >

through that mess of trash to drag it out. We thought somehow that we would get great fish steaks from under that armored hide. We spent thirty minutes chopping around on that beast with knife and hatchet before we decided that we weren't that hungry—yet.

We fished and hunted and floated at our leisure for the next two days, rolling out and swimming alongside the boat when we got tired of sitting, or wandering off through the woods when we found clean high ground. I wonder now that the water didn't turn us blue when we went swimming, but evidently the sun and air were warm enough to make the cold water comfortable. And perhaps our blood was thicker and more circulateable then. I wonder also why we didn't catch something fatal from drinking Neches River flood water for five days. I remember once coming on a dead hog, bloated and floating in a drift, and our concern was to quickly grab our water jug and fill it upstream from the hog. We later discussed the high probabilities of other dead beasts being upstream from our filling point.

We had decided early on that we were not going to make Beaumont and still get back to school in time to finish the spring semester. We knew that there was at least one bridge between Diboll and Beaumont and it was not even half way and that we had floated for several days and had not gone under a bridge.

In the late afternoon of the sixth day we rounded a bend and finally saw the bridge on Highway 69 ahead of us. We pulled up on a nice high and dry sand bank near the bridge and pitched camp and learned that next to camping on a mud island, camping in the sand is almost as bad. It gets into everything—clothes, food, guns, teeth, eyes, ears, etc. In spite of which we enjoyed the camp and were excited to be back in civilization, with cars and people whizzing by over us.

The next morning we walked a mile down the highway to a country store and filling station and had a soda pop and candy bar that restored us to the ways of the modern world. We learned that the bus to Nacogdoches came through at ten. We therefore committed our faithful boat to the current of the river, stuffed everything we had into our warbags, and napped on the side of the road until the bus came.

< 9 >

On the Neches in the spring of '47.

We made it in, ducklings and all, and our loved ones were happy to see us. We talked about the trip until we had worn out all our friends. Every time we get together now we talk about it. I've been all over the world, and Hubert fought in later wars and jumped out of supersonic airplanes, and that trip still stands as a part of our lives encapsulated in a piece of time as pristine and complete in itself as a classic short story. As we think of it now, forgetting the pitch and sand and mud and mosquitoes, it defines what to both of us is the core of existence—to live in, on, and as a part of the great outdoors, to wrap woods and water about one's self and be at one with nature, to be our childhood's perception of heroic Daniel Boones, camping in the wilderness, living off the bounty of the land.

I warned you not to bring up the subject. And if you ever get in a conversation with Hubert Mott, for goodness' sake don't ever mention river boating to him or he will talk your ear off.

My carrying on about Mr. Hill's trapping story doesn't mean that it is the best in the book. Really, I mentioned that woodsman's story

<10>

just so I could have an excuse to put my own in. I enjoyed them all and you will recognize and remember that these are some of the best papers we have heard at meetings over the past three years. Paul Stone came down from Yale and presented his very interesting paper on J. Frank Dobie at the Uvalde meeting in '89. His paper prompted me to retrieve an unpublished outdoors sketch by Dobie on deer hunting. At the same time I got out Bertha Dobie's essay on Frank's interest in grasses. Bertha had planned to come to the 1972 TFS meeting in College Station and present that paper, but she got sick and Wilson Hudson read it. Two papers destined for use in the TFS history now under way—on Dorothy Scarborough and Ben Mead— were fortuitously presented at recent meetings. Charles Shafer's prison language lexicon is, I believe, a valuable contribution to studies of folk speech. These and so many more! We honor the contributors for the time they spent, the interest they had, the articles they wrote. This book is filled with the bounty of Texas, as were XLVIII books before it.

The Texas Folklore Society thanks William R. Johnson, recent past president of Stephen F. Austin State University, and Patricia Russell, Chairman of the Department of English and Philosophy, for continuing financial and moral support.

I particularly thank Carolyn Satterwhite, the Society's secretary and the assistant editor of this publication.

The Bounty of Texas is dedicated to all those hunters and fishermen who still fantasize about living off the bounty of the land, particularly to those outlaws I go to the woods with: Luther Lowery, Bill Clark, Pat Barton, Wink Barbin and Chuck Davis.

Francis Edward Abernethy
Stephen F. Austin State University
Nacogdoches, Texas
February 1990

<11>

Model-T Ford with the day's catch of soft-shell turtles — and daring diving-girl decal on front window. *Courtesy Mrs. Florene Hill*

R·A·HILL
The Bounty of the Woods

[There are times and episodes in our lives that define ourselves to us and with which we define ourselves to others. They might not be the largest or longest or most productive but they are the most vivid. Thus, when Russell Arden Hill of Llano, Texas, decided in 1983 to write his memoirs, out of seventy-three exciting, traveling, work-filled years, Rusty Hill chose two years of his youth to explain himself to posterity. These were his years as a trapper and hunter, when he lived off the bounty of the woods, when he and the land were both young and surging with life.

Rusty Hill left the woods when the Depression knocked the bottom out of the fur market and never went back to it as a living. During the Depression he worked in the East Texas oil fields, he followed the wheat harvest, picked berries, and worked at any job he could to support his mother and his brothers and sisters. He got into construction work in the shipyards, stayed with construction during his Navy hitch in WWII, and continued after the war, building bridges, dams, and plants all over the United States. He and his wife Florene and three sons lived an exciting traveling life until he had a heart attack in 1964, after which the family moved back to Llano. Rusty Hill stayed active during these last Llano years as a "creative woodworker" and with a bait shop for the fishermen of the Llano River.

In 1983, when Rusty Hill was seventy-three, he decided to write about all this rich long life. And he wrote about what to him was the richest part of it, what he wanted most to be remembered by, what remained most vivid in his mind of many memories—when he lived as a trapper and hunter, strongly and vigorously, off the bounty of the woods. Editor.]

<13>

A *Panther in the Cold*

IN THE late fall of 1927 four of us were trapping and hunting on the Rio Grande down river from Candelaria, below the rim of the Chinati Mountains. We awoke to about two to three inches of new snow, and as we needed meat badly, a hunt was quickly organized. Frank Rhoades and I were to go up the Rio Grande. Mancel Maddox and Jim Brewer were to go down the river, and each party was to circle back under the rim rock of the Chinatis. In each party, one of us carried a .22 rifle and the other a .30-30 rifle, so we were ready for anything from rabbits to bear.

After a while I spotted a covey of blue quail huddled under a bush, and slipping up on them from behind a small mesquite thicket and using .22 CB caps, I killed ten with my first eleven shots. On the twelfth shot a quail stuck his head up just as I shot, and I got him and the one I had covered. Now I know you think this is a tale for the Liars Club, but the secret is not to hit a bird in the head because then he flops and flutters around all over the place and the rest take flight. Put the shot just at the butt of the wing, and he just drops and doesn't move and the others don't get nervous. A CB cap makes hardly any noise and using a single-shot rifle makes the interval about right. Anyway when the head-shot bird busted up my stand, I had a mess of birds.

About that time I heard Frank whistle, so I gathered my game and looked him up.

Frank had found the tracks of a big mule deer going up a draw and showing pretty in the snow. We took the trail while keeping watch up ahead for any steam the deer's body might put off, for it was beastly cold. Of course we didn't know just how cold it was, so we just pulled our collars up and went on. After a while Frank spotted the deer's breath coming from behind a big boulder, and figuring out which way he was facing, he began his stalk while I stayed on guard with the .22 rifle with longs in my gun. Frank shot too far back, and the deer broke out in a high lope. He wasn't bleeding much, but with the snow we didn't need much sign for trailing.

We followed the wounded buck through a draw straight up to the Chinati rim. Then the draw turned sharply left, so I took the .30-30

<14>

and left Frank with the .22. I cut across the bend in the draw to try to head the buck before he could top out.

I beat him to the rim rock and slid down into the bottom of the draw that had now become a steep-sided little canyon. About the time I hit the bottom I heard the crack of the .22. Dropping all caution, I went plunging down the hill to get to where I could see up either side in case the deer broke free.

The canyon ended in front of me in a wall with a four-foot opening that dropped off on the other side about five feet to the trail below. When I got to the opening I could see the buck stretched out dead lying in the trail and just beyond him lay a mountain lion, equally dead.

Frank said that the panther had finished off the wounded deer before he got there and was prepared to guard the kill. When it appeared that the lion was going to attack him, Frank decided to take his one shot with the .22 rifle and then fight it out with the gun stock if necessary until I got there. Luck or not, the .22 bullet went right through the heart of the lion, and he only gave one short hop. Lucky for me too, because the way I was traveling, I would have leaped through the hole in the wall and landed astraddle of the lion, and I'm sure that would have smarted quite a bit.

Frank was so excited he couldn't even help skin the deer. He wanted to carry the lion out whole! I finally got him to gut the lion, and we took one quarter of the deer meat and the lion and started for camp, which was about six miles away. (Later we dug that .22 bullet out of the lion and saved it, and I still have it today, all these years later.)

Down in the bottom of this canyon it was a cold twenty degrees, but out of the wind it was a hard pull to the top and we raised a sweat! When we got out on the fan at the bottom of the draw and into the full force of the wind, the sweat turned to ice. We were hung blue with cold before we got to camp, and it must have been three hours before we warmed up enough to respond to the rest of the camp's questions. In fact I forgot my quail until the next morning. They froze solid!

Jim and I brought in the rest of the deer next day, and when we got back to camp meat was cooking and sure smelled good. However, when I found out it was panther, I took my name out of the pot and

<15>

cooked myself some venison. The other guys swore it was good and eventually ate the whole cat. I didn't try even one bite. I have seen those boys eat just about anything that could be killed in this country—'coon, 'possum, armadillo, turtles (both soft and hard shelled). When I was young, I didn't go for that stuff. I was hardly able to eat a chicken!

Later that week we went into the store at Candelaria, and they told us that on the day of that big hunt the temperature had dropped to six degrees! If I had known that, I'd have stayed in camp by the fire and missed those things that are still fresh in my memory fifty-three years later.

Frank got $50 bounty on that lion, and in those days that was good money.

We soon had all the country within fifteen to twenty miles trapped out and hunted out, so we packed up and went to Marfa to sell our furs and resupply.

A Panther in the Camp

WE THEN moved inland from the Rio Grande to the top of the Chinati Mountains. Our camp was in a beautiful spot in a grove of live oaks just at the top of a draw, but below the top of the main backbone of the mountains.

About a hundred yards down the draw a big spring came flowing out of a crack in the rock into a rock basin holding hundreds of gallons of water. All the creatures for miles around watered there, and all kinds of tracks appeared every night. We brushed the sand clean every night. That is, whoever got the last bucket of water did, as everyone had a turn at this job. We found that a big mountain lion was watering there every fourth night, so we took turns sitting up watching to try and kill him. He never showed up as long as we watched, and for several days after, so he was more or less forgotten.

Then came the night Frank was to get water, but he forgot it until someone made the comment that if the camp caught fire the first thing to burn would be the water bucket. Frank got a kerosene lantern and the water bucket, and started picking his way down the path to the spring.

<16>

Now, growing out of the rock and leaning across the pool at the spring was a big cottonwood tree which shaded the spring at all times. In a little while after Frank left for the spring there came the damnedest clatter from down there you ever heard. It sounded like someone stomping a bucket in a pile of dry brush, first one side of the canyon, then the other. Then Frank passed through the camp like a falling star, but he got his brakes on when he got out of the light on the other side, and swinging around he bounded back to the fire and collapsed on his bedroll. He was white as a sheet and drops of sweat as big as watermelon seeds were pouring off him, even if the temperature was way below freezing.

His clothes were in rags, and he had some deep as well as shallow cuts and scratches from his ankles to his eyes. He was trembling like a leaf, and his eyes were bulging out like peeled grapes! Well, we got him wrapped in a quilt, as he was shivering and shaking all over, and in ten or fifteen minutes calmed him down a bit. He told us that just as he dipped his bucket in the water he heard a noise in the tree, and he held the light up to see what it was. He saw this mountain lion just as it jumped on him and knocked him head first into the water, lantern and all. Scrambling out he stepped in the bucket and after shaking it off legged it for the camp. About halfway up the draw he and the cat met head on, and the lion dragged him almost back to the spring. He broke loose and took the side-hill route back to camp!

Well, the next morning we all went down there, and after reading all the tracks and signs we concluded that the lion was at the water when Frank approached the spring. Hearing him, the cat ran up the sloping tree trunk and lay watching, while Frank stooped to get the water. Frank was too good a woodsman to miss the least noise, or maybe he sensed or smelled him, and when Frank raised the light it blinded and scared the cat and it fell on him. The terrified cat ran up the draw toward camp, but there we had a big fire, so he turned back and still blinded by the fire light, he met poor Frank again, and indeed did roll him back a ways! Then he and Frank took opposite hillsides, and began to tear through the brush, cat claws, cedars and stuff, making a hell-of-a-racket and scaring each other half to death!

Frank never did accept that explanation but held to his first conclusion that he was attacked twice, and those deep scratches were claw marks, even though some of them contained pieces of wood and

<17>

sand in them. Anyway, we never saw cat tracks there any more, and after we fished the kerosene lantern out of the spring and bailed out the basin, I thought the water always tasted oily, like kerosene.

The Cast of Characters

WE NOW picked up three more trappers. Our buddies and lifelong friends had come to join us, so we had to move camp into a more densely populated country, both in fur and people. Now all these men in camp were experienced mountain men except me, but with these tutors I was well on my way.

There were seven of us now: Grandad Maddox, Uncle Allen Crider, Frank Rhoades, Jim Brewer, Mancel Maddox, and Rex Ellington, Flo's brother, and myself. So here I will add a little summary of the character of these men. You know that to be so close together over the years in isolated spots, as we were for so many months at a time, we all knew each other like an open book and could almost read each other's minds or moods just by looking at each face. So here goes, but remember, I loved all these men. We were buddies.

Old Grandad Maddox was sixty-seven years old and looked one hundred. He was stooped almost ninety degrees, and his hands and feet were knotted and gnarled. His long face and long yellow beard made him look somewhat like a goat, and being older, we all looked to him for advice. He was a welcome addition to any camp because he always took over the cooking, wood gathering, and water carrying and did his trapping right around camp.

"Uncle" Allen Crider was tall, slightly stooped, slow moving and talking, about sixty years old but not showing it much. He sported a Wyatt Earp mustache and could trap the smartest coyote. He hunted and trapped for bounty mostly (not furs)—rogue bears, wolves, cats—anything with a price on it.

Frank Rhoades was my mentor, and he took me as his apprentice. He was past fifty years old, but ageless in every way. He had never been to school, but read everything. He was self taught. His ability with math would confound a computer. You could never learn his methods because he didn't understand them himself, but if you spoke of two sets of numbers, instantly he had the sum and could find the

<18>

results of division, subtraction, or what have you. He was a whiz at this. Born and raised in the Big Thicket of East Texas, his knowledge of animals was almost complete. His trapping was slow and plodding, but once over a territory it was clean.

Jim Brewer was tall, red-headed, fiery-tempered, contrary, always ready to take the other side, a good enough trapper, excellent hunter and fisherman. He always looked calm but was at times very excitable. For instance, he and I were hunting meat for the camp one day, and he was carrying a new .30 Remington game master (That is a pump rifle.). We walked into a draw and suddenly jumped out eight mule deer. They went straight up the draw and turned up the mountainside. Well, Jim never fired a shot. I killed the first one, and looked around to see why he wasn't shooting, for he should have downed at least one. And there he was, drawing a bead on them but instead of shooting he was pumping the cartridges out onto the ground! The deer were gone by then, and I stood there laughing at him. He didn't like that and wanted to know what I was laughing about. I asked why he didn't shoot, and he pointed out that he had killed the deer by the tree and said that the gun had jammed after the first shot. By then I had picked up all six of his cartridges, which was all the gun held. I held out my hand and none of them had been fired. He turned red as a beet and swore that the rifle must hold seven cartridges, but there was no way it could be done. He never admitted to buck fever or being shook by having a whole herd of deer jump up right underfoot, and I'm sure he'll always believe the gun jammed. He even had our gunsmith, Mancel, tear the gun to pieces to find what happened, but a Remington rifle will not jam.

Jim was a fearless climber, an excellent pecan thresher. He was careful and thorough and a tough taskmaster for whoever worked for him. He and I were almost inseparable and played poker on the halves. He was always matching me in foot races. We played all comers at dominoes, marbles, or whatever. We especially loved to get someone into a shooting match. We never lost many card games except to a marked deck of cards, and then we'd try to find and learn the mark and break the gamblers who put in the cold deck.

Mancel Maddox was Grandad Maddox's son. He was our gunsmith, financier, the man with the money, the adventurer, the planner and plotter, and the tradin'est man you ever saw. By the time we had some

< 19 >

furs in camp he usually owned part of them by lending money or for fixing guns or for the use of some equipment of some kind. You would have to be the first one to say that he was fair; he just had that trading spirit built in! He used his money to buy things that he knew we were all going to need. The rest of us never thought of these things until we needed them. We were charged a modest fee for using the things he had the foresight to have.

Mancel was my best friend, and I loved him as a companion and as a fishing and hunting and camping buddy. His word was his bond. All the collateral one needed from him was his handshake. People always went to his little gunshop to trade or have guns fixed, and a lot of people just went there to talk and visit. He was a good talker and had that gift of gab that drew people to him. Nothing fazed him, either talk or praise; and if you were arguing with him, in a little while you would find yourself agreeing with him! Why, Mancel was the only man I ever knew who got credit at a United States Post Office! He could take a broken pocket knife and start trading, and by the next week he could have a twenty-three jewel Elgin pocket watch and a milk cow and calf. He did not smoke or drink, but he was very good at all kinds of games, cards, including dice, but never gambled or bet on anything. He never uttered a curse word in his life. In exasperation he might say "dadgum," or when he would get up on a cold winter morning and charge from his tent to the camp fire he would rub his hands together and say, "Great suffering balls of cat dung, but it's a cold morning!" This alone made him unique in a camp of hunters and trappers. Mancel was not a violent man. He was very soft spoken, calm, cool, and collected. If anyone had any argument with him, he could talk him out of being mad and make him sorry he ever was in the first place. Everyone in Llano liked and respected him and his parents. Their house was always open for a good cup of coffee or a complete meal if you happened to drop by.

Rex was twenty years old and a true Ellington, and he was Uncle Allen Crider's protégé, and a real good student he was. Rex had lived most of his life in the woods and rivers and could catch more fish than all of us together. He was a mix of Cherokee, Cajun, and English. He was small, waspish, fiery tempered, and foul mouthed, but he and I were firm lifelong friends. I suspect I too had some faults, but he never pointed them out to me. I loved him dearly and felt a great loss at his death.

<20>

Jim Brewer and Mancel Maddox at camp with hides and a freshly trapped beaver and bobcat. *Courtesy Mrs. Florene Hill*

In this winter of 1927, I was seventeen, skinny, freckle-faced, and had long reddish-black hair. I was all skin and bone with just enough meat on my frame to hold the bones together, but I could run a twenty-mile trap line and have time to move and reset five or six traps a day. Usually by the time I had been on a place three weeks I had all the game within my reach. I was competitive, slow-tempered, far thinking, and a diabolical schemer. I was not quarrelsome, but I was always ready for anything.

And I am now the last of this bunch who lived in those early days by the bounty of the woods and rivers of west and central Texas.

Frank Rhoades and Jim Brewer with a catch of furs. *Courtesy Mrs. Florene Hill*

Mrs. Epps and Mrs. Crow

ON THE 3rd of January, 1928, we loaded all our stuff on our Model T's and moved inland to the Davis Mountains.

By the night of the 5th everyone was established. Uncle Allen and Rex were to go to the Rock Pile Ranch to trap for a lobo wolf with a $500 bounty on his hide, and also a lion with a $250 bounty on his hide. I'm sure this would make a good story, but Uncle Allen was so close-mouthed and Rex so apt to exaggerate that I don't know if I ever heard the truth of that hunt or not. I'll just say that they got both the wolf and the lion and came back with the money and will let it go at that!

<22>

Jim and Frank went to the apple farms, while Mancel, Grandad Maddox, and I went to the vegetable farms to trap for small varmints.

A Mrs. Epps came to the camp one day wanting someone to trap on her ranch for some chicken-eating critters, so I took the job. I moved into a snug three-sided shed, set up my camp, and went to work setting out traps. By nighttime the next day, I had forty traps set, and the next night (or late evening) I had caught twenty-one furs: four fox, three coons, two bobcats, one wolf, five ringtails, and six skunks.

Mrs. Epps had chickens roosting in trees as far as a fourth of a mile from the house, turkeys all the way from her back door to the creek, lambs in the sheds around the barn, and pigs, too. It was easy living for the varmints, all of which were tree climbers except the wolf and he liked pork and lamb! So it was a Sunday dinner everyday for everyone except Mrs. Epps.

Now for all woodsmen in those days it was early to bed and early to rise so on the fourth or fifth night there, I was all bedded down in my soogans, or bedroll as it is called now, and was sawing logs by nine-thirty or so. Then the night was shattered by such screeches and screams as one is ever likely to hear. They turned my blood to ice and caused goose bumps to rise a half-inch all over my body. There was a light at the back of Mrs. Epps house, and that seemed to be the center of the commotion. I jerked my pants and boots on and headed that way like the hounds were on my trail. I arrived to find Mrs. Epps in her flannel gown, barefooted and with a shot gun and a kerosene lantern. She was screaming for me to come, and it seemed like minutes before she realized I was there.

She thrust the shotgun into my hands and I held the lantern up. She kept screaming about an owl among the turkeys. I got the shine of his eyes and blasted him with double-O buckshots. Maybe you can imagine my consternation when a one-hundred-thirty pound mountain lion fell almost on top of us! Mrs. Epps dropped the lantern with a scream and with a couple of twenty-foot leaps was in her house with the door barred, looking out the window. The lion was stone dead, but I think Mrs. Epps thought he was going to eat me, and she wanted to be safe in her house to enjoy the sight.

The next morning she came out bravely enough, and we loaded the lion onto her Model T Ford pickup and to town she went. That

<23>

evening late she brought me the $50 bounty that was paid for mountain lions and told me she had left the cat at the taxidermist. Later I found out she had sold him the cat, but it was all right with me, as I was just glad to be alive and free! If she had had close enough neighbors to hear her that night and come to her rescue and found her screaming and me holding onto her, they might have took it for what it seemed to appear and "saved" her by putting a bullet in me!

In about ten days I had Mrs. Epps' place trapped out, and as I bundled up my stuff to go, Mrs. Epps offered me a steady job to get me to stay, but no deal. I was committed to the "free life" and had to go, so she loaded me and my stuff and hauled me back to the camp where Grandad Maddox and Mancel were. During the ten days I was at the Epps ranch I had gotten 103 pieces of fur, more than the other six trappers altogether. I was real proud of myself, and before nightfall that day another widow lady had come to get me to trap her place. Mrs. Epps had told her about me. Mancel and the others thought this was very good for me, as I was young and needed the experience of trapping alone.

When we first started out, Mancel and I agreed that he would finance my part of the trip for half of my catch. As I was now going to Mrs. Crow's place to trap and would stay there and eat with her, Mancel and I divided my furs, and I took my part to Mrs. Crow's place with me.

Mrs. Crow was as nice looking as Mrs. Epps was homely. She was also very outspoken and positive, so when she told me (after we got to her place) to come on in and draw up a tub of water and bathe and take those filthy trapper's clothes I was wearing to the barn and put on these clothes that belonged to her late husband, I gave her no lip. I was soon soaking in a real bathtub in 110 degrees water. I shaved the fuzz off my face with a razor I found there and combed my shoulder length hair, and helped it curl some. Mrs. Crow was delighted with the results, and when I admitted to a knowledge of Forty-Two she called some neighbors to come over, and we all played Forty-Two until midnight.

Early the next morning I began my trapping circle, and I soon saw that I was again in a veritable zoo and the first night's catch proved it. At the end of the three days' trapping I had fifty-eight furs, and at the end of eight days I had 121. On the ninth day I pulled up my traps

<24>

and high time too, as I only had a few scattered catches in the most distant traps.

The next morning all the trappers gathered at the Crow ranch, and we loaded up to head east to sell our furs, regroup, and plan the next chapter in our lives. Mrs. Crow didn't want me to leave and offered many inducements and fringe benefits if I would stay and work for her. She pointed out how young I was and that I was wasting my life with such a "foul smelling" bunch, but I kissed her fondly and left in a hurry. What she offered was indeed the good life, but I didn't realize that for years.

It was now beaver and muskrat season so we moved on to finish out the years' work of trapping.

Mancel Gets Credit at the Post Office

WE PULLED into Toyahvale, Texas, early in the morning, and mailed our furs to "Taylor Fur Co." in St. Louis, Mo. We all had plenty of money, what with the bounties and the sale of our first catch in Marfa. Jim took the train home as his wife was expecting a baby. Rex, Frank, and Uncle Allen went up to New Mexico and trapped down the Pecos River for about two hundred miles. Grandad Maddox, Mancel, and I headed west and intercepted the Rio Grande at Indian Springs, south of Sierra Blanca, and trapped down to Ruidoso, about one hundred miles as the river flows. Beaver were very hard to catch, but we managed, with hard work and perseverance, to get about thirty blanket-sized pelts.

Muskrats were easy. We got about two hundred of them and about two dozen mink before we got to the store at Candelaria, where Mancel went in to buy a few articles of food. Now, when we outfitted the first time to go west it was in Llano and things were very reasonable: tall cans of milk, five cents each; salt bacon, eight cents a pound; oatmeal, five cents a pound; sugar, four cents a pound; soap, two bars for a nickel. But at Candelaria things were more than double in price. Considering its isolation maybe it didn't seem too bad to me, but Mancel began to bargain slowly and whittled the prices down. The storekeeper also bought fur and had several hundred on hand.

<25>

Mancel Maddox setting a trap. *Courtesy Mrs. Florene Hill*

So Mancel offered to buy them, and finally bargained for them for $815, which took most of the cash we had.

After leaving there we had only gone a ways down the road when we broke a spring on our Model T, so when we got to Ruidoso and then sent to Marfa for another we were really short on cash. We made up a bundle of selected furs to mail out so's to get some money, but we didn't have quite enough money to pay the postage on them, so Mancel haggled with the Post Master about an hour and finally got credit at the Post Office for $2.30. That was the only time in my life I've ever known this to happen. We stayed there and waited, and on the third day the mail hack brought the spring for the car and a money order for the fur. And now came another problem. The Post Master didn't have enough money to cash the money order, so we finally settled it by taking the money he had on hand, and another

<26>

money order for the remainder. These little towns along the Rio Grande were very isolated in those days of 1927 and 1928.

March 1928, was now upon us, and it was time to head east so we shoved off to meet Rex, Uncle Allen, and Frank in Llano. The check from Taylor Fur Company was awaiting us, and we quickly settled up and dispersed temporarily.

It was now around March 15th, and Rex and I went to give part of our money to our parents. I gave three-fourths to my parents and Rex did too. We kept one-fourth for ourselves, and we had plenty to outfit ourselves for spring fishing. Oh, we were busy young men in those days when a man could be free. So finding our mutual buddy, Whistle, free for the time, the three of us went fishing. Well, he brought us good luck for awhile, and we sold our fish as fast as we could catch them!

Selling fish caught in the rivers of central Texas was illegal and we knew it, but the game warden's mother was a steady customer of ours, and so were some of the best people in town. This was a law that we very much resented and thought should be abolished. We thought we were supplying a demand and ploughed right on until Whistle got caught. He could not make them believe that he really was selling a piece of string, and that the fish on the end of the string were just an accident. So to jail he went.

Charlie Buck and the Pearls

AFTER A few days we finally broke Whistle out of jail, and all three of us headed west to the Concho River. There we met an old mountain man called Charlie Buck. He was camped with his wife and three stepdaughters, who were about twenty, sixteen, and ten years old. They were gathering mussel shells, opening them for pearls, and selling the shells to a button factory in San Angelo. There were no plastic buttons in those days. They were made of wood, shell, bone, or leather. Mussel shells brought pretty good money if they were opened, dryed, and hauled to the factory. Mussels also develop pearls, and a freshwater pearl in perfect form is very expensive and eagerly sought by jewelers. Even the not-so-perfect ones brought good money.

<27>

Buck wouldn't take us into his camp, but we had our own outfit, so after getting him to agree to sell our shells for us we located a long shoal of big, black, river mussels, and we went to work. We were down river a ways from Buck's camp. The water was icy cold, as it was still March, but on the first day Whistle and Rex got eleven pearls. I got only one. I had put out four fish lines of about two hundred hooks and had busied myself making corn pone, so I earned my third of the pearls anyhow.

Old Charlie Buck was the genuine article. He had been a scout for the cavalry. A one time squaw-man, his beaver trapping had almost depleted the state of Texas of beaver until the game department closed all streams to beaver trapping except the Pecos and the Rio Grande. He was now old and looked like a living skeleton. I think he had consumption. He coughed and spat constantly. He did no work—his wife and stepdaughters did that—but moped up and down the river hunting squirrels or sitting against a tree just smoking, coughing, and spitting. Charlie Buck was considered a bad man to have any kind of dealings with because he was entirely without scruples or conscience. Rumor said that he was a coldblooded killer who had, when younger, hired his gun or knife to the highest bidder. All I know was it sure gave you a chill to be busy at something and have him "ghost" up behind you and utter that low growl which passed as his voice. Charlie Buck could stroll through a thicket that would turn a deer and never make a sound. He never stepped on a stick or rolled a pebble, and when he was on a hunt all coughing ceased until it was over.

But Whistle, Rex, and I were young, and we would take a chance if we could make some money. Besides, he had three stepdaughters.

Well, in about three weeks of steady work we had a big bank of shells, seven tons it turned out later, and just over three teacups full of pearls. Now, old Charlie Buck always dropped over to our camp to try and buy any pearls we found, but being wise to him we never showed him any but a few inferior ones called "buttons" or "slugs." We kept the good ones buried under our bedrolls, and we would cuss our luck constantly when we were near him. But he watched us all the time, and being an expert mussel gatherer he knew almost exactly how many pearls, slugs, and buttons that many shells would produce. I was very leery of him. Well, as I said, his wife and those

<28>

girls did all the work, and they never had much to eat except mussels, fish, or squirrel. They had no other meat, bacon, or white bread, only corn meal and what few wild greens they could find, such as poke greens and lamb's-quarters. Whistle and Rex used to sneak down to their camp at night and take food we had left over and trade with the girls.

One evening Old Buck came to our camp and was trying to buy our pearls, and when we denied having any at all he called us many descriptive kinds of liars and stalked out of our camp mighty upset. I saw right away that we were going to have to leave our camp or maybe shoot the old buzzard. So after supper Rex and Whistle took what biscuits, bacon, and potatoes and jelly we had left over, and bragging what a good trade this would make down at Old Buck's camp, they left. After they took off I got worried, so I dug up the pearls and put them in the almost empty coffee can. I made up a pack of our remaining food, leaving out just enough for breakfast. I then moved my bed about a hundred feet from the others so the boys wouldn't wake me when they came back to camp.

Well, I was jerked from a sound sleep by the blast of a ten-gauge shotgun and another and another, on a diminishing scale, so I knew the race was going away from me. I knew we were in for it, too, so I grabbed my rifle and six-gun, rolled my bed and tumbled our provisions into a sack. Then I quickly rolled up Rex and Whistle's beds and made up two packs and faded into the darkness! Within seconds the boys ran into camp grabbing up the packs I had made and their guns. I gave a little whistle and led the way out of the river bottom.

Well, they were badly shook, saying Old Buck had tried to kill them, but I knew better as Old Buck had never missed anything he shot at in the past sixty years. I also knew that he was just at the edge of our camp as they came running in, watching to see if they dug up any pearls! He knew I was out there somewhere, not knowing if I would kill him or not, and the boys not wasting time to hunt the pearls probably saved our lives.

We walked the twenty miles into Christoval by daylight. I picked out six nice pearls, and we sold them to the local jeweler as soon as he opened his store. Though they were worth much more and all of us knew it, we accepted $150. Then we bought a complete change

<29>

of clothes, ate the last of our grub and caught a bus for Waco, it being over 150 miles east. We were sure we'd made a clean getaway.

We got a hotel room in Waco and spent a couple of hours sorting and matching pearls. Some of them were pink, some shaded to blue, some almost purple. Some were pear shaped. In fact a great many of them were, and we had lots of buttons, that is, half pearls, and lots of ugly misshapen slugs. Among the slugs I noticed several that were more or less star shaped, and thinking how I could mount them as earrings and on necklaces, I traded my share of the buttons for all the slugs.

We took the pearls to several jewelers and got such low offers we decided we would take them to Dallas. Late that evening, however, a couple of Jewish men came to see us, and after about three hours of matching, sizing, and color coding, they offered $2,100, but quickly settled for $2,400 when we argued about it. They paid us in cash and were almost gone when I thought of the slugs and buttons. I showed them how I thought they could be used, and they paid me $140 for the whole lot. Then they gathered up all the stuff and were gone so quickly I never could have given a description of either one of them.

I have often pondered their actions. They knew where we were, what we had, and I'm sure knew the offers we had refused. They just came in, shook hands, muttered a couple of unpronounceable names, sorted the pearls, paid in cash, and left. Were we cheated? Were they cheated? We would have sold for a lot less, and they didn't look like jewel merchants. Maybe they had a racket of their own too deep for country kids like us to fathom. Anyway we were in the chips, and I'll have you know that was darn good money for three weeks, then or now!

Whistle and Rex bought new suits and all the trimmings, and dressed in their finery, they went out on the town. I bought me a money belt, and putting all my money in it but a few dollars, I headed back for the Concho River to see about all those mussel shells we had stacked up. By the time I got there, they were all gone and so was Old Buck. I went to the button factory and found that Old Buck had sold nine tons of shells two days before. I had a good idea where to look for him, so I set out for Llano. Sure enough, I found him camped on the Llano River right near town.

<30>

Charlie Buck greeted me like a brother and before I could get my mouth closed had handed me $125. Then he launched a plan to cut a big willow tree thicket which was in the middle of the river and make it into willow porch furniture and sell it in Llano and surrounding towns! Well, I found myself being accepted as a full partner. He stored my bedroom in a lean-to, and before I knew what was happening, I was eating dinner and feeling like I'd been hit over the head with a bung starter! Every time I opened my mouth to object to something, I was hushed by a wave of the hand and inundated with more schemes. I never knew there were so many ways to "live off the land." Well he talked so much and painted such a rosy picture that I accepted and fell asleep from exhaustion!

Making Willow Furniture for Charlie Buck

WILLOW FURNITURE making was hard work but Old Buck was a master craftsman. With me cutting the willow wands (the long slim willow branches), Old Lady Buck sorting them as to size, and the girls stripping bark from larger trees to be used for lacing and tying, the work went like a prairie fire.

The Rhoades lived down the river too, and the furniture making drew them. Frank Rhoades and his father, Uncle Jerry, joined in with us. With all of us making the furniture, Old Buck started taking it from house to house and place to place selling it. The first day he sold six sets. This included two chairs and a settee. Now, this was porch furniture, as everyone had a porch in those days, and in the early evening the family would sit on the porch in the cool. Well, he divided this money with me but none for his wife and the girls. The Rhoades were good, quick, and thorough furniture makers, so the girls and I had to get faster in order to keep them busy. We were making furniture faster than he could sell it, so Old Buck called a halt, saying it had to be sold while it was still green, because when it dried it might warp. Frank and I started going to more distant towns, and we sold all we could take.

Well, we returned a few days later to find everything in an uproar. Old Buck had been arrested for raping the youngest of his wife's girls. He had tied her up in the willow thicket, and a fisherman had heard

<31>

the child screaming and crying, and following the sound he had almost beat Old Buck to death with a club. The fisherman got the sheriff and they had Old Buck and the whole family in jail. Buck got a ten-years-to-life sentence, but as it turned out three years was life for him.

Buck had several thousand dollars on him when he was arrested, so Frank and Uncle Jerry took that and got the wife and girls out and bought them a house to live in. The older girls were married soon after, and the young one started to school, the first of any of her family ever go to school. Frank, Uncle Jerry, and I split up the furniture money and gave half of it to the old lady.

Float Trip on the Llano

FRANK BOUGHT the truck from Buck's wife, and we outfitted for a floating trip down the Llano River. We got Uncle Jerry to drive us to Junction, seventy-five miles down the road to the west, and we launched our canoes and went off on a trip down the river.

Well, the middle of July is blazing hot in Central Texas, and this was about July 10, 1928. We would drift down the river from around 3:30 or 4:00 A.M. until somewhere around 8:00 or 9:00 A.M., or until it started getting hot. Then we would pull up in the shade of one of the tall bluffs, which were all along the river, and rest and poke around. We hunted arrow heads and flint knives, and we found hundreds of them. We could have sunk the canoe with rub stones which the Lipans and Comanches used to grind acorns into a kind of meal. These stone slabs all weighed over one hundred pounds each, so we noted their whereabouts, intending to pick them up later. Of course we never did, and floods changed the landscape, even if we had ever tried to go back years later. But we were young, and things like that were soon forgotten as we went on to other things.

In some places there were deep overhangs, which showed signs of being used for shelters for maybe hundreds of years. By scratching around in these caves we found flint axes and spearheads. We gathered a lot of this stuff just for fun, but in the 1920s no one we knew was interested in Indian artifacts. Instead we fished, hunted, and cut mussel shells for pearls. We didn't find but one or two pearls,

<32>

as the Llano River didn't produce mussel shells or pearls like the Concho River did. We only cooked once a day and ate the other meals cold! Talk about lazy! We needed a squaw or two to make an Indian Chief look like a workaholic!

A man's nature soon rebels at this sort of life, however. Upon seeing that all the pecan trees which lined the banks of the Llano River from end to end were loaded with pecans, and as it was now August, we hauled out the canoes at London. We phoned Pinki's grocery store in Llano and left a message for Jim Brewer to have Uncle Jerry Rhoades bring him up in the truck, which he did. Uncle Jerry went on home and Jim rode with us in the canoes down the river for the next thirty miles. We located a beautiful pecan bottom, and looking up the rancher we bought the pecans on the trees, paying him cash for them. Then we stacked the canoes, and the rancher took us to Mason where we again called and had Uncle Jerry come pick us up.

Threshing Pecans on the Llano

W E W E R E soon busy outfitting ourselves for the fall's work—threshing and picking up the pecans. This included a need for two large tents, as both Jim and Frank were taking their families. Jim and Alice had four kids and Frank and Mary had seven, and neither one of them even thought of excluding me or Mancel. So the planning started, and after much haggling and brain wracking we all decided who would stay in what tent and what groceries we would need. Mancel pointed out that he only wanted to camp with us and that he would do the hunting and some fishing and furnish his own grub. After an O.K. and a handshake all around, we loaded up and were off.

Our camp was in a downright beautiful place. All the tents were in a circle under the trees, and in the center we made a fireplace of limestone that wouldn't pop when it got hot. We made some willow chairs, built a big, big table, and the campground looked like home.

In early September pecans begin to open, so we all fell to with good spirits. Everyone was fat and sleek except Jim and Frank. No amount of food ever raised their weight, nor did the lack of food ever

<33>

seem to reduce them. We truly lived on the fat of the land along with about ten pounds of beans everyday! But everyone was happy and everyone was expected to do his part of the chores, which everyone did, including the children. We ate wild greens, wild onions, and fish, squirrel, rabbits, turkey, venison, quail, duck, and we even killed several hogs. We always killed the hogs far away from camp, because hogs ran on open range in those days and were considered valuable property. I had a quail trap set well back in the brush, and set lines for ducks on a sand bar where the water was only one or two inches deep. You stretch the line real tight and weigh it down in several places, then put hooks on short stagings and bait them with grains of hominy. The ducks peck the hominy and get hooked. Ducks rest in shallow water so foxes and other varmints can't slip up on them. Sometimes I'd get a duck on every hook. We ate everything, as hard working kids seem to have hollow legs.

Now all predators were subject to regulations, and we could certainly be classified as predators, so the game warden harassed us constantly. We accepted it as one of our God-given rights to live off the bounty God had provided, so we considered the game warden to be an enemy to us and to all free people!

The game wardens would rear up around camp at all kinds of times. They always believed they had us dead to rights eating illegal meat, but our meat cache was further away from camp than anyone who was used to riding in a car ever liked to go on foot. We always kept a lookout on top of a high bluff at meal time and never brought any more meat to camp than we could eat at one meal. In fact, that would have been hard to do as all those kids in camp worked hard—up early, to bed late—and they never left a scrap of food on the table at any meal. They liked anything cooked any way.

We finally broke the chief game warden down. Jim went to the meat cache one day and found there was only enough left for that meal. He brought the flour sack it was in back to camp to be washed, because after it had been used it was always bloody and stiff. After removing the meat he just tossed it over into the trailer with the pecans and we all forgot about it. But the warden drove into camp just after sunup the next morning, and the first place he looked was in the trailer. Sure enough, there he found the bloody sack. You may know a big smile came over his face and he said, "Well, I sure have

<34>

you now." But Henry Rhoades, who was about six years old at that time, was sleeping in the same trailer, and he raised up and said, "That's where my nose bled last night." Well, you can imagine our surprise, but no one said a word. The warden was mad because he knew he couldn't start an argument with a six-year-old. He got back in his car and left so fast his car wheels threw sand all over camp, and he never came back again.

No one had coached Henry to lie, nor had any of the other kids been coached. We just concluded that Henry was a born liar, and that could well be, as he is an old man now and still lies. Henry's never been cornered in a lie and can tell some of the most outlandish tales you ever heard. And just when you think you have him in a tight crack, he comes back with a tale you almost believe! It's uncanny. You soon quit trying to catch him in a lie, for with his nimble wit and quick tongue, he soon leaves you far behind.

Of course, this was all before radio and television. Why, even a telephone was a mystery to most people, although we had used a phone several times. There were very few in most small towns, and most country people wondered how you could talk on a wire if it didn't have a hole in it for the voice to go through!

While I was in school I had a teacher who stressed reading with expression and accent, so at night in camp, I'd read to all these people from pulp magazines. They all loved Westerns, so we'd get *Wild West Weekly* or *Western Story* or *Ranch Romances*. These magazines always had several good stories, usually one to be continued in the next week's copy. Everyone would listen with rapt attention. There was always a story of a range detective named George Crumb, and, boy, was he tough. He always got his man.

In early November the first winter storm howled down on our camp. The wind beat all the remaining pecans off the trees and windrowed them, so we gathered them in easily and quickly. The women were beginning to get anxious to get back to town to buy the kids some school clothes and put them in school. And what used to be such a beautiful camp was now dreary and cold. The men all wanted to get outfitted for the winter's trapping too, so we broke camp and headed for Llano.

The Winter of 1928-1929

TO OUTFIT for the 1928-29 expedition looked easy, but now both Frank's wife and Jim's wife were expecting another child, and after buying school clothes for all the kids and restocking both pantries in each house, we were a little short of money. This was disappointing to both Jim and Frank as they both wanted to be self sufficient, but the only thing that had changed was that they now had a truck, so once again we all had to pool our resources. Frank, Jim, Mancel, and I were all destined to stick together.

I held out some money and got me a job at the local turkey-killing-and-processing plant. They were packing the turkeys for the Thanksgiving holiday that was just a short time away and everything was hurried. I worked twelve days with only two breaks of four hours each to sleep. We finished up at ten A.M. on the twentieth of November, and Mancel picked me up at the packing plant. I had made $196.00. That paid my part of the outfitting and I had some money left over.

We camped at Live Oak Draw, which is the site of old Ft. Lancaster near Sheffield. There I did some catching up on sleep and then we went on to Ft. Stockton. I shopped for sugar, salt, soap, cloth, needles, thread, cheap shirts (at that time thirty-five cents each), socks (two pair for fifteen cents), and other stuff I thought I might trade to Mexicans from across the river. They were the poorest people you ever saw and needed everything. Unless they slipped across the river, their nearest stores were almost a hundred miles south. If the Border Patrol caught them on this side, it could mean the death penalty, depending on who the patrolman was.

Although I was outfitted for river camping, the others decided we ought to trap in the Chinati's and in the Capote Mountains, just to be onery I thought. However, we located one of the best camping places we ever had. Do I seem to like every camp better than the last? If I do it's not far from the truth. Here we had a fine grove of live oaks with a solid rock wall to the north, topped by thick cedars, and with water in a flowing stream from a spring on the west. A wide break in the eastern mountains let in the first rays of the rising sun to help warm us up in the early morning. To the south was a wild jumble of canyons and ridges, one after the other, extending for many miles.

< 3 6 >

The Mystery House and the Treasure Road

ON THANKSGIVING day Jim and I decided to explore to the south and look for some good trapping country. We started up a wide canyon which opened just across from camp. It soon pitched up sharply, and when water had eroded the ground badly we soon saw that we were following what appeared to be an abandoned road, where it crossed bare rocks. Wheel ruts were cut an inch deep here. We had been thinking we were the first white men to come this way, only to find out we were latecomers indeed! The road had not been used for scores of years. Oak trees about six inches thick were growing between the ruts, and oak trees grow mighty slow in that land of so little rain and so much cold.

Over this ridge and around a sharp bend we saw the most unexpected sight of a lifetime! There stood a rock house in perfect repair. The roof was thatched with lechuguilla, a kind of dagger-like plant indigenous to this land. In the house, which had been abandoned for many decades, were piles of oxen shoes, nails for oxen shoes, three yokes for oxen, along with many kinds of farm implements. Just back of the house was a field of about sixty acres enclosed by a rock fence eight-feet high consisting of two rock walls three feet apart and filled with sand, dirt, and small rocks. Its height made it deer proof. This was really a colossal work and took a lot of time. We could find no clue to the identity of the builder, although we later inquired all over the country.

The nearest and maybe best clue we found was in Shafter, a silver and gold mining town about twenty miles east of there. Mining had ceased there in World War I. I asked some of the old Mexican men if they knew anything about the rock house, and a couple of them did remember a man who used to bring fresh pinto beans, corn, winter squash, and other produce to sell. But they never knew where he came from, so if it wasn't that man who lived on the farm, who was it?

The wagon road continued south, so we followed it until we finally lost it in a maze of small canyons about eight or nine miles from the rock house. Where it could have been going is a mystery, because just at the top of the ridge where we lost the trail, the

<37>

mountains broke off in a cliff maybe a hundred feet high and continued to fall in big steps to the banks of the Rio Grande maybe thirty miles away.

Having now topped out we circled west, and keeping in the mountains we examined every pass and trail for varmint signs. We found the land to be fairly well populated with both large and small animals. Jim gave me his part of the country as he was older, and it was too broken and too far for him. I was eighteen then and could stand the hard country.

I lead us in a circle to the east, and just as the sun was about to go down we hit the head of our home canyon. Jim called for a rest so we set down on some rocks and rolled cigarettes. I was facing east and could see our camp. I saw Frank go for a bucket of water and Mancel starting a fire, so I remarked that we had better hurry and get our name in the pot for supper. Jim said it would be a long time before we ate as camp was about six or eight miles behind us. Seeing that he was lost, I went along with him, but pointed to the fire in our camp and asked if he thought we could get a cup of coffee there. He was happy that we had seen this camp so we hurried down, and it was dark when we got there. Jim didn't recognize the camp until he saw Frank and Mancel. He couldn't have been more stunned if it hit him in the head with an axe. He drank lots of coffee, but didn't eat much and went to bed early. He didn't go to sleep but tried to figure out how we got back to camp. He never figured it out, and he never went that way again.

We told about our round and all about the rock house and wagon road, and immediately the others decided the road was to a lost gold mine. While we were making inquiries about it, one man in Marfa got real interested and asked lots of questions as to the exact location. Well, Jim's best descriptions would put the location many miles off, and then I grew cagey and backed him up. In fact, we took the hunt even further afield, thinking we might search the whole mountain range later. But we never did and I doubted anyone except a well trained tracker could ever find the location again. Ranch men then and now never go back in there. They use the cattle's love of salt to lure them out of those deep and far away places when they need to work them.

<38>

A Den of Wolves and a Bounty Problem

FRANK AND I took a round checking trapping territory one day, and we were going up a fairly large and deep canyon which ended in a circular bow. We were tracking a really big wolf and wondering where he could have gone when we discovered a crack in the east wall of the canyon. The wolf's trail went into the crack, so even though it didn't look big enough to pass through, we followed into the worst jumble of rocks and boulders you ever saw, some as big as an automobile, and some as big as box cars and bigger. All the dirt and small rocks had been washed on through the opening leaving rocks stacked topsy-turvy. Frank found a way to climb to the top of the pile, and I was to follow the wolf's tracks into his lair. So holding my Colt .41 before me I slid carefully into the dark passageway, slowly, and I do mean slowly, for I'd rather follow a panther into his den than a wolf. A wolf will not growl or make any sound before jumping on anything, but a panther seems to use his loudest burst of sound to fix his prey as he makes his leap.

Well, my eyes began to get used to the gloom, and I thought I saw glowing eyes up ahead. I let go with a squall to Frank that I was on him. The eyes blinked out and as fast as you can think came the crack of Frank's rifle and then an unexcited, almost conversational noise saying, "I got him; come on out."

The quickest way out was the way the wolf went, so I scrambled that way in a hurry. I found a tunnel about the size of a barrel and dropped down to enter it. Well, imagine how it feels to be elated to the bursting point, and in a flash—so fast your brain and nervous system can't act—have a set of jaws wide enough to take your head off open up within inches of your face, with teeth as long as your little finger! I pee'd my pants! What happens is your body goes on automatic. Without conscious action, the gun was in the right place, actually half way down the throat, and I blasted away so fast it sounded like raking a stick down a picket fence. That's what Frank said. I didn't know because I jerked my head back so fast I almost tore it off on the rocks above me.

The next thing I knew I was out in the sun and Jim was tying a bandana so tight around my head I couldn't blink my eyes. It seems Jim and Mancel were out meat hunting and heard Frank's shot when

<39>

he killed the big dog wolf and had drifted in our direction. They were close by when I shot it out with the bitch wolf, and even though it took a lot to excite either of those guys, they did get busy when they knew I was in that rock pile with a lobo wolf! They had dragged out me and the bitch both and had bandaged up a gash behind my ear. Frank and Mancel were busy bringing out eight pups about the size of housecats. The bounty on lobo wolves in Presidio County at that time was $150, so it looked like a good day's work.

Now, Frank, who had the most experience with bounty hunting, cautioned us not to kill the pups. By the time the two old wolves were skinned I was ready to go, and each of us taking two pups, we went back to camp. The wolf pups were no more afraid of us than dog pups. They got to where they ran to us every time something startled them. We had brought a roll of net wire with us to fence our camp with because sometimes an old cow will chew a tent up and ruin it in one day. The least they can do is crap all over everything, and the most they can do is get a rope wrapped around a horn and run off with the whole thing! In some places wild hogs will invade and can ruin all your food in minutes. As we had seen no sight of livestock near camp, we used the wire to build a large pen for the wolf pups. We brought in enough varmint carcasses to keep them well fed.

Frank took the two wolf hides to Marfa and got the bounty. Instead of telling anyone about having the pups, he just pointed out that the bitch had pups, probably big enough to take care of themselves. Her tits showed that she had suckled eight pups so the Cattlemen's Association offered Frank a flat fee of $1,000 if he could get all the pups, but only $25.00 each for baby pups. One of the Association members ran the mercantile store, so Frank made a big show of buying a pick and shovel and even inquired about borrowing a good dog, so if we found them we could dig them out of their hole. Fortunately he left town before anyone could come up with a dog.

About a week later we killed and skinned the pups before we got more attached to them, and Frank led us through this story we were going to tell of how we diligently searched and located and dug out the varmints. After we got it all straight and down pat, off we went to Marfa to see the cattlemen.

Well, the cattlemen wrangled around about paying the bounty, and a couple flat refused to put in their part even though they had

<40>

around fifty members and their share would only have been $25 of the $1,300 they had offered as bounty. Some thought $1,300 was too much for a stinking ignorant trapper! The other members kept their word and paid the $1,000, as cattle at that time (before the 1929 crash) were high and they could afford it.

Well, Frank was mad, and before he left town he found out where the non-payers' ranches were located. When he got back he wrote to Rex and Uncle, who were off trapping wolves under government contract. He asked them to save alive a pair of young wolves. We soon had a letter back from them asking us what to do with the pair. They now had two nice young tame wolves caught in New Mexico. Frank and Mancel went to Taos, New Mexico, to get the pair and then took them to the Scruggs Ranch, shot a fat calf, and turned the wolves to feeding on the carcass. In two weeks the pair had set a pattern of killing a calf every fourth day.

Scruggs sent word to us right away that he wanted us to trap on his land, but we sent word right back that him being so tight, we were afraid he might want half the furs we caught. Boy, he was enraged and came blustering into our camp armed with a Colt .45 automatic, but when he was met by four men as well armed as he was it had a very calming effect on him. Frank told him why we wouldn't trap for him and further that he hoped the wolves ate all his cows and him, too. Then picking up a 1903 army rifle he invited Mr. Scruggs to leave our camp. And light a shuck he did, quickly!

Setting Up Shop on the Rio Grande

HAVING NOW depleted the fur and game in a twenty-mile circle, we moved down the river to the Rio Grande where the Capote rim and the river came together. There was not really room enough there for four trappers. One line up the river and back under the Capote rim and one line down and up to the rim completed two circles, so Mancel, for a share of the catch, agreed to take care of the camp and set a few traps right around camp. Frank and Jim agreed to that, so I took the trade goods I had bought in Ft. Stockton, moved across the river on the Mexico side, stretched a little tent up, and opened a store.

< 4 1 >

In a very short time I had several customers who just appeared out of the brush. We visited some and before long I was about half shot on pulque, a drink the Mexicans make from the maguey plant. It is not cooked but is like drinking whiskey mash or green home brew right out of the crock. Men and children came in first, but when the women and girls (who were peeking through the brush) saw that I had some cloth and had opened a big box of hard candy, they shyly and little by little came into camp.

These people are usually badly treated by the Texans and would have good reason to be unfriendly had they found a Texan across on their side of the river. However, I speak a respected Castilian dialect, and I greeted every man as if he were a Spanish "Grandee" and every woman as if she were at least the equal to the Virgin Mary. Being very polite to all comers, I was soon drinking and trading like mad. The third day I was almost out of goods to trade, but I found that some of the people wanted shotgun shells. They were not allowed to own rifles or pistols but could own single-barrel shotguns, if they were of good character—and if the Rurales didn't decide to hang them anyway, just to cheer up their men.

The trappers on the other side of the river were not doing much good, and it now being near Christmas the cold winds were sweeping down the river, which flowed north to south here. Most of the weed seeds and other natural foods were used up, so the fur bearers were moving, some to hibernate. Jim, Frank, and Mancel decided to head for home.

I bought all the supplies we had left over and started trading again with the Mexicans. Word had gone out that I traded for furs, tanned goat hides with the hair on, tanned deer hides made into buckskin, also wool ponchos and serapes. In a few days I was out of goods to trade but had pretty well traded with all comers. So I gathered all my stuff and borrowed a couple of pack jacks from a Mexican who had become my drinking buddy and companion, and we ferried all this stuff across the river. This young man had one leg off below the knee. He had no crutches or anything like that to help him walk, but he used a pole about six or seven feet long, and using it like a vaulting pole, he could sure cover ground. He wouldn't come across the river to the American side, but waited for me to unload his jacks and

<42>

return them to him on the Mexican side. We split our last bottle of pulque and embraced. I promised to return soon, but I never did.

I had traded for more than a hundred furs. Most had been skinned starting at the mouth and turning the skin inside out without making a single cut in the hide. After having scrapped all the fat and flesh off the skin and allowing it to almost dry, the tanner turned the hair side out and then stuffed the hide with grass. I had fox, coon, ringtails, lined skunks and little spotted skunks, a few coyotes, and even three coatimundi hides, which must have been carried a long way from deep inside Mexico. I lumped all these particular skins to a taxidermist in Alpine for seven hundred dollars. This, with my part of the bounty on the lobo wolves and the fur I traded for, upped my cash to near $1200.

Frank and Jim had over $700 each, and they decided to hurry home before New Year. Mancel and I packaged all our flat and cased fur and mailed them to Taylor & Co. in St. Louis, Mo., and gave Ft. Davis, Texas, as our return address. We also wrote to the postmaster at Ft. Davis that if we didn't call for it, to hold our mail for thirty days and then forward it to Llano. I took my serapes and ponchos to the dry cleaners in Alpine to have them cleaned and pressed, and in answer to a casually put question I replied that they would be worth about eight or nine dollars each. I had eleven in all so I was most surprised when the tailor offered me ten dollars a piece for them. I was now down to twenty-two well cured goat hides of many colors. So I made a deal with Mancel, and we went up to Taos to sell these skins to an Indian artifact store where they made beaded buckskin vests and felt-backed rugs for the tourist trade.

A blizzard came howling out of the north, and it pushed us south back to Texas at full force. We were back in Van Horn by early evening, and we holed up in a hotel there. The winds through Guadalupe Pass were soon up to sixty miles an hour and all traffic stopped.

Mrs. Crow and Mrs. Epps Show Up Again

M A N C E L   W A S signing in at the desk in the hotel lobby when in came Mrs. Crow, my ranch friend and Forty-Two partner of

<43>

the year before. We hurried to get hot coffee for her. Maybe some know this already, but the reason no one drove cars when it was really cold was that cars in those days didn't have heaters in them. Mrs. Crow had spent Christmas with her mother in El Paso and was on her way back home. We soon had a Forty-Two game going. The game broke up about midnight, and she and I talked and she hired us to trap her place again. This was now New Years Eve day, 1928.

Mancel had become good friends with a lady who was iced in with us, and they were looking forward to the New Year's dance. Mrs. Crow was in a hurry to get back to the ranch, so she and I decided to push on. Mancel was to come later. We got hot bricks, lap robes, and a thermos of coffee, and set out for Ft. Davis and the Crow Ranch.

We had no trouble at all on the road, but when we got to the ranch it was a shambles. Mrs. Crow had hired a Mexican family for the year around, but they had gone off visiting and the weather had prevented their return until several hours after we got there. Now, everybody who keeps goats has to have sheds to protect them from the weather. You don't have to gather your goats because they will always come in during bad weather. So while everyone was gone, a panther had invaded the sheds, and though he only ate parts of three or four goats, he killed over sixty, and the ones that he ran away from the sheds froze to death.

Mrs. Crow had lost several thousand dollars worth of angora goats, and when the Mexican family who were supposed to look after the ranch drove in I thought she was going to kill them. She tongue lashed them so bad they turned around and left like they were dodging bullets. I got hold of the gun she had and kept her from shooting. Then I told her I would track and kill the panther and she quieted down. The next day we went into the Ft. Davis post office and found that almost everyone had lost most of their goats to lions and the cold. Some of them had lost cows that were in a weakened and poor shape. Taken as a whole, Mrs. Crow had actually fared better than most.

Mancel came in that day and said that we had gotten our check from Taylor Fur Co. It was the last good price ever got for fur, for that winter of 1929 and spring of 1930 everything went to hell. *The depression had hit!* The next time fur was to bring a good price was 1975,

<44>

and by that time Mancel, Frank, Jim, Grandad Maddox, and Uncle Allen Crider were all a long time dead.

With the trapping money we already had and because of the cold, Mancel was ready to head for home. I explained to him that I was obligated to trap the panther for Mrs. Crow, and while we were talking Mrs. Epps drove up and wanted me to trap varmints at her place. I told her I couldn't, so Mancel said he would. The four of us worked out a deal to trap all the predators for these and two other ranches. Mancel was to stay at the Swift ranch, and I was to stay with Mrs Crow.

Mrs. Crow hired another Mexican family for the ranch, and they had a border collie dog. The very next morning this dog was barking near the barn, and sure enough had the goat-killing panther treed. I shot it through both shoulders, and it was dead when it fell to the ground. Within minutes Mrs. Crow was on the phone telling everyone the news. In due time all the neighbors came over, and Mrs. Crow cooked a big dinner and everyone enjoyed themselves.

The cat was an old female and was in heat, so Mancel and I took out the female assembly and what urine the bladder contained and made up trap bait. It was good bait too, and we caught two young male panthers the next week. We used horses and that sure beats following a trap line on foot. You can't run any more traps on a horse, but you don't leave so much man scent and always seem to catch more fur. In three weeks Mancel and I had caught more fur on these ranches than all of us did down in the Big Bend country. The fur season was now over, so we shipped all our furs to Taylor Fur Co., giving Llano as our return address.

Gambling at the End of the Season

BY FEBRUARY 2, all trappers, bounty hunters, and mountain men were back in Llano and everybody had money. The lazy cheap-John gamblers and hangers-on were swarming around, trying to get some of the fur money. Three of these hustlers had bought a case of cards and had spent many weeks carefully opening each deck and, using a type of marking ink put out by the K.C. Card Co., had marked every card from the ace to the deuce. I am sure they

<45>

spent countless hours dealing and practicing reading the backs of cards where the mark was.

All of our crew was soon back in town. Llano was noted for its trappers, pearl hunters, and fish poachers. Llano was also known for its deer poachers, some of whom killed thirty or forty bucks during the season and sold them to out-of-town hunters who couldn't or didn't kill their own. All of us did this sometime, and some all the time. Frank had one son who killed sixty or so each season and uncounted number of does from which he only took the hams and back straps and sold the meat up and down the countryside.

But, back to the gamblers. We played in a few games, but not liking the way the game was played we dropped out. We knew that the cards must be marked but not where. It made no difference how often a new deck was put in the game, it was always the same. We knew they had marked a whole case of cards and then had taken them back to the drug store where everyone traded. Finally after much searching we found the mark and soon we knew it as well as the gamblers. Jim and I teamed up on them then and broke their bank several times before they gave up. They had bought queer dice too but shooting out of a cup made it impossible to control dice, so we beat them badly and they moved on.

April was upon us and we were sort of out of it. Frank was a blacksmith and tool sharpener and could work most anytime. Jim got a job driving a transfer wagon, called a delivery truck nowadays. Mancel was a gunsmith. I drifted out and got a job on a pipeline. On a pipeline job, board and room was $1.50 a day, work or not. When your money ran out you were run out of camp.

Working on a Pipe Line

THEY ADVERTISED that South Texas was where the sun spends the winter, but a couple of days after I went to work down there it began to rain. I had enough money and had paid for two meals, and I was packed and ready to go further on when the superintendent bawled, "All out!" Only twenty men made this muster. He explained that they had a break in the line at Sabinal and that it was bad and that everyone ought to get all the clothes he

<46>

owned and put them on. He said they had rain coats in the supply tent and to get one and get on the supply truck.

The big truck was a Bulldog Mac that would only go about thirty miles an hour but could haul any amount of weight. If it had any springs at all, they would only activate after five tons, which we weren't. We had about seventy miles to go in freezing rain and on this springless, flat-bed truck. Most of the space was taken with tools, an extra joint of pipe, an extra collar, and lots of picks and shovels. The cook came out with a box of sandwiches, and I was able to get my hand in the box and grab two before they melted in the rain. We then headed for Station C. After ten miles everyone was wrapped in ice, and except for hands, feet, ears, noses, and the rest of our bodies, we were almost comfortable. After twenty miles everyone was so stiff and cold that we couldn't feel a thing.

We rode for hours before we stopped. We stomped around to loosen up our frozen joints, and then we stumbled into the cafe where the truck had parked. Once inside it seemed we were being roasted alive. Being so cold and then going into so warm a place made your skin prickle and hurt. Coffee, "left over from yesterday" and so strong it would float an anvil, began to take its effect and everyone was finally able to sit down and eat a good meal. All too soon we were ordered on the truck again and were soon at the scene of the oil break.

Oil was everywhere and shoe-top deep, so at least there was no doubt about where to dig. Some of the supervising crew built a bonfire, but all us peons crowded them out so they put it out. Everyone started swinging a digging tool to keep from freezing. The work dragged because when you dug a hole it soon filled with water, but if you left it a few minutes it would freeze over. We had to dig a canal to channel the water away.

We worked all night and half the next day before they brought food. We felt like galley slaves. Working twelve hours at full speed takes lots of fuel, and the Humble Pipeline Co. did finally bring plenty of food, which we swallowed like capsules. By night and after digging up five joints of pipe, we had found the break. It was a pulled collar. Twenty men, all tired and worn out, can hardly back out a joint of twelve-inch pipe, but by midnight it was fixed back together and back filling was started. Now that the job was finally done the

<47>

rain and sleet finally stopped. We loaded up and pulled out for our camp at Poteet.

We had worked under the very worst conditions for fifty-four hours, with no sleep and only two meals, but after eating a big meal and sleeping about ten hours we were ready to go again. We were a bit stiff and had some peeling from frost bite, but after learning we were to be paid a full seventy hours everyone was happy. For seventy hours' work we got $35. Compare that with two days' wages today in 1980. That was top wages in those days, but it was all money, not these cigar-coupon wages we get today.

The End of the Good Free Life

HAVING AUGMENTED my wages with some good hands at poker, I decided to go home for a few days. It was a good thing too. My dad, who worked on the railroad, had had a bad heart attack and was in the railroad's company hospital in Houston. My mother was frantic, what with nine other kids and no money coming in. After I got there I found out that the Humble Oil Co. was going to build a plant and refinery right there in town, and as I was getting known by now as a "construction stiff" I had a job within an hour. I'm sure that nothing could have heartened my mother more. I had some money and gave it to her to help out. I still had some money in the bank at San Angelo, and also in Amarillo, but I just left that in, maybe to put to good use some day.

My mother had ten children. I was the oldest, almost nineteen. The youngest twin boys were four months old, and I had never seen them. There was another boy and six girls between me and them, the ages and sizes pretty close. So we sent Mom to Houston to see Dad. She only stayed the weekend and came back very depressed. A week later they brought Dad home with a railroad doctor. I got home from work at five that evening and spoke to the doctor briefly. He said that Dad wanted to see me and that I'd better hurry.

I went in and Dad said, "I'm sure glad to see you, boy. I was wondering what would happen to all these kids, but your ma says you have taken ahold of things."

I said, "You know me, Dad."

<48>

"Yes, I do" he said.

That was Dad's last breath, and that was the end of a free life and time for me. It takes a lot of money to keep up a family the size I inherited. While the young ones were growing up, the old ones were sending home the results of broken marriages. Well, there never could be too many for Mom and me, but it was always close.

The '29 Crash came soon after Dad died, and the refinery we were building closed down and never did open up. There was no work anywhere. I didn't bootleg any more because I couldn't stand the thought of hurting Mom if I got caught and sent to the pen. We were rescued by the East Texas oil strike, and for a year or so I worked twelve to sixteen hours a day in the oil fields. Then oil went to ten cents a barrel, the companies quit, and I went home dead broke.

During those hard years of the Depression I did anything I could to get by. One year Grandad and I cut wood on the halves because nobody had any money then. Grandad was seventy-six but a hell of a man, and he cut more than I did every day. In three weeks we cut thirty cords of wood, walking two miles to work and back. We ended that job when I split my foot with an axe. Crippled as I was, I went to work threshing pecans for Louis Grenwelge. He was a slave driver, but he brought my pay up because we were paid by the pound and I threshed six hundred to a thousand pounds a day. When threshing was over, Mancel, Frank, and I headed out to the headwaters of the Llano and San Saba rivers to trap for the rest of the season.

The Thirties were hard times, but all of us in Llano worked together at anything we could get and survived. Then came Pearl Harbor and World War II and everybody went off to service or the defense plants. They were spread all over the world. Some came home after the war; some never did. Nothing was ever the same after that. Old Llano and a way of life we enjoyed and expected changed drastically. The days I write about are now gone forever, just memories.

<49>

Elmer Kelton

ELMER KELTON

Fiction Writers Are Liars and Thieves

Banquet address to the Texas Folklore Society
at Lubbock, April 1, 1988

SOMEONE has said that fiction by definition is a lie. By extension this means that fiction writers are liars. In that context I will admit to it, and go a step further. I will say that fiction writers are *thieves*.

We steal stories wherever we find them, disguise them, paint them up like car thieves in a chop shop, then present them as our own. We watch people and steal their characteristics, give them to our fictional characters and call ourselves creative.

The beauty of it is that it is not against the law. Readers seem to see no harm in it. They'll even pay us well for doing it . . . now and then.

So I stand before you tonight confessing my sins, and even telling you a little about how I've done it.

Dr. C. L. Sonnichsen once said that if you steal from one source you are a plagiarist. If you steal from ten sources you are a researcher. If you steal from fifty sources, you are a scholar.

My crime is much greater than that.

For instance: *The Time it Never Rained*:

Charlie Flagg is the middle-aged rancher who serves as the main character in *The Time it Never Rained*. He struggles through the long seven-year drouth of the 1950s, gradually losing a little here, a little there until he has lost most of what he owns, except for his dignity and his self-respect.

Many people have asked me if I modeled Charlie after their fathers. My mother believes he is modeled after *my* father. They are *all* right. I used so many things from so many people that Charlie Flagg is a little of them, but in total he is none of them.

<51>

Page Mauldin is another major character in the story, Charlie's best friend. Charlie is a small rancher, owning a little land, leasing some more. He is as big as he wants to be, nowhere near rich, but comfortable. Mauldin, however, is driven by ambition to be the biggest rancher in West Texas, and he just about is. But he is leveraged to the hilt and has his operations scattered all over the country. His size and his debts make him a lot more vulnerable even than Charlie, and eventually he loses everything.

To a very substantial degree, I modeled Page Mauldin after a real person, one of the biggest ranch operators in West Texas in the 1940s and well into the 1950s. I knew him fairly well. Eventually, like Mauldin, he lost almost everything he had.

When the book came out, I was a little nervous that he would recognize himself in the story—I didn't see how he could possibly miss the connection if he read it. One day I ran into him at the San Angelo auction. He said, "I just read your book." I thought, "Oh God, here it comes."

He said, "You know, I sure did enjoy it. That old Charlie Flagg was just like me."

He never tumbled to the fact that he was Page Mauldin, not Charlie. And you can believe that I never told him any differently.

Fiction writers share one advantage with painters: if they don't like something where it is, they can move it.

In my mind, I set *The Time it Never Rained* in the area around Eldorado, south of San Angelo. It had many of the kinds of settings I needed, a good combination of ranchlands and farmlands. Now, Eldorado is a nice town, and I have had a lot of friends there, but it doesn't have all the features I needed for my story. As an example, the book opens in the courthouse, and I wanted a nice Victorian courthouse, not a plain square type like Eldorado's. So I just moved the 1880s courthouse from Paint Rock down to Eldorado, which I called Rio Seco in the story.

The Eldorado wool warehouse didn't quite fit the needs of my story, either, but there is a big one down at Sonora that was just right, so I moved it.

<52>

There is a little scene in the book where Charlie pauses in the warehouse to look at a coyote that has been badly stuffed. His legs are all out of kilter, his eyes are bugged out. His body is shaped like a square bale of hay. At his feet is an ironic little sign: "Bitten by a Boston wool buyer."

Actually, I saw that one time in a wool warehouse in Eden.

The story has a coyote hunt. Cowboys are supposed to be wild, but you've never seen wild riding until you've seen a bunch of sheepmen after a coyote. I've known some pretty good cowboys who would back off and check it to them.

The coyote chase in my book gets pretty wild, but it is no wilder than one at Barnhart that inspired it. I remember people talking about that one for a long time.

It got some riders spilled. The airplane used in the hunt came down too low and bumped a wheel against the cab of the pickup. Luckily no one was hurt. However, my dad was on a coyote drive north of Crane one time when the pilot piled up his plane and was killed.

In the real hunt at Barnhart, they never got the coyote they were after. Late that night, long after everybody had given up and gone home, two frightened wetbacks ventured up to a neighboring ranchhouse, looking for food. They had seen that mass of horseback riders and pickups and the airplane bearing down on them. They thought they were being hunted by all the border patrolmen in the world.

They dug deep down in some brush and hid while the whole procession passed by, almost on top of them. No one saw them.

They were still lying there an hour or so later, terrified, when they saw the coyote come up out of his hiding place just a little piece away and trot off triumphant.

I used that in the story.

There is a scene in which Charlie finally is forced to sell the last of his beloved cows. He has called out a cow trader from Rio Seco to bid on them.

I based that scene fairly heavily on watching my father dicker with an old Midland horse trader named Big Boy Whatley. Dad enjoyed the challenge of trading with Big Boy. If you washed out even with Big Boy, you were in the big leagues.

<53>

One time Big Boy brought a young horse out to try to sell him to my father. He had a great story to tell. The horse was broke gentle as a dog. He knew how to watch a cow, and you could rein him with one finger. Pitch? No sir, he had never pitched a jump in his life. Why, even the womenfolks could ride him.

I used to wonder about Big Boy's womenfolks.

A cowboy named Happy Smith decided to try the horse. We've had space shots that didn't get as far off the ground as that horse threw Happy.

Dad chewed Big Boy out a little. "You told me that horse wouldn't pitch, when you knew damned well he would."

Big Boy calmly said, "That's the way I sell horses."

I also based the trader character to some degree on a sheep buyer and commission man who used to live in San Angelo. He could get awfully enthusiastic when he was trying to sell something, but he couldn't find one good thing about something you were trying to sell him.

One time he was on the telephone at the feedyard, trying to sell a string of sheep. He painted them up something grand. "Straight four-year-olds they are, but they got teeth like a yearlin'. Conformation? Why, they're big and smooth and thrifty, as good as ever walked. And wool?"

He got so carried away with himself that he laid down the telephone, spread his hands about a foot apart and declared, "I tell you, they got wool on them this long."

I have taken a lot of abuse for the final chapter of that book. It seems that most readers would rather have had the story wrap up with a good rain, and everybody happy. But life isn't often that generous. The rest of the book was patterned after life, and I thought it would be a betrayal to have it end with all the loose ends tied up neatly and all problems solved.

Those of you who have read the book know that it ends with a big rain, all right, but there is an ironic twist. It is a cold rain that catches Charlie's Angora goats fresh out of the shearing pens. Freshly-shorn Angoras are extremely sensitive to cold rain. They can chill down and die in a matter of minutes. There is a bitter joke in the ranch

<54>

country that shearing time always precedes the last cold rain of spring and the first cold rain of the fall.

Anyway, the rain comes, and Charlie loses most of the goats that have made it possible for him to survive the long drouth with a little something left of his former holdings.

It is an all-too-common incident for people in the goat business. Every one of them who has been at it some years can tell you a story. I modeled *my* story somewhat after a true article written in the 1930s by San Angelo agricultural columnist Sam Ashburn, about a loss suffered by his friend Tex Ward. That article was considered so graphic that it was once reprinted in a journalism textbook. Sam Ashburn had been dead for perhaps thirty years when I wrote the final version of *The Time it Never Rained*, but I visited his widow and asked her permission to do a little gentle plagiarism. She seemed very pleased that someone remembered Sam's work.

An old friend of mine named Leo Richardson, at Iraan, was one of the best sheepmen I ever knew. He told me a story once about the time he was trying to get a start in ranching for himself, working for cowboy wages, saving every dime he could and investing in goats. With three or four years' savings he finally built up a fair-sized bunch, only to lose almost all of them in one cold rain.

Leo was one of the many models for Charlie Flagg. When the book first came out, we happened to be in one of our periodic drouths in West Texas. Leo told me he had read all but the last chapter. He was saving that one to read when it finally rained, because he felt sure it would rain in the last chapter of the book.

I didn't have the heart to tell him how the book was going to come out.

The Good Old Boys:

THIS IS another example of literary license—moving things around. In my mind I set the story around Paul Patterson's original home, old Upland in Upton County. I changed the name to Upton City to allow me a little freedom with the facts, which is every folklorist's prerogative, not to mention fiction writers'.

<55>

A homestead was an important focal point of the story. For it, I used my grandparent's old homestead about twenty miles north of Midland and a good sixty miles from the scene of the story. I did it that way so I would always have a clear mental picture of the setting.

I have moved more things than Red Ball or Mayflower.

Hewey Calloway is the main character. The scene is 1906, Aught Six, the oldtimers would have called it. Hewey is a drifting cowboy 38 years old, going into middle age and the automobile age and not happy about either one of them.

When I was a boy on the McElroy Ranch east of Crane in the 1930s, these cowboys would come through every so often looking for work. By that time they usually seemed to be driving an old Ford or Chevy coupe instead of riding a horse, but otherwise they were pretty much the same as they would have been 30 years earlier, when my father was a boy. To some degree Hewey was patterned after them, along with a healthy dose of imagination.

I dedicated the book to a bunch of the original McElroy Ranch cowboys I had known. In one way or another, most of them had a little of Hewey Calloway in them. Or vice versa.

In the story, Hewey had just spent the winter feeding cows up in the snows of the Sangre de Cristo mountains of New Mexico. Now that summer is coming on, he is on his way down into hot West Texas to visit his brother and his family. Now, that tells you that Hewey is not totally in charge.

Brother Walter had once been a drifter like Hewey, but he has married and settled down to raise a family on a small shoestring homestead. Walter's wife Eve has affection for Hewey as a brother, but she is appalled at his lifestyle and his lack of responsibility. She is always worried that he will lure her husband or her young sons off to that same way of life.

If my grandparents were still living, I suspect they would find a lot of themselves in the characters of Walter and Eve. A lot besides just the use of their homestead for a setting.

There is another character in the book who is a kindred spirit to Hewey. His name is Snort Yarnell. He is something of a rounder, a good cowboy who gives not a thought to the consequences of anything he does.

<56>

To a large degree I modeled Snort after a cowboy named Bellcord Rutherford, who worked on ranches in the Midland-Odessa country. Every oldtimer in that country can tell you a dozen Bellcord stories. One of them concerns the way he got his nickname. I have heard several versions, but the most likely is that when he was a boy he wanted a rope, so he climbed up into the bell tower of the church and took the bell rope. Ever afterward, he was called Bellcord.

I also borrowed just a little from an old cowboy and famous roper of the 20s and 30s and 40s named Bob Crosby. Crosby was a big, rough but honest fellow who had no pretensions about him.

It is hard to overstate the esteem in which he and others like him were held in those days in the ranching country. In their environment, they were the equivalent of movie stars or rock stars.

I remember once when I was eight or ten years old, and Bob Crosby was going to rope in the Midland rodeo. My Uncle Ben took us kids over to meet him and shake his hand. I couldn't have been more awed if I had met the president.

Bob Crosby kept his fame in perspective and did not let it alter his chosen lifestyle, which was Spartan.

There is a story that he was once to be a star attraction at some rodeo. The town leaders decided to throw a big to-do for him as soon as he hit town. They prepared a barbecue and a whole blow-out, which they would kick off as soon as he checked in to the local hotel.

They waited and waited, but Bob Crosby never showed up. The barbecue got cold and the beer got warm, and the committee got egg all over their faces. Time came for the rodeo, and Crosby never had checked in. Everybody went down to the fairgrounds to start the rodeo without him. They found him camped down there with his horses under the shade trees, waiting for the show. Hotel? What did he need with a hotel? He wasn't going to be in town but three days.

He used to tell a story about the time he hurt his leg somehow. It got infected and must have verged on gangrene, because the doctor said it had to come off. Crosby did not agree with that diagnosis. The Lord had issued him two legs at birth, and he intended to check two legs back in when his time came.

So he went home and treated himself. He made up a poultice of horse manure, applied it to the wounded leg and wrapped the whole thing with an innertube.

<57>

It had a negative impact on his social life. But he saved his leg. I had Snort Yarnell tell that story in the book, on himself.

There is another character in *The Good Old Boys*, an old drifter who comes along a few chapters into the story. Of all the characters I have ever used, he probably comes about the closest to being lifted right out of real life and put in a book just as he was, or at least as I saw him. In the novel he is a senile old ex-trail driver on a wornout black horse. He comes by Walter's and Eve's homestead for a handout; he is what used to be called a chuckline rider, which meant riding from one chuckwagon or line camp to another, taking a meal or two and then moving on.

He is not given to spoiling good water by immersing his body in it, so he has a fairly ripe aroma on the downwind side. Walter welcomes him with traditional West Texas hospitality, but Eve feeds him on the porch and tries to stay upwind.

When I was a boy in the 1930s, I saw an old man just like that. He used to come by my grandparents' little ranch a couple of times a year, riding an old horse, drifting across the country to visit kinfolks.

Folks said he had been a cowboy in his time, but his time was long since past. I vividly remember watching him ride up and ask my granddad if he had any tobacco. Granddad didn't use it, but he invited the old man to stay for supper. He always did, and found a place for him to roll out his blankets and stay the night.

At the time, being just a kid, I thought the old man was a romantic figure out of the colorful Old West. I marveled at his freedom, being able to roam wherever he wanted, when he wanted. It was a good many years before I was old enough to realize the tragedy of his situation.

One day he got down from his horse to open a wire gate a few miles up the lane from my grandparents' ranch. He suffered a heart attack and died there in the gate. There was irony in the fact that he had spent his younger years an open-range cowboy, and he died in the middle of a barbed-wire fence. He died the same way he had lived: all alone.

I used him in the story as a metaphor for Hewey, 25 or 30 years down the line, if he did not change his ways and settle down. In the book I had him die just as he died in real life.

<58>

The only big liberty I took with him was that I moved him back thirty years in time, and changed his name.

The Hewey Calloway of my book could have *been* the old man I saw when I was a boy.

That is a side of the cowboy story that not many people write about, or talk about. Most cowboy stories have a strong tinge of romanticism. It spoils the mood to tell about cowboys getting old and lonely and sick, to tell of them spending their final years stove up, living on social security in some poor little house in town, or in a nursing home, bored, broke and hurting.

But I have seen it happen too many times, to too many of the best.

That is why you can laugh at the surface humor in *The Good Old Boys*. But you can cry a little too, at the sadness beneath.

I used the same theme in a little different way in *The Man Who Rode Midnight*.

Stand Proud:

I HAVE probably caught more flack from critics about *Stand Proud* than about any of my other books. Many of them disliked the main character, old cowman Frank Claymore, because he is so hard and unyielding, proud and stubborn and at times a little mean.

I didn't intend him to be any plaster saint. I meant him to be stubborn and difficult, because he had lived through a life that had made him that way. I tried to show that in the story. Some of his life was based on real history.

We fiction writers often borrow from real historic personages, though we may not call them by their true names, and we weave a certain amount of fiction around them. For instance, in *Stand Proud* you'll find a good bit of Charles Goodnight, under the guise of Frank Claymore. I am not the only one who has borrowed liberally from Goodnight. Ben Capps did it with his *Sam Chance*. Larry McMurtry did it in *Lonesome Dove*.

I guess a lot of us owe some royalties to the Goodnight estate.

One of the points J. Evetts Haley made in his biography of Goodnight was that Goodnight had no particular allegiance to the Confederacy, and he joined the frontier Rangers as a means of

<59>

avoiding service in the Confederate army. Deep down, he remained sympathetic to the Union.

My Frank Claymore shared that feeling with Goodnight. Scouting the frontier for Indians was preferable to fighting against the Union. In that service, however, he was bound under the orders of other men, and their folly got him into the disastrous battle of Dove Creek, which happened in real life just west of present San Angelo. A group of Confederate irregulars and civilian militia tied into a migrating band of Kickapoo Indians. Like Custer, they sadly misjudged the strength of the enemy, which in reality was not an enemy anyway but a friendly tribe. In short, they got whipped unmercifully. A lot of men died for nothing, and a friendly tribe of Indians turned extremely unfriendly. They became a scourge along the Mexican border for a good many years afterward.

In the story, Claymore takes an arrow in his stomach. The arrowhead stays in him the rest of his life, a constant reminder that following other men's orders can get you killed. He makes up his mind that from now on, nobody will ever again be in a position to tell him what to do. He will do what he damn well pleases, whether right or wrong. Sometimes he is woefully wrong, and he suffers for it.

There is a scene in the book where Claymore, out scouting, rides up on a hill and looks down into the most beautiful valley he has ever seen. He has a hard time tearing himself away, and the valley stays in his dreams until some years later when he is able to return to it and make it his home, which he holds—or tries to hold—against all odds.

Some years ago an old man named Ira Bird, in Coke County, told me a story about his father. He was a boy at the time of the Civil War, not quite old enough to go to the army but old enough to serve in a Ranger company scouting the Indian frontier. One day, while on a scout, he rode up on a hill and looked down upon what now is called Yellow Wolf Valley, in the western part of Coke County. It was a magnificent sight, for the valley was black with buffalo.

The scene haunted him for years, and in time he was drawn back. He found the valley and settled there, and his descendants still live in that valley today.

Like that valley, the story haunted me for years. I kept hoping for the right circumstances to come along so I could use it in a book. I finally did.

<60>

The Day The Cowboys Quit:

SOME OF you have heard me tell about the part an elderly ranchwoman named Rachal Bingham played in my writing *The Day The Cowboys Quit.*

The book was loosely based on the cowboy strike at Tascosa in 1883. In real life the cowboys lost the strike. Many of them stayed around, taking up land, running cattle of their own. The big ranchers regarded some of them as thieves. They hired Pat Garrett to ride around over the country, be seen and perhaps scare some of the undesirables into leaving. Garrett was by that time famous for having killed Billy the Kid.

I had a character roughly based on Garrett, but I could not bring him to full life. He seemed just a flat, two-dimensional villain, like Jack Palance in the movie *Shane.* The story had a hole in it where that character was concerned.

One day I interviewed an elderly ranchwoman named Rachal Bingham at Spur, and she told me a story about an oldtime gunfighter named Pink Higgins. Higgins had been a good friend of her father's. He was well up in years by the time Mrs. Bingham was grown and married Al Bingham.

The ranchers there had been suffering some rustler problems and hired Pink Higgins to stop it. One day he met one of the main suspects, a cowboy, on horseback in the middle of the road. They both drew six-shooters, and the cowboy came out second. He was buried where he fell.

A headboard was put up to mark the grave, but cattle kept rubbing against it and knocking it over. Al Bingham decided finally that it would be a good idea to put a little fence around the grave to protect it from the cattle. He put some posts and wire and lumber in his wagon and started.

Before long, who should he meet but Pink Higgins? Higgins asked him where he was going. Bingham couldn't lie to him. He told him he was going to put a fence around that grave to protect it. He sat nervously then, wondering what Higgins' reaction would be.

Higgins thought about it a minute, then said, "That's a good idea. I'll go help you." He turned around and helped Bingham put a fence around the grave of the man he himself had killed.

<61>

I interpolated that into my story. Suddenly the gunfighter, called Lafey Dodge in the book, came alive as a real human being with more than one side to his character. I think that one scene helped make the book. And I owe it to Mrs. Bingham's story.

*
* *

Several years ago John Graves was speaking to this group. He said you should never tell a fiction writer a story you want to use yourself, because he will pre-empt it, give it a few twists and make it his own.

I have always tried to be honest in most ways, but when it comes to good stories, I am as big a thief as you'll meet. What I've told you tonight is by way of being a confession.

If you have been watching me, you have noticed that all day long I have been taking notes.

Meetings of the Texas Folklore Society are like having the doors of Neiman-Marcus flung wide open, with no cashiers and no guards on duty.

And you thought I came here just for the fellowship.

<62>

JOYCE ROACH
ROBERT FLYNN

A Sense of Place

BOB: If you're from Chillicothe, Texas, sometimes you get the feeling it's not a real place. It's one of those hallucinations folks have. Like Albuquerque. People have heard of Albuquerque, although everyone knows it's not a real place. "Chillicothe," folks say. "Never heard of it." "Have you ever driven from Fort Worth to Amarillo?" "Lots of times," they say. "Then you drove through it." "Never saw it," they say.

Maybe the reason Chillicothe isn't real is because Chillicothe doesn't have much reason for existence. The only reason it's there is to give folks from Vernon and Quanah something to feel superior about. It's not a real place like Jacksboro that has a history, and a fort, and a courthouse. The Green Frog Cafe.

JOYCE: Yes, it's true. Jacksboro is superior. You mentioned driving through Chillicothe. One could not and still cannot drive through Jacksboro. One must drive around it. In addition to the other amenities you have just named such as Fort Richardson, the places known for fine cuisine and a courthouse, the town is built on a square. You simply cannot trust any town that is not built on a square. A square speaks of antiquity, of stability, and the shape of a town's personality.

BOB: Yeah, but if you were from Chillicothe you didn't have to put on airs. You didn't have to pretend you knew how to spell Chillicothe. No one else knew either. Not even the politicians could pronounce it.

JOYCE: We knew how to spell Jacksboro and we knew how to pronounce it. The word was misspelled however. It is spelled J-A-C-K-S-B-O-R-O, but the correct pronunciation is "Jackspur" as in "the spur belonging on the boot of Jack." That is why the town was so

<63>

Proof that Joyce Roach's Jacksboro has a town square. *Courtesy Joyce Roach*

named. We were educated about such historical matters early in Jacksboro. We were smart.

BOB: In real places like Jacksboro, smart kids rode to school on long buses. Dumb kids rode to school on short buses. In Chillicothe, everybody rode a short bus.

But Chillicothe was better than Jacksboro because when you told your folks there was nothing to do, they didn't argue with you. They couldn't find anything to do either. Dad used to spend whole days straightening fence staples. "What're you doing, Dad?" "I'm straightening these staples." "Don't they have to bend over the bob wire?" "I'll bend them back when I get ready to fix the fence."

I've spent whole days watching Dad straighten staples. I'd get awfully hungry before Dad would stop so Mother could fix us something to eat. Then we'd go to the house and watch her slice onions. She also sliced tomatoes but with onions you had participatory viewing. I guess those were the happiest days of my life, watching Dad straighten staples all day and then watching Mother slice onions. And it was educational. It prepared me for watching television.

JOYCE: Watching staple bending and onion peeling. That is— narrow. In Jacksboro, we watched each other and we listened and that was truly educational, hands on learning, you know. I first learned my colors from people. Mondays were big days. We inspected each other's wash on the line and reported if the socks were *gray*. I heard a man say once, "Oh, some widows do look good in *black*." The

<64>

widow Jones wore *red* soon after her husband's death, and the con-
soling deacons said she had a peace that passed all understanding. All
boys had *green* teeth, and *black-dog* breath. And the Ag boys said Mrs.
Jacobs' Sunday dress was the color of chicken-do. (We didn't use the
S word except *shucks, shoot,* and *ah, shaw,* and who wants to say
chicken-shucks or *bull-shaw.*) That meant the color was a kind of a
cross between *yellow* and *green* with some *brown* thrown in depending on what the chicken had been pecking and where. Never wear
white shoes before Easter nor after Labor Day. But you don't have to
wear shoes at all from June to August, if you don't want to. And
many-colored rainbows proved to me that God always kept his
promises and that Jacksboro, which was neither on a river or a lake
and certainly not situated on a low place, would never again be
destroyed by flood—at least the square never would, which was all
that counted.

You might not have had anything to do in Chillicothe but we
certainly did. I had my hands full just learning my colors.

BOB: You may have learned your colors, and I do admire your
chicken-do dress but you don't seem to recognize any shape but
square. Chillicothe didn't have a square. Infrequent visitors looked
in vain for what was generally known as town. "Where's town?"
"You're standing right in the middle of it." "But where is it?" Like
Oakland, there was no "there" there. Chillicothe was long. But not
very long.

Chillicothe doesn't appear on post cards because by the time they
wrote Chillicothe there was no room for Texas. And no one ever
sent a telegram.

Chillicothe has a road sign. They hired a painter to paint the road
sign, but he was one of those painters who moved his lips when he
read. Since no tourist ever slowed down when they got to Chillicothe
the painter put the sign longways, parallel to the road so folks would
have time to read it as they passed by. Which was okay except that
the whole town was between the L and the O.

JOYCE: Chillicothe is certainly a strange place, a rectangular
place, a strung-out place. What did you do for entertainment?

BOB: For entertainment you could go to church and be told you
were wicked or you could stay home and feel good about yourself. We
were Baptists. We couldn't feel good about ourselves even when we

<65>

stayed home. So a lot of Sundays we just went to church. Ministers could be entertaining though. Especially Brother Whatley whose favorite sermon was on the sin of fornification. Everytime he said "fornification" he wet his lips. He made it sound so appealing that boys dropped out of school and joined the Marines so they could get fornified.

JOYCE: Regular Sunday church wasn't especially entertaining to me, and I was a Baptist too. I had to look to other churches for entertainment. Revivals were about as much entertainment as we could hold up to, but since revivals happened in the summer time we had a spell to recover. We got a look at the ways of the heathen brothers and sisters in other denominations. I liked it when the Methodists entertained.

BOB: I went to the Methodist Church one time. The sons of bitches were singing our songs.

JOYCE: You know, don't you, that the Methodists were responsible for all those bloody songs? Oh, I know we Baptists sang them and tried to pretend that Fanny J. Crosby wrote everything, but I found out later that it was the Wesley boys who were responsible for all that bloody business. You remember—"Alas, and did my Savior bleed;" "Are you washed in the blood of the Lamb?" "And that thy blood was shed for me?" "There is a fountain filled with blood drawn from Emmanuel's veins." And what about "Blessed Assurance" which says "born of his spirit, washed in his blood?"

BOB: Joyce, Fanny Crosby wrote "Blessed Assurance."

JOYCE: Well, it doesn't matter who wrote it. The Baptists had a right to blame somebody else for something some of the time.

Testifying was even more entertaining than revival music. At revival time, the preacher would call for the testifying and then anyone who wanted to could get up and tell about the sinning he had been doing and how Jesus had washed away his sins, in blood, of course. None of us children ever testified because we were too young to know about hard sinning, but we could tell from the testifying that we had a lot to look forward to.

We played games too, for entertainment. And not just at church. Didn't you play games in Chillicothe?

BOB: We played Mumbly Peg and Blind Man's Butt.

JOYCE: Spin the Bottle, Knocking for Love, and Post Office.

<66>

BOB: Those were girls' games. We played Hide and Seek, Red Rover, and Pop the Wimp.

JOYCE: Hearts, Rummy, Dominoes.

BOB: We didn't go in much for games, but we had mysteries. Our biggest mystery happened in the high school cafeteria. There were always two things on your plate you couldn't identify. One was a meat and one wasn't.

Of course when things got real dull we could always go to the big city for entertainment. We used to go to Vernon at least once a month. In Vernon you could spend all day in the White's Auto just looking around. My Dad used to take me for walks through the town. The court house to use the toilet. The gin, the grain elevators. The court house to use the toilet. There's something about being in the city that excites the kidneys.

One time Dad took me for a walk in the Vernon cemetery, only it wasn't called the Vernon cemetery, it was called the Yamparika cemetery. That should have told me something right there. City folks named their cemetery after a perfume. We got to looking at the gravestones and there were angels, and woolly lambs, and petrified trees. And some of the stones had stories on them. We got to reading the stories about how God came and got Aunt Martha and took her away. It got dark while we were reading about God coming and taking Aunt Martha, and scary, and the angels started looking like maybe God sent them to take me away and I got scared.

I got to looking around to see if God was coming after me and a little dog jumped on my leg. Only I didn't know it was a little dog. Today I know it was a poodle, but Chillicothe didn't go in much for poodles. If a dog didn't look like a dog we didn't believe it was a dog. We were Christians.

This dog didn't look like a dog; it looked like one of them woolly lambs and I thought it was going to drag me into a grave. I didn't say much about it to Dad. I just ran. I ran across a U.S. Highway. I ran down the main street of town. I ran through a latched screen door. Leaving a permanent impression.

My Mother was mad. At my Dad. "You let my little boy run across the highway?" Mother yelled at Dad. "You let him run down the street?" "You let him run through a screen door?" Mother was pretty

<67>

sure it was Dad's fault. "Why didn't you stop him?" she screamed. "I couldn't catch him," Dad said.

JOYCE: See there! It has to do with towns built on a square again. If you had a square in Chillicothe, you wouldn't have to run through the screen door. You could have run around the square. There would have been plenty of folks to stop you. You could have got help. Maybe somebody would have counseled you, guided you, violated you. Maybe the Ku Klux Klan would have been in the midst of a burning, and you would have had a light to see by. You wouldn't have had to run plumb through a screen door. You would have been calm when you got home. You would have known that nothing in the cemetery was as death defying as life on the Jacksboro Square.

BOB: In Chillicothe the most death defying thing we had was Algebra. The only people who took Algebra were girls who were interested in comparative shopping. Chillicothe is a farming community, and farming is as death defying as anybody wants to get.

JOYCE: Chillicothe was just a hick farming town strung along the highway between rows of cotton or something. Jacksboro was a ranching town. Ranchers are superior to farmers. Naturally, I think it has to do with horses. Farmers walk behind horses, and when you spend your days behind a plow looking at a horse's rump and trying to keep from stepping in something, it affects the way you perceive the world. But when you get to ride the horses, people look up to you. They have to even if you're four feet eight. I grew up riding horses and thinking I was taller than I really was. Some kids rode their horses to school. They tied them and let them graze on the playground. They took those animals home foot sore and limping because all of us had run out and ridden them at recess, jumped them over the see-saws, or run them in a figure eight around two merry-go-rounds. That kind of training will improve the quickness in both horses and children. Jim Bob Arnold used to get his horses in shape for the round-up by letting his two boys bring the animals to school for two weeks before he gathered his steers off the range. When he did get his herd bunched, he let the Ag boys and us girls too take their pick to show at the Fort Worth Stock Show. The judges at Fort Worth had to look quick at the Jacksboro entries because the animals were so wild that it took three to get them in the ring, three more to get them out of the ring, and three to run them down when they broke for the

<68>

carnival midway. Generally, the Ag teacher just pulled the rig to one of the midway gates and waited out the show there. He never knew whether or not anybody won a ribbon. He did know that every single year he went home with more cattle than he came with. That was a kind of victory, sure enough.

BOB: You were quite a girl, Joyce. In Chillicothe girls didn't know they were the opposite sex. We didn't know it either. They smelled like boys. They dressed like boys. They talked like boys. We called them little heifers. Sometimes we called them gophers. "Hey, little heifer, wanta gopher a ride? Well, saddle up the horses while I take a leak off the back porch."

JOYCE: When I got to high school I discovered I was a girl. Up until that time, it was hard to tell. Riding horses and trying to rope steers on the Midway does nothing to establish in your mind that men and women have different functions in the world. It didn't take me long to get the hang of it in high school. Anybody and everybody who was a girl could be a cheerleader. I feel a civic duty to share and perhaps instruct you by means of quoting some Jacksboro cheers: "Purple socks, white socks, Football shoes; We'll give Chillicothe the Football blues." Or—"Big dog, little dog, flop-eared pup; Jacksboro Tigers, eat 'em up!" Or—"Chillicothe Bob, long and tall; He can pick cotton, but he can't play ball!" And another—"Harry James, Betty Grable; Come on, boys, let's show 'em you're able!"

BOB: Those are certainly morally edifying and ennobling, Joyce. Thank you for sharing those pearls with us swine. We didn't go in much for public screaming at Chillicothe. We were too dignified. We didn't spell out Chillicothe on the football field either. Not enough kids in school. We did spell C.H.S. But had to use lower case. Even then we had to use two dogs to make the seat of the h. They were good though. To be sure they didn't go running off, they brought in a couple of trained watch dogs that never moved. They guarded wherever they were placed. It worked great for halftime, but they couldn't get them off the field, and the whole second half had to be played around them. No problem though, neither team ever got to midfield. And when the game was over they picked them up with a front end loader and took them to the gin.

JOYCE: Life was pretty plain in Chillicothe. Can't you name a few good things about Chillicothe?

<69>

Robert Flynn with the spires of Chillicothe in the Background.

BOB: There were a lot of good things about Chillicothe. For one thing, everybody was famous for something. I was the first in my class to get pimples. And the last to get rid of them. I became the patron saint of the socially inadequate.

JOYCE: That is embarrrrassing. You were embarrassing. I don't remember being embarrassed about anything. Everything I did was done out of a sense of knowing that I was right. However, everyone in town got embarrassed about me every summer at revival. Revivals had a strange effect on me. I don't know whether it was the music or the testifying or the preaching or what, but every time the minister asked for people to rededicate their lives, I went running off down the aisle, at every church, at every revival to give myself to whatever the Lord needed me for. I knew God was calling me and that He could help me learn whatever it was I needed to know. I bit off more than I could chew a time or two and got in a jam, especially that time the preacher called for those who would rededicate their lives to looking after murderers and escaped lunatics at large who were known to be camped on the Brazos River. I was standing at the front already by the time the preacher got down to the particulars and about how we were to have our bedrolls and horses and camp gear ready by sun up. About all I heard was "Tonight we camp on the Brazos de Dios." It took me awhile to get sorted out just what we were going to do after we camped.

BOB: Like you, Joyce, I thought the Lord had something special for me to do. I thought he wanted me to discover beauty. It was pretty clear that I was going to have to leave Chillicothe.

JOYCE: Chillicothe isn't a pretty place, that's for certain. I have driven through it and looked between the L and the O. There aren't any trees in Chillicothe. Jacksboro is in the Western Crosstimbers. That means that there are trees, mostly oak, interspersed with rolling prairie. Trees make people feel more sure of themselves. When people have trees to get in they have a place to hide. In Chillicothe there's no place to hide. Decent people need to have secrets and a place to do things in secret. People from Chillicothe, from the Plains, are bound to be too open, too obvious, too honest, too friendly, don't you think?

BOB: I've certainly always been too honest. And I've been my share of friendly. Chillicothe is just big enough you can't forget a name. Myrtle Bailey. I always tried to forget her name. And telephone number. Somebody wrote her telephone number on the end of my belt. Everytime I put on my trousers and started to buckle my belt there it was: "When things go wrong call Myrtle Bailey." Myrtle

<71>

Bailey fixed flats down at the Conoco and drove the wrecker, and when I started driving, Dad wrote her name and telephone number inside my belt. I still think of her sometimes when I buckle my belt, and remember the way she could blow up a truck tire without using a pump.

The only person who ever forgot Myrtle Bailey's name was Brother Patrick. Brother Patrick had been pastor of the Baptist Church for thirty years. He had been there so long he sometimes mistook grown children for their parents. He had been pastor so long he didn't have to have help for eulogies and he didn't bother with wedding rehearsals. Until he married Ben Tooley and Sue Beach.

Old Brother Patrick looked at the two youngsters before him and got a little confused. He was pretty sure that Ben was a Tooley. You could always tell a Tooley, but you couldn't tell them much. A name came to him. David. No, David was the groom's father. Or uncle. Scott. Scott Tooley. No, Scott was a Dismuke. The Tooleys and Dismukes had married each other until the only way you could tell them apart was that the Dismukes drove Fords. The Tooleys wouldn't be caught dead in anything but a Chevrolet. There was one divorce when the new couple couldn't agree whether they would buy a Ford like his father or a Chevrolet like her mother. But usually when a Tooley and a Dismuke got married they joined the Plymouths.

The crowd in church was getting restive while Brother Patrick wrestled with the name of the bride and groom. The groom fidgeted like he was ready to bolt from the church, and the bride was on the verge of tears. Brother Patrick began a halting homily on the sacredness of marriage, hoping the names would come to him. Sue Beach. He was sure of the bride's name. Or Shirley? He was certain he had the right family but was Sue the mother or the daughter?

The congregation was getting impatient, the bride and groom were eyeing each other, ready to call the whole thing off. Brother Patrick knew he could delay no longer. In his desperation, he whispered a prayer and the answer descended like a dove. He would get the names from the bride and groom. Turning to the groom, he asked, "In what name do you come to be married?"

The groom's eyes rolled back in his head. No one told him that question was going to be on the exam. His agile brain raced through the lecture his mother had given him about honeymoon finances,

<72>

the speech his father had made about motel etiquette, the Chillicothe high school Fight song, the creed of the Future Farmers of America, back to the summer he went to Vacation Bible School. "I come," he said, "in the name of our Lord Jesus Christ."

In desperation Brother Patrick gave up the game. "What does your mother call you?" he asked.

"Puffen," said Ben Tooley.

"Puffen," Brother Patrick said, "do you take —" The bride's first name had slipped completely from his head. "Do you take this Beach to be your wife?"

The affair was such a disaster that afterwards at every wedding, for as long as Brother Patrick was pastor, the bride and groom wore name tags. There was even a ceremony where the best man got to remove the bride's name tag from her bodice. Men who had married women from outside Chillicothe had to explain the custom. But in Chillicothe the name tags became so popular that some Methodists wore them at their weddings. The Methodists, though, went in more for plastic rather than the traditional mother of pearl.

Weddings were among my favorite times. What were your favorite times?

JOYCE: My favorite time was the Depression.

BOB: In Chillicothe we didn't know when the Depression began. We didn't know when it was over either.

JOYCE: During the Depression, nobody had anything, but we all had such a large share of nothing and we all had nothing in equal proportions. Nobody had more of nothing than any other person had of nothing, and so we all had plenty. And when you have plenty, then no one wants for more. My daddy had a job, my mother was my mother, and I was an only child. We could hardly keep up with the schedule for the week. There was church twice on Sunday, well, really four times, if you counted Sunday School and Training Union and once Wednesday or twice if you counted Girls Auxiliary or Royal Ambassadors before prayer meeting. There was school every day. Girl Scouts met on Thursday afternoon. UIL practice in softball or play practice or extemporaneous speaking or poetry reading took up the spring. Football and band when we could field either a team or a band took up the fall. Ice cream socials and horseback riding every day filled up the summer unless you broke it up with a camping

<73>

Joyce Roach and Robert Flynn. "Somewhere out yonder we'll find that perfect place, and we'll name it Chilliboro! . . . or Jacksicothe?"

trip or two to the Brazos River to hunt lunatics. Every other minute was taken up with scripture memorizing or Bible study to help fill in the gaps in our educations.

Sometimes we tried to rest up a little. Mostly we rested in the summer time lying out in the yard on a quilt beneath a highway of Milky Way stars. The full moon gave you a general idea about how far up heaven was, and the dark ground which held my body and those of my playmates marked down as far as any of us thought about going. Outer boundaries changed with whatever mental images we conjured brought on by ghost stories, songs with four-part harmony, family sagas, recounting of brave or tender lovers, dirty jokes, word games, how Ruth said, "Whither thou goest," and little Samuel said, "Speak for thy servant heareth." I first heard the line, "I have seen the

<74>

world in a blade of grass," and later knew that I could not see the microcosm in a blade of grass. I did, however, know the world contained on the perfect square of a family mosaic quilt or a courthouse square and knew that latitude and longitude were ample enough to reveal the universe, were at the very least as big as the universe.

My second favorite occasion was World War Two. World War Two only confirmed my good judgment about the Depression. We knew joy collectively and sorrow too. Even our soldiers from Jacksboro went as a group into battle because they were a National Guard unit. Collectively they went overseas and disappeared collectively as a part of the Lost Battalion in the jungles of Burma. And as a town we waited somewhere between life and death, lost and found, anticipation and dread until the Lost should reappear. But we waited together.

I even learned that the world is not square but round in Jacksboro. Down on my knees beside my grandmother as she prayed and I repeated the lines after her, I learned that the world stretched beyond the square and only became rounded with the journey from self. I became acquainted with the Japanese, "those slanty-eyed, runty Japs," who terrorized my Uncle Fred at Iwo Jimo or when he found himself pinned down on the beach in a snow storm dressed in Navy-blue winter gear. I learned too of those "boot stomping Hitler-Germans" in Africa with Rommel, the Desert Fox, who thwarted my Uncle Glen, the Odessa Oilfield Giant. And from the same heart's words I learned "forgive seventy times seven"—two lessons at the same time and from the same mouth of a grandmother whose last name was Hartman.

In other ways I learned two lessons which always live side by side in a small town—the best and the worst.

And I learned about triangles. God the Father, God the Son, and God the Holy Spirit; thesis, antithesis, synthesis; triads, triarchy, triaxial, tricycles. From Jacksboro I early found the Texas triptych—Texas fact, fiction, and folklore.

I learned my colors and my shapes; squares, rectangles, triangles, and that one meaning of round is "without sharp edges." Jacksboro taught me all I need to know or ever needed to know. All the lessons came from a sense of place and being appropriate to that time and

<75>

place no matter how it might look to someone else because you couldn't help yourself.

Maybe it is true that you can't really go home again. But you carry home with you over the years for better or worse. Sometimes home hangs like an albatross around my neck and "with a glittering eye" I must speak of Jacksboro and "all those who dwell therein." At times, I exorcise the pain and sometimes, as if by the telling, I speak the place into existence like Brigadoon. The sense of that place and those people is never very far from my mind and rises both bidden and unbidden to haunt, to comfort, to terrorize, and to charm, to find its way into my words both written and spoken.

BOB: The best thing about Chillicothe was everyone was your family. They may not have been your friend but they treated you like family. They spoke when they passed on the street. They waved when they passed on the road. They stopped if you looked like you needed help. And if you were in trouble the whole town was on your side. Wherever I may be in the world, I know that in Chillicothe folks still sing about "A Hill Far Away."

JOYCE: My favorite song is "Softly and Tenderly."

BOB: Why?

JOYCE: Because it's about home and heaven. I think heaven will surely contain some of Jacksboro and Chillicothe, or I won't go. And when the song says "Come home, come home; ye who are weary come home" I know The Father had Jacksboro and Chillicothe in mind.

BOB: Bless our towns, bless our homes, and bless all those within them.

<76>

PAUL CLOIS STONE

Brush Country, Vaqueros, and Hamlet's Ghost
J. Frank Dobie and the Magic of a Tale

THIS YEAR marks a quarter century since J. Frank Dobie's death. Last year was his and Walter Prescott Webb's centennial year, an occasion marked by the Texas State Historical Association's special issue devoted to these two. That particular issue of the *Southwestern Historical Quarterly* (Volume XCII, No. 1) was all the more important in the study of our region, and I would argue, in the nation's cultural history because of the insightful though critical reappraisal of Dobie by Professor Don Graham of the University of Texas at Austin. Though I disagree with a number of his conclusions on the "whither Dobie" question, I cannot disagree with his approach. The Dobie persona needs to be distinguished from the record of Dobie the scholar, teacher, and author. However, that is not a simple task. In fact, it is quite a difficult one considering it is the Dobie persona or legend, combined with the written record, which will be a permanent part of American cultural and literary history, not to mention our folklore.

Professor Graham's critique of the Dobie mystique gave us a new look at the criticism of what I call "Dobie culture" which Larry McMurtry advanced twenty-one years ago. I think Graham can be paraphrased as follows: McMurtry found Texans' near exclusive adulation of Dobie, along with Webb and Bedichek to be a bit much. Appreciation of the three, Dobie in particular, was limited geographically, and by strong implication, intellectually. He wrote "The world outside never heard of Bedichek, hasn't read Webb, and isn't particularly interested in Dobie. The world inside doesn't read much and doesn't read well, but the three were loved and honored here. Their merits as men were long ago confused with their merits as

<77>

J. Frank Dobie

<78>

writers . . . and few of the people who loved them had any skill in judging books."[1]

There is no question that Graham also thinks a much clearer distinction must be made now between the Dobie legend and his actual successes as a writer. I found McMurtry's criticism unsettling then, and I find it even more so now.

Another of McMurtry's observations quoted in part by Graham: "[Dobie] has had the largest audience of any Texas writer, but at that it is an audience composed primarily of middle-aged nostalgics, and it will probably not outlive him much more than a generation."[2] It is not clear whether McMurtry's objection then had more to do with Dobie or the so-called "middle-aged nostalgics," or, as Professor Graham suggests, at McMurtry's having been snubbed by Don Pancho. Whatever the case, McMurtry's observation was that of the boy from Archer City, tired of men who read next to nothing, or thought they were supposed to read nothing but J. Frank, who has himself discovered the wide world of Norman Mailer, Flaubert, and Terry Southern, and thereby finds himself distinctively happier in the new, better read urban Texas than in the company of nostalgic cow men. In fairness to McMurtry, he did have a point.

Given my own experience as an observer of American culture and a student of Western history, I take a different view regarding the disposition of the Dobie legacy. From my perspective it has seemed that a general sense of Frank Dobie's importance in the formal national academic community has grown since 1964 and that it will continue growing in the twenty-five years to come. Frankly, I am in the academic program I am in because of my interest in Dobie and what his life and work tell us about American history. This is not said to denigrate other Texas or Southwestern writers, but it is true that others do not, and have not commanded the constant attention and respect that Dobie has in my university, Yale. That is said without chauvinism but with respect to the claims that Yale can make to being one of the leading centers for the study of the American West.

It's also been my experience in attending three of the Elko Cowboy Poetry Gatherings and similar events to observe that Dobie is now more recognized across the North American West as a major, once-in-a-century representative of the "cow country" cultural experience than was the case a quarter century before. Among cow

<79>

people, an audience Dobie unapologetically wrote for, and, of course this is the title of his last book, his influence is undiminished. One example is singer Ian Tyson's composition "Murder Steer," based on a chapter in *The Longhorns*. Another is Don Edwards' song and recitation, "Stompede," which relies verbatim on different texts from the same book.[3] Listen to some of the Dobie material my friend from Weatherford used: "The air is still and hot, the sky becomes overcast, as sheet lightning begins blinking along the horizon ... The two herders stop and listen. The cattle and the night are too quiet ... At that moment, the lead steer of the herd awakens, rises to his knees and looks around. He gets to his feet and turns to smell the approaching storm ... Then, almost at once, on every tip of five-thousand horns appeared a ball of phosphorescent light—the Fox-Fire, St. Elmo's Fire."[4] I contend this is pretty good. There is some magic here.

Nevertheless, the problems which students of intellectual, cultural and for that matter, emotional history, find in Dobie are ones which will not go away. In fact, they should be studied with a far more critical eye than has often been the case in the past. However, as we do that, I think we need to bring with us an implicit criticism of ourselves as readers and of our culture as one which, in many ways, has lost a sense of the mysterious and of wonder in nature including our own nature as human beings.

I want only to say a few more "academic" things about Dobie, since this is a paper about folklore and not about history, and I must apologize that some of this is about me. Buster Welch says that he is not a horse trainer, that he doesn't know that much about training horses for cutting horse competitions. He says of himself that he's a cowman, that what he does know is something about instinct, intelligence, and emotion and something about the interaction between human beings, animals, and their environments. Of course, Buster Welch is a horse trainer—most would say the very best, but he differs from some other trainers and cutters because of where it is he understands himself coming from intellectually and historically. Buster Welch's comment is a recognition of the richness and the mystery of millenia of herdsman culture, for which there is no comparison in even the richest cutting horse futurity. That is the point of his disclaimer.

<80>

I am a historian in training, and for the past two years my attention has mostly been devoted to research and studying historiography. This is basic professional training. However, there is another aspect of this training which is outside of the institutional process. Reading and remembering, hearing and remembering, and thinking about what is worth remembering and trying to hear, has been an important part of this. In attempting to discover, and in some cases define, major themes in Western history, whether land use, regional literature, cultural pluralism, gender issues, or education and urbanization, I find that there is no way not to include Dobie.

That is where Dobie's importance is so clear. Like him, or not, what he stands for or not, he's similar to Frederick Jackson Turner. He is always there and always part of the discussion, both of the history of this country and the question of what kinds of transformational experiences go into making an American.

Turner viewed the frontier as the dominant factor. Dobie did not think it was that simple. For him, the frontier might change a person, but not nearly so much as the stories which a frontier experience either gave birth to or itself changed in small or great ways. For Dobie, the underlying human truths were apparent in stories. This is a remarkably sophisticated realization.

In the 1961 publication of this society, Dobie wrote: "I accept without reservation the ghost in Hamlet but reject the Holy Ghost as a metaphysical superstition."[5] His context is a story he learned from the vaquero Santos Cortez which had to do with a *bulto*, a "ghostly bulk."

That essay, "Storytellers I have Known," was reprinted and sent out by the Dobies as a Christmas card that year. I first read it this past May while doing some research on the career of Henry Nash Smith. Smith, interestingly enough, figures into it since he was along with Dobie on the 1933 trip to Mexico which resulted in some of the material for *Tongues of the Monte*.

I was struck by Dobie's metaphysical pronouncement and doubt, and though not surprised, also not persuaded or moved. My first impression was that this was a little like the newly agnosticized college freshman rejecting the idea of a personal God.

However, Dobie was talking about something else. Of Cortez he says, "(He) believed in ghosts. That's where the intellect of a

<81>

sophisticate comes in." Here again my reaction is varied. It is tempting to substitute the word "sophist" for sophisticate. Is Dobie to be trusted on theological matters more than Augustine, Aquinas, Paul Tillich, or for that matter, Thomas Merton? I do not think so, and at the risk of sounding elitist I do not see why Cortez's spirituality should command more respect than any of these worthies. I've always looked for a statement in Dobie's published or unpublished work analogous to Kenneth Rexroth's realization that Tertullian, Ignatius of Antioch, and Augustine were every bit as intelligent as Eugene Debs and Clarence Darrow. I have not found this in Dobie yet, but I keep looking.

Nevertheless, Dobie's statement cannot be understood on the superficial level of my first reaction. His is an affirmation of the magic of real experience, the real "spiritual" experience of a story being told and heard, over rather dry, and perhaps meaningless doctrine. It is a statement about folklore and the ghostly presence it can command or invoke, not about social assumptions derived from theology or denominational tradition. The difference is that the former conveys some sense of life and vitality; whereas the latter might not. One has to do with people's lives, in many cases as they are being transformed, and the other, with assumptions about what truth is supposed to be.

In the text for a speech which was prepared for but not delivered at the regional writers conference in Corpus Christi, June, 1955, he wrote: "The inner lives of human beings of the West have not yet been treated. Contrast *The Virginian* with Owen Wister's journal made while he was gathering data for writing."[6] Santos Cortez's bulto was to Dobie quite real. It was the shadow of an inner life.

Did Dobie write successfully about the inner lives of Western People? No, but I think he was always on the verge of doing so. On the other hand, perhaps he did; it is simply that we do not have the sophistication to understand how he was attempting to do it.

For him the inner life was a ghostly presence directly connected to cultures which were themselves conscious emanations of regional history and memory. This presence had to do with home. It was in this context that Hamlet's ghost and the brush country bulto were of equal importance. I believe he has been seriously misunderstood in this regard.

<82>

In the mid Fifties, Dobie, returning from a trip to England was entertained by the Yale Collection of Western Americana, which was then housed in Sterling Memorial Library. Archibald Hanna, the curator of that collection, had arranged for the visit. Dobie, speaking to Professor Howard Lamar, remarked that as he woke in London the first morning of that last trip he wondered to himself why he had been away from home so long.

Where was Dobie's home? What did the word mean to him? Surely it was more than a place, Live Oak County or the house in Austin. Home was some place in the spirit of a people interacting with a landscape, either natural or man-made, a landscape with a history which haunted them. In many senses he was at home in that place where a story is formed. One of his major influences was the body of English literature, and I think in some way he wanted to be an American Addison, to be able to present a people to themselves, if not by describing their manners, then by telling their stories.

Dobie, like Santos Cortez and Hamlet, understood the beautiful terror of a haunting presence, a presence which could be a culture or the inheritance of many cultures. In his diary from his student days at Columbia University, 1913-14, he wrote: "Tonight with Mary and Woods I went to see Forbes Robertson in his American farewell representation of *Hamlet*. All in all it was the greatest dramatic performance of the greatest poet I have ever seen."[7]

This theme emerges again some forty years later. In his unpublished article "Panther: Hunter and Fellow Mortal," he wrote: "At the scent of the morning air, the panther, like Hamlet's ghost, always has to vanish."[8]

As a writer, Dobie's real voice, the voice of his inner life was like that panther and like Hamlet's ghost. It was an archetypal image of a past which seemingly flees from the light and the present. On the basis of my reading of quite a few Dobie manuscripts, letters, and fly leaf inscriptions over the past two years I'm convinced he was a man of the nineteenth and not the twentieth century and that efforts of his own and those of others, including Bedichek, to make him more "contemporary" were what most hindered his talents as a writer.

Thanksgiving night, 1913, Dobie attended a Metropolitan Opera performance of *Parsifal*. He wrote: "(I) thought it the most sublime music I have ever heard. All day I have been in a kind of sad dream,

<83>

shunning noises, and hoping that there is a personal God . . . Few know what longings and loveliness come with such feelings." Is this the same writer of the 1961 "Storytellers I Have Known?" In some ways I think it is a more mature one, one more easily transformed in spirit by the great theme or story—one more willing to participate in the magic of that experience. However, that is not something he completely lost.

Dobie also wrote of Santos Cortez, "(He) would explain that he was bored with talk about cow tracks, bogged down cows, some vaquero's horse that got a thorn in his knee and things like that. He wanted conversation. Conversation generally consisted of his encounters with deer, men and ghosts."[9]

The extended quotation states that these stories reminded him of John A. Lomax's collection of cowboy songs and ballads and inspired him to collect traditional tales of Texas, the Southwest, and Mexico. By no means, though, were these tales just of cow tracks, cow bogs, and thorny-kneed horses. Dobie was consistently after that mystery contained both in a tale and in the telling of it. The same TFS article contains a paraphrase of Charles Badger Clark's poem, "The Glory Trail," and the Nicene Creed, which directly addresses the sometimes supernatural sources of a good story: "After having received, high up in the Mogollons, among the mountain tops, *authentic tidings of things both visible and invisible*, I went to Santa Fe on the road to Texas."[10]

What is present here is a much more profound and deeper sense of spirituality than has been commonly credited to Dobie. He is most reminiscent of Joseph Campbell in that the story is viewed as the thing which both creates the language and, in turn, the culture.

This, I believe, is the real task in studying folklore. Dobie understood that, and in most cases I do not think we instinctively do. Our "generic culture," as cowboy poet Baxter Black calls it, has done countless awful things to the basic human sense of awe, or terror and wonder which are, at times, virtually the same thing. To look for the greatest mystery or secret, claimed the Renaissance Hermeticists and Neoplatonists, one needed go observe the trivial, to study the commonplace and contemplate the obvious. Dobie turned to the stories of Nat Straw, John Young, and George Saunders, and to tales of gold nuggets the size of oranges lying in Mexican canyons which only a few poor fools and dreamers are permitted to see. Saunders and

<84>

Young, men who were called *vaqueros* as well as cowboys, were symbols of a herdsman culture in transition. The word vaquero describes part of that transition. The treasure and lost-mine stories were small but bright reflections of the great story, the quest of Parsifal for the Grail.

Dobie's place in literary and cultural history is secure because of this. The pity is that it was not a quality which was as developed in his literary style as it could have been. There was only one *Tongues of the Monte*, after all.

However, that is not entirely his fault. Many of Dobie's friends were encouraging him to develop other qualities as a writer, good qualities, perhaps more practical or modern ones, but nevertheless other qualities. It was his mother, I have recently learned from Wilson Hudson, who first insisted he stop living in the past.

As a writer Dobie was at his best when searching for that inner spark of vitality which can only be found in the past, a past which, like the panther, might flee the morning but is always present in the reality of shade. Far from being a threatening presence, Dobie found it to be a strengthening one. As Po Campo says of Deet's ghost in *Lonesome Dove*, "The dead can help us if we let them, and if they want to."[11]

Notes

1. Larry McMurtry, *In a Narrow Grave*, Encino Press, Austin, 1968, 31.
2. Ibid., 44.
3. Ian Tyson, *Ian Tyson*, CBS LP FC 39362, 1984. "'The Murder Steer' is based on an actual tragic event that occurred in west Texas nearly a century ago and was recounted in J. Frank Dobie's *The Longhorns*. The players in this real-life drama were Fine Gilleland, representing the Wentworth and Dubois outfit, and Henry Harrison Powe, a one-armed Confederate veteran-turned-rancher. And of course there was the disputed yearling bull (technically not a steer because he did not receive the requisite and customary range surgery) that was emblazoned with the word *murder* to mark the grizzly incident. The phantom longhorn that allegedly materialized for several years in bunkhouse windows and dusky thickets of the Big Bend country lives on in this quintessentially western Tyson original. 'Ghost Riders in the Sky,' watch out."—Jay Dusard in the album liner notes.

<85>

4. Don Edwards, *Songs of the Cowboy*, Sevenshoux Publishing, Weatherford, Texas, 40.

5. Publications of the Texas Folklore Society, *Singers and Storytellers*, Southern Methodist University Press, Dallas, 1961, 4.

6. Manuscript, Southwest Writers Collection, Southwest Texas State University, San Marcos.

7. Dobie, Columbia Diary, unpublished manuscript, Southwest Writers Collection, Southwest Texas State University, San Marcos.

8. Manuscript in the Southwest Writers Collection, 20.

9. *Singers and Storytellers*, 4.

10. Ibid., 13.

11. Larry McMurtry, *Lonesome Dove*, Simon and Schuster, New York, 1985, 770.

J. FRANK DOBIE

Curiosity in Deer

WHEN I went to manage my Uncle Jim Dobie's big Olmos ranch in La Salle County in 1920, I associated with more deer than I have associated with anywhere else. More than once, riding around, I counted one hundred or more in one day. At that time the custom of big ranches down in the brush country was to feed venison to the hands a good part of the year.

Along in the fall I kept seeing a pair of bucks nearly every time I passed a certain dirt tank in the San Casimero Pasture trap. I drove an old T-model Ford without any top. One day before I started out, the cook at the ranch house told me that we needed meat. I knew that on the way home I was going to pass by the tank where I had been seeing the two bucks and thought I might get one. I did see them, but they saw me first and galloped off into the brush of a small hill maybe two hundred yards away. I felt sure that they would not go far. I got out of the car, took my .30-30, and with the wind in my favor circled through low scattering brush to get a view of the far side of the hill. When I got around, moving cautiously, there, about one hundred yards away, stood one of the bucks. I am a poor shot, but I broke his neck. He was a heavy ten-pointer and packed lots of tallow. After gutting him, I picked up my rifle and started back to the car to drive it as near as I could to the carcass.

I took a direct route back to the car instead of walking in the circuit I had made away from it. Only thirty or forty yards from the carcass, I was walking along a narrow, dim trail through thick high brush when the second buck and I met face to face. He literally fell over himself, fell to the ground in a kind of somersault as he tried to run around in the narrow passage. Two or three steps behind him the brush was sparser, not more than breast high and mingled with

<87>

prickly pear. Scared is no word to define his condition of fright—but he did not know exactly what had scared him. His curiosity, mixed with masculine fighting spirit, was so strong that he was not going to leave without satisfying himself about what had scared him. He wheeled facing me not more than twelve feet away. While he was tumbling over himself getting away, I had advanced two or three steps, my movement, I suppose, unseen by him. I could have counted, almost, the hairs in his eyelashes.

He was blue-black, and like his mate, as fat as a mutton. Like his mate also, he had ten points, heavy beamed, wide-spread antlers. He was snorting, and the wind was coming out of his lungs with such force that it shook the black-chaparral leaves in front of him. He lowered his head a little and raised it. He was planted on the ground like a cow pony squatting down to hold a roped steer. His instinct was to charge, for he was still not sure what had scared him.

Now I stood transfixed in wonder, gazing at him while he gazed at me. I was not making any breathing sounds, however, as he was making. I had my rifle leveled on him, ready to shoot in case he charged, but I did not want to shoot. It was a hottish October day, and I had all the meat headquarters had any use for. We did not stand thus more than two or three minutes, I suppose. The fine buck, finally comprehending that what had scared him and what now faced him was the deadly enemy of all deerkind, wheeled and in a second or two was out of sight.

Along in December following I was riding horseback one late evening in a fine mist that cut visibility down to a low point. I was riding a big, sorrel, hard-mouthed horse we called Pilón, because he had been thrown in as a *pilón* (something extra) with a herd of steers Uncle Jim had bought. The young deer, coming yearlings, had mostly cut off from the does and were bunching together, as is their habit in good deer country. While I was approaching the wide sacahuiste (salt grass) flat that spreads out on both sides of the Nueces River in this part of southern Texas, I saw two or three yearlings in scattered mesquites that edged the sacahuiste.

I saw them before they saw me and reined Pilón to a halt. One of the yearling deer must have seen me just as the halt was made. He, or she, moved forward to see what that looming object in the mist might be. The move was made cautiously, slowly. The other year-

<88>

A curious deer. *Courtesy James C. Kroll*

lings in sight also moved a little closer, all very much interested. At the same time other yearlings I had not at first seen began emerging from the brush and mist. Pilón did not make a single move, and I didn't either. He must have stood, while I sat motionless, for ten minutes. By the end of that time between fifteen and twenty yearling deer were standing in a semi-circle facing us. Once in a while one would stamp his little feet in petulance, as if to say, "Why doesn't this thing satisfy our curiosity? What is it?"

The light was getting dimmer, for it was growing dusk. Presently a young fellow on the left point of the circle got a whiff of human scent. I suppose he got a whiff. He wasn't more than thirty feet away. Away he went, and away went all his companions.

*
* *

Young deer have more idle curiosity than mature ones. One winter day I was hunting in Uvalde County, a Mexican boy with me to help carry the bag if I killed something. The weather turned misty, and about noon, after a round afoot, I came back to the car and drove off a dim ranch road to some big live oak trees that would shelter us

<89>

while eating lunch. We built a fire. The damp wood gave off a heavy pleasant-smelling smoke.

While we were squatting down eating and drinking coffee, I saw two yearling deer approach. I warned the Mexican boy not to move. The yearlings had not seen us, I think; they had seen the smoke and perhaps smelled it. They came slowly, stopping often. They came so close that I could have chunked one with a stick of wood. They wanted to find out what the smoke was. It is their nature to distrust, fear anything strange; it is also their nature to investigate it.

Another time, late in the day, I was walking for pleasure in a pasture near Kerrville. On the side of a wooded hill I saw two deer not far below me in trees and brush. They saw me and became alert about the time I saw them. I stopped, my body blended with a tree, before they had a sure view. For minutes they stood, eager for some revealing movement that I would not make. Then they moved so that I lost sight of them. They were south of me and the wind was from the south. I had no idea that they were circling to get a smell of the thing they had seen. I remained absolutely still. Ten or fifteen minutes later I heard a snort—the deer "whistle"—to the northwest, looked and got one fleeting glimpse of a rapidly moving flag. Smell had given them the information they were after.

I stood still at dusk beside a wide tank of water and watched a doe on the other side all but have a fit from curiosity about my presence. She stamped and jumped up and down, having a "regular conniption fit." "What is it and why doesn't it move?" her actions asked. Here was an intruder, she knew, perhaps human. She did not know about guns and the lack of safety from them in clear space—something most old bucks and many wise old does know. Any deer wise from experience would have left, but this doe had more curiosity than caution, and she was certainly irritated at being baffled. I tired of her antics and walked away. My motion satisfied her curiosity and with a snort she sprang into the brush, where she should have gone when she first discovered me.

One time I was driving in a topless T-model Ford along the brushy rim of a dry lake. The road was rough and I was going slowly when I glimpsed a doe and fawn back in the brush just off the road. I had my Kodak, wanted a picture, and stopped, letting the engine idle

<90>

while I remained seated. Presently a yearling deer that I had not seen walked out into the clearing near the car. He was soon followed by a spotted fawn I had seen. It is not usual for a yearling to stay with its mother after she fawns, but here doe, yearling and fawn all were.

The doe kept making a low bleating sound, telling her young ones to come back. But the yearling knew more than his mother. Nobody was going to boss him. I could not see the doe, but her voice told me how anxious she was. The yearling had no doubt seen and heard the car. Now, out in the open, maybe fifteen yards to the rear, he could hear the engine and smell its fumes. The fawn was not old enough to have much curiosity but wanted to experience something with the yearling adventurer. It would not heed the mother's warning either. The low bleats were not continuous but were repeated several times. The yearling stamped his front feet, came closer, stamped more. Neither the car nor I made any response. Finally the yearling's curiosity subsided. In his way he must have concluded that the car was a part of the landscape. He began grazing on a low weed that grew more abundantly on the lake soil than on higher ground around it. The fawn was still with him; the doe, still invisible, had ceased to bleat. The yearling had satisfied its curiosity, and when I drove away, he made a short move to one side but was otherwise indifferent.

<91>

Bertha & Frank Dobie at Paisano by Edgar Kincaid. *Courtesy Southwestern Writers Collection, Southwest Texas State University and Bill Wittliff*

<92>

BERTHA McKEE DOBIE

The Pleasure Frank Dobie Took in Grass
Read by Wilson M. Hudson at the
1972 TFS meeting in College Station

WHEN Librarian John B. Smith telephoned to invite me to the serious festivities of this day and to speak briefly on the life of J. Frank Dobie I replied that the subject was large. More specifically, what should I talk about? "Whatever you wish," Mr. Smith said. "But the program has to go to the printer. I'll put 'J. Frank Dobie' down, and then you can limit it as you choose."

I have restricted the subject to the pleasure Frank Dobie took in grass. It's not, I think, inappropriate to this occasion. Mr. Jeff Dykes and Frank Dobie were friends. Both were great practitioners of what Frank delighted to call "the art of conversation." They knew how to tell tales and to laugh at them. Both built libraries on Texas and the West. Both knew a good deal about the political, economic, and ecological history of the state in which they were born. Mr. Dykes was a professional soil conservationist, Frank, an amateur. Their friendship was rooted in the soil of Texas and knotted with a blade of tough grass.

During Frank's childhood on a Live Oak County ranch grass seems not to have kindled his imagination. The brush—that vast, all but impenetrable tangle of bushes, low trees, and cactus did. His writings contain no recollective passage on grass to set beside the eloquent description of brush in *A Vaquero of the Brush Country*. The coarse, wiry sacahuiste through which he guided his horse the year he managed his Uncle Jim's ranch out west in La Salle County was, however, something beyond the means to an economic end. He enjoyed it.

<93>

The period of which I speak today came much later with the purchase in 1952 of a small ranch in Burnet County which we named Cherry Springs for it's wild cherry trees and clear-flowing springs. From the front porch was the kind of prospect Frank liked best, a meadow, or what might become a meadow. It had been a field, but for years had not been cultivated. Weeds and the special weeds we call wild flowers covered it. Bunches of little bluestem, seeded by nature from an overlooking hill where that grass grew abundantly, were scattered over it. In his first spring of ownership Frank had seeds of buffalo grass and side-oats grama, many bags of them, broadcast over that old field. In his eagerness he would get down on his hands and knees to look for sproutings. He went to Waco to visit R. C. Mauldin, a botanist who raised native grasses or seed, and was thrilled to see what native grass had done to restore old wornout land. In a letter to Frank Mr. Mauldin wrote, "I am saving several kinds of grass seed for you. Some are just samples." Frank took friends and family over the hills that comprise the greater part of Cherry Springs Ranch and pointed out the native grasses: the dominant little bluestem, some side-oats grama, here and there a clump of hairy grama, and beside sloughs tall, handsome Indian grass. Three-awn needle grass through which we walked to a maidenhair fern bank on Fall Creek did not need to be pointed out. It introduced itself. Wilson Hudson, a friend to whom Frank gave side-oats grama seed and a few roots of Indian grass to put in his back yard, tells me that he still has a few plants of side-oats grama and until the past summer, when drought became severe, had Indian grass.

This was the period during which Frank wrote, "No matter what improvements are put on ranch land, its essential worth consists of the grass it grows and nothing else. The combination of the practical and the beautiful in grass is singular. The sight of a turf, whether of short grass carpeting the earth or tall grass waving in the wind, restores my soul. A valley of green grass is beautiful in the way that mountains, sea, and stars are beautiful."

When Frank was hospitalized in the fall of 1957 our nephew, Edgar Kincaid, Jr., wanted to do something for him that he would really like. Edgar decided to bring in grasses from Cherry Springs. He and I drove out together. While I looked for wildflowers and found a rare ladies' tresses orchid, he cut little bluestem from the hillslopes,

<94>

tall Indian grass from moist places, side-oats grama, windmill grass, and perhaps other sorts. All were in full head. Edgar put them in an artillery shell Frank had brought back from the first World War and took them over. When Frank left the hospital some weeks later, he gave his florist's flowers to nurses, but the grasses in the brass artillery shell he had us bring home. They were not thrown out until spring.

Frank sold Cherry Springs and bought a place nearer to Austin. This retreat he named Paisano for the bird that is also called roadrunner and chaparral. Here also the dominant grass is little bluestem. One day during this period Frank and his friend Glen Evans were returning to Austin from a deer and wild turkey hunt on Ralph Johnston's Rancho Seco in Medina County. At Blanco, where they stopped for lunch they saw an exhibit of grass paintings by Vivian Caswell, a local ranchwoman. Mrs. Caswell later showed these watercolors at the Witte Museum in San Antonio, where I saw them. The day of the Blanco stop they were new to Frank. He had just come from a ranch where the restored turf was heavy with curly mesquite and buffalo grass, but the picture he chose to own is of the little bluestem. He hung the picture on a closet door—the only available wall space—of the downstairs room where by that time he worked and slept. Now it hangs in the Dobie Room at the University of Texas in Austin. From it an observer's eyes travel to an earth-colored Indian bowl filled with little bluestem grass from Paisano.

<95>

Dorothy Scarborough. *Courtesy The Texas Collection, Baylor University, Waco, Texas*

<96>

SYLVIA GRIDER

The Folksong Scholarship of Dorothy Scarborough

DOROTHY SCARBOROUGH is best known as the author of the controversial novel, *The Wind*, but her scholarly reputation rests on her work as a folklorist, especially as a collector of Appalachian and Black secular folksongs. Scarborough's interest in collecting folksongs lasted throughout her lifetime, starting when she was a child in Waco. Some of her earliest childhood memories were of going out into the cotton fields with her father and listening to the Negro field hands sing while they worked.

As an adult, Scarborough embarked upon a career as a professional academic. After completing her B.A. and M.A. degrees in English at Baylor, she taught for a year in the public schools of nearby Marlin, Texas, before returning to Baylor in the faculty of the Department of English.

In 1910, weary of the "undergrad grinds," she took a leave of absence from Baylor in order to travel abroad and study literature at Oxford University. During that year the Texas Folklore Society was founded and immediately upon her return to Baylor she joined the Society, ultimately becoming a life member. She published her first scholarly article, "Traditions of the Waco Indians," in the first publication of the Texas Folklore Society in 1916. This was a local topic to which she never returned, focusing her attention exclusively upon the study of literature and its folklore adjunct, ballad and folksong.

In 1914, Miss Dottie was elected President of the Texas Folklore Society, and for the first time the annual meeting was held away from the University of Texas campus when she hosted the meeting in the spring of 1915 at Baylor, in the Carroll Library Building. Her presidential address was entitled, "Negro Ballads and Reels," and there was standing room only that evening to hear the concert of

<97>

Negro folksongs performed by Black students from Paul Quinn College in Waco. This presidential address, which she never published, was the first public statement of her interest in Negro folksongs. The fieldwork for this program was conducted almost exclusively in Waco, where she spent much of her free time "wandering about in the suburbs of South Waco, in the Negro section, dropping in at various places." (*On the Trail of Negro Folksong*, 43) She collected Negro versions of traditional Child Ballads as well as African chants and familiar ditties, some unprintable according to the Baptist standards of the day. She was not particularly interested in the sacred songs, which she felt had been sufficiently documented.

A few years later, after she had moved to New York City in order to complete the Ph.D. and become a member of the faculty of Columbia University, she and a Baylor colleague who was a professional musician, Ola Mae Gulledge, began to hold evening soirees at which Miss Gulledge sang Negro folksongs and accompanied herself on the piano while Scarborough provided a scholarly commentary on the backgrounds, meanings, and possible origins of the various songs.

Concerned with all aspects of Black secular folksong, these two friends also made a special visit to one of the nondescript brownstones on New York's West 46th Street, where they interviewed the famous "Father of the Blues," W. C. Handy. As Scarborough later wrote, "Blues being widely published as sheet music in the North as well as the South, and sung in vaudeville everywhere, would seem to have little relation to authentic folk-music of the Negroes. One might imagine this tinge of blue to the black music to be an artificial coloring—printer's ink, in fact. But in studying the questions, I had a feeling that it was more or less connected with Negro folk-song, and I tried to trace it back to its origin." (*Trail*, 264)

Handy quickly verified her hunch regarding the folk origins of the blues. He explained to her, "Each one of my blues is based on some old Negro song of the South, some folk-song that I heard from my mammy when I was a child. Something that sticks in my mind, that I hum to myself when I'm not thinking about it. Some old song that is a part of the memories of my childhood and of my race. I can tell you the exact song I used as a basis for any one of my blues. Yes, the blues that are genuine are really folk-songs." (*Trail*, 265)

<98>

Scarborough published a report of this interview with Handy, "The 'Blues' as Folk Songs," in *Coffee in the Gourd*, PTFS II (1923), one of the very first published acknowledgements of the folk roots and relationships of the blues as a folk musical idiom. She also included a description of the visit in *On the Trail of Negro Folksong*.

Throughout her early years teaching English and creative writing at Columbia, Scarborough was busy not only writing fiction but also collecting and annotating secular Negro folksongs. She printed up a request for folksong tunes and texts and mailed the flyers to friends and acquaintances throughout the South, including the presidents and superintendents of all the Negro secondary schools and colleges. She also contacted her friends back home in Waco and Marlin, and they sent her fragments and variants for years to come. Her sister, who lived in Richmond, Virginia, also helped with the project, especially when Miss Dottie spent most of her summer vacations there.

In 1925, Harvard University Press published *On the Trail of Negro Folksong*, a landmark collection based on Scarborough's years of fieldwork and correspondence. While Scarborough was still teaching at Baylor, the distinguished Harvard literary scholar, George Lyman Kittredge, had come there to lecture. Kittredge, of course, was influential in the founding of the Texas Folklore Society because it was he who had suggested the idea in the first place to his student at Harvard, the cowboy-folksong collector John Avery Lomax. Scarborough met Kittredge when he came to Texas and maintained contact with him. Through Kittredge's influence, the prestigious Harvard University Press agreed to publish her folksong collection. Kittredge kept close watch on the progress of the book and even read the proofs to make sure of the quality of Scarborough's scholarship and literary style.

He needn't have worried. The collection was impeccably researched and also somewhat innovative because of the literary quality of the lengthy narrative descriptions of the informants and of Scarborough's collecting adventures and techniques. This narrative is interspersed with the texts of the songs, some of which are musically transcribed. The ten chapters encompassed an introductory essay and an analysis of the role of the Negro in transmitting traditional songs and ballads, as well as separate chapters on Negro

<99>

ballads, dance songs or "reels," children's game songs, lullabies, songs about animals, work songs, railroad songs, and blues.

On the Trail of Negro Folksong was favorably reviewed throughout the country, and Scarborough's reputation as a folksong authority was quickly and firmly established. Black scholars and performers were impressed with the quality of her work and consulted with her frequently whenever they were in New York City. She became a frequent radio speaker on the topic and lectured widely, including at a meeting of the Modern Language Association when her friend and fellow folklorist, Louise Pound, was the first woman president of the MLA. She also spoke to such groups as the Dixie Club and the Texas Club of New York. As a token of her expertise she was asked to write the entry on Negro folklore for the 1937 edition of Encyclopaedia Brittanica.

Her most famous work, The Wind, was published almost simultaneously with Trail, in 1925, and her autobiographical novel, The Unfair Sex, was serialized in the magazine, The Woman's Viewpoint, beginning in December of that auspicious year. Although Trail had taken her years to complete, The Wind was written in a matter of months. The year 1925 thus marks the peak of her career, and she had to choose between being a novelist or an academic folklorist. The decision must have been a difficult one, because in the "Afterword" of On the Trail of Negro Folksong she had written, "I hate to say good-bye to this book. Writing the last words in it would be downright grief, if it were not for the fact that I may some time spend a sabbatical year loitering down through the South on the trail of more Negro folksongs, before the material vanishes forever, killed by the Victrola, the radio, and the lure of cheap printed music." (Trail, 282-283) But she never did seriously return to the collecting and documenting of Negro folksongs.

However, just because she devoted all of her time to writing novels did not mean that she had abandoned folklore entirely. She became a literary pioneer and innovator in the use of folksong stanzas to foreshadow and progress the plots of her novels. Negro folksongs are an integral part of her extended personal essay, From a Southern Porch (1919) as well as her first novel, In the Land of Cotton (1923), and she once quipped that she found that "readers were more interested in them [folksongs] than in anything I could write." (Trail,

<100>

11) In *The Wind*, she used stanzas from both traditional cowboy songs and Negro folksongs. She continued to utilize this technique in her later novels.

As all fanciers of Texana know, one reason *The Wind* is regarded as such an important early Texas novel is because of the uproar its publication created in Sweetwater, the town where the novel was set.[1] In order to appease the citizens of Sweetwater, in 1927 Scarborough accepted the invitation of the West Texas Chamber of Commerce and the Sweetwater Rotary Club to deliver the dedicatory address for the new Sweetwater Civic Center Auditorium. She chose as her topic for this speech, not *The Wind* but rather a discussion of the relationship of Negro folksongs to the Scottish and Old English ballads of Europe.

Scarborough's career as a novelist collapsed after the publication of the disastrous novel, *Can't Get a Redbird*, in 1929. She had informally agreed (i. e. with no contract) to write this novel for the Southern Cotton Growers Association as propaganda supporting farm collectivization. She also made the tragic decision to submit the manuscript to a committee of Co-Op executives, none of whom had any real literary training or critical sense regarding literature. The result is a heavy-handed attack on the tenant farming system, weighed down with lengthy technical descriptions of all aspects of the cotton growing industry. Scarborough took a semester's leave of absence from her teaching duties in order to conduct the research necessary to write this book. The most unfortunate coincidence, however, was that the publication of the book coincided with the 1929 stock market crash and subsequent national economic depression. The bottom fell out of the cotton industry, and Scarborough and her publisher, Harper's, were left with a large press run of books that nobody wanted to buy. The book was an artistic and financial failure.

Scarborough's literary reputation never recovered from this debacle. Family responsibilities as well as financial difficulties associated with the Depression combined to extinguish Scarborough's creative spark. Her last novel, *The Stretchberry Smile* (1932), was only mediocre. Because she needed the money she contracted with Harper's to write a nonfiction children's book entitled *The Story of*

<101>

Cotton (1933), which was more memorable for the woodcut illustrations than for the writing.

In an attempt to salvage her career, Scarborough turned once
again to the topic that had first brought her national recognition,
collecting folksongs. This time she decided to collect Anglo ballads
instead of Negro folksongs. In 1930 she was awarded a research grant
by Columbia University, which became the infamous Project 41.
With a specially built portable Dictaphone, she set out once again to
collect folksongs. Her collecting forays into the "hills and hollers" of
Virginia and the Carolinas were eminently successful, and she
gathered texts, tunes, and notes by the trunkful. She returned to New
York City with her booty, and in 1932 was awarded a sabbatical
during which she travelled once again to Europe and spent a few
quiet months in Italy writing the first draft of her second collection
of folksongs. Upon her return to the United States, she contracted
two professional ethnomusicologists to transcribe selected tunes
from the wax Dictaphone cylinders, which were worn out completely as a result of this tedious process.

A Song Catcher in the Southern Mountains is much more professionally presented than the somewhat gregarious and chatty *On the
Trail of Negro Folksong*, although the narrative descriptions of the hill
people and their lives are one of *Song Catcher's* strengths. The book
is divided into three main sections: Background, Ballads, and Songs.
Transcribed tunes and a brief essay on their modal aspects form a
special appendix. Extensive comparanda and informant data are
noted throughout with the texts. Although she was working on this
project during the depths of the Depression, Scarborough was able to
convince Columbia University Press to undertake the expensive
project of publishing the collection with the musical transcriptions.

Finishing the manuscript of *Song Catcher* revitalized Scarborough
and she began to write fiction again. She signed a contract for a series
of short stories with the *Saturday Evening Post* and began outlining
and plotting a historical novel about the Battle of the Alamo. Then,
unexpectedly, in November of 1935 she died in her sleep from
complications of the flu. The night she died she had been working
on corrections of the galley proofs of *Song Catcher*.

Two years elapsed before *Song Catcher* was finally published
posthumously in 1937. The delay was caused in part by the press's

<102>

financial problems but the main complication was litigation threatened by one of the ethnomusicologists and one of the informants. Both demanded changes in the manuscript, which of course had already been set in type. Such changes were almost prohibitively expensive at this stage of publishing so the press negotiated with these women for months and finally published the revised book, withstanding a tremendous financial loss as a result of the delays and alterations.

In spite of the controversy over the musical transcriptions, the book has won a solid reputation among subsequent generations of folksong scholars. In fact, after it went out of print with Columbia, it was reprinted in 1966 by AMS Press because it was regarded as such a valuable collection based on solid fieldwork.

Scarborough's reputation as a folklore pioneer and scholar is based on these two folksong collections which bracket the beginning and end of her short career. She planned to compile at least three more books from the texts and tunes she collected in Appalachia, and had she lived to accomplish that project she would probably be regarded as one of America's foremost folksong collectors instead of a popular woman novelist who also collected folklore.

Notes

The biographical data in this paper are drawn from the following collections:

The Dorothy Scarborough Collection, Texas Collection, Baylor University.

Project 41, *A Song Catcher in the Southern Mountains,* Columbia University Press Papers, Columbia University.

1. For further information, see: Grider, Sylvia. "The Showdown Between Dorothy Scarborough and Judge R. C. Crane." *West Texas Historical Association Yearbook* 62 (1986): 5-13.

<103>

Ben Carlton Mead
1902-1986
Courtesy Jack Duncan

<104>

ROBERT J. DUNCAN

Ben Carlton Mead:
Portrait of an Artist

AR T I S T Ben Carlton Mead didn't just belong to the Texas Folklore Society. He was one of its own. Ben became acquainted with the Society when he met J. Frank Dobie in about 1929. Soon he was attending Society meetings and illustrating Dobie's books. In 1932, he drew the first paisano that was used as the Society's emblem. It graced the title page of *Tone the Bell Easy* (PTFS X) and still appears periodically in Society publications. (See title page.)

Mead led an interesting life. He grew up in the Texas Panhandle when it was still virtually a frontier. He was a newspaper sports writer, a commercial artist, an art teacher, and a well-known western artist. He illustrated dozens of books, working in Texas, Chicago, and New York. He participated in archaeological digs in the Big Bend. He published several articles and worked for years on a history of the Panhandle. Ben painted numerous public murals. He designed a large billboard, still prominent on the Dallas downtown cityscape, that features a real waterfall. He even appeared in a television episode of "Gunsmoke."

Ben was a meticulous artist. He did careful historical research to make his work authentic. Additionally, he was one of the most vigorous, free-thinking, optimistic, and imaginative people I have ever known. He was also one of the most articulate and, of course, artistic.

Ben was born at Bay City, near Matagorda Bay, on November 21, 1902. His father was in the lumber business, and the family was constantly moving.[1] The Meads were living in Galveston on August 17, 1915, during a hurricane that killed 275 people. It was almost as severe as the "West India Hurricane" that swamped Galveston Island in 1900, killing thousands. However, in the intervening years,

<105>

the protective seawall had been built. Also, people who had lived through the 1900 cyclone paid a lot of attention to the warnings in 1915, so the death toll was not as bad as it could have been.

The storm hit before daylight. The Meads barely escaped by finding shelter in a brewery. Ben said: "The pilot wheel of a Mexican schooner was in our front yard [after the hurricane had passed]. The ship's captain had tied himself to it. His body was still there. My father gathered us together and we headed west."[2]

The Mead family settled in Lamesa, on the Staked Plains. Lamesa was at the end of the tracks. Ben had vivid recollections of those pioneer Panhandle days: "The same railroad company [Santa Fe] planned a new route southwest from Lubbock and its terminus would be in the vicinity of the Blythe Ranch forty-five miles northwest of us. Here a new town would be born. Since we were the nearest supply point, it was our windmills, lumber, barbed wire, hardware and paint that would go into the birthing process, freighted laboriously over a three-day trip by a little wagon train of three double-team rigs, repeated many times. We were already calling the place Blythe, but later its official name became Seagraves."[3] "Our lumber was freighted . . . through sand, shinnery, and miles of prairie dog towns. Antelope skimmed the horizon; deer sometimes mired in the wet sands of dry, salt-crusted Cedar Lake. The teamster's son, my age, and I thought it a paradise. We roamed far from the wagons, hunting rabbit, doves, quail, prairie chicken, and curlew, to cook in the iron skillet at sundown. . . . These things shaped my memories and influenced my interests in the years to come."[4]

During Ben's teenage years, the Meads moved to Tulsa, where Ben took his first art lessons. Then they moved to Amarillo. While in high school, Ben painted theatrical posters and stage scenery and worked as sports editor for the *Amarillo Daily News*. He graduated from Amarillo High School in 1923, rode to Chicago on his motorcycle, and enrolled in the Art Institute. He came back to Texas in July of 1924 and married his high school sweetheart, Maida McAfee. They returned to Chicago, and Ben continued his studies for two more years. He studied illustration under Jerome Rozen and Charles Schroeder.[5]

In the mid-1920s, the young couple returned to Texas, and Ben became a designer for Sunset Advertising in San Antonio. Soon he

<106>

opened his own studio as a freelance commercial artist. By 1928, Ben was moving toward specializing in illustration; he designed the dust cover for *Stories from the History of Texas*, published by the Southwest Press in Dallas.

In the spring of 1929, Ben read in the newspaper that Carl Sandburg was coming to town to give a lecture. Ben took his wife and daughter to hear Sandburg. Mead had never heard of Dobie. Dobie introduced Sandburg to the audience, and Ben was even more impressed with Dobie than with Sandburg. Ben instantly took a liking to Frank Dobie. The next time Ben was in Austin, Dobie invited him over to his home on Waller Creek. At their first meeting, Dobie asked Ben if he could draw a windmill. Ben said that indeed he could, that he had been drawing them since he was four years old. Dobie ranted about some Brooklyn artist who had been hired by his publisher to illustrate one of his books. The fellow could not get a windmill right despite several attempts, and Dobie doubted that he had ever seen one. Ben showed Dobie what he could do and got the job of illustrating *Coronado's Children* a Literary Guild book-of-the-month.[6]

Frank Dobie and Ben Mead became good friends, and Ben always visited him when he came to Austin. In 1931, Ben joined the Texas Folklore Society and attended his first meeting, which was held at the Witte Museum and the Menger Hotel in San Antonio. That was the year that he illustrated *On the Open Range* for Dobie. In later years Ben was called upon again to illustrate Dobie books: *I'll Tell You a Tale* in 1960 and *Cow People* in 1964, which included an annotated sketch that Ben gave to Dobie in 1938. Ben told me he had no idea how highly Dobie had regarded his illustrations until years later when he read Lon Tinkle's biography of Dobie, *An American Original*. Tinkle says, "He [Dobie] was delighted with Ben Mead's work and felt that 'it [*Coronado's Children*] is going to be the best illustrated book dealing with the West since Remington.'"[7]

Mead made thousands of sketches of western objects to use later in illustrations and paintings. When he was sketching a horse skeleton near Fort Davis in 1928, several young boys on horseback stopped to observe. One of the boys looked at Ben, then looked at the decomposing carcass. He said: "Mister, you're going to have trouble selling that picture, I betcha."

<107>

The kid who made the remark was sitting on a saddle that had a huge round saddle horn—almost as big as a grapefruit. Ben wanted to sketch it, but the boy had to go home to do his chores. Ben had finished the skeleton sketch, so he followed the boy home. The boy's father came out and introduced himself. He was a banker by the name of Walter Bloys. When Ben asked about the unusual saddle, Bloys said that his father had bought the saddle in Honey Grove, Texas, in 1882. Interestingly, the father was the same Reverend Bloys who was the circuit-riding preacher who founded the famous Bloys revival campground near Fort Davis.[8]

Later Ben had an art show at a gallery in San Antonio. George W. Saunders, who founded the Old Time Trail Drivers' Association, had gone to the exhibit with some of his womenfolk, but he stood in the doorway and would not enter. Ben went over and invited him in. As Saunders started to say he wasn't interested in art, he caught a glimpse of Ben's charcoal sketch of the Bloys saddle. He got very excited and said, "That's the old-time apple horn saddle, like I used to ride when I was a boy!" He came in and became an art lover. He and Ben became friends, and Saunders gave Ben many western objects to paint from. The sketch of the horse skeleton was used in *Coronado's Children*, and the saddle sketch wound up in *I'll Tell You a Tale*.[9]

In 1930, Ben went to work as staff artist at San Antonio's Witte Museum. In those early Depression years, Ben did everything from painting habitat background scenes to doing carpentry work making exhibit cases; from helping with the reptiles to going on archaeological expeditions in the Big Bend. On one trip to the Terlingua area, Mead made a plaster cast of a huge Indian petroglyph that was over ten feet long and four feet high. It was displayed in the entrance to the Witte Museum from 1931 to 1962.[10]

In 1932, Mead, Dudley Dobie, and Colonel Martin Lalor Crimmins went on a camping trip in the Big Bend, where they caught rattlesnakes to be milked for venom serum.

Colonel Crimmins had attended medical school and was within weeks of graduation when he quit to join Teddy Roosevelt's Rough Riders. After a heart attack at 55, he retired to San Antonio, to a peaceful life of catching rattlesnakes and milking them for medical science.

<108>

Dudley Dobie was the school superintendent in San Marcos. Ben said Dudley lived near the outskirts of town and was "kind of farmerish" at heart. He raised chickens and a few pigs, and kept a milk cow.

The three travelers built fancy, well-ventilated boxes to hold the snakes safely. When they left San Antonio, they decided to take three of Dudley's fryers to cook and eat on the way. Since the snake boxes were empty, they used them to hold the chickens. At night, they would feed the hens corn from roadside fields and hobble them so they wouldn't stray far. After a couple of days, they made the mistake of naming the chickens and thinking of them as pets. Then they couldn't bear to kill them, so they had to keep the captured rattlesnakes in tow sacks.[11]

Chris Emmett, in his biography of Crimmins, *In the Path of Events*, describes the trip this way: "In San Antonio, the retired Colonel soon attracted kindred spirits, three of whom were Ben Carlton Mead, of the Witte Museum, Henry B. du Pont of Wilmington, Delaware, and the ubiquitous Dudley R. Dobie, of San Marcos, Texas. One June 28 [1932], the quartet left San Antonio 'for Big Bend to find things of interest.' For two weeks they sketched, wrote, inspected caves, 'drank the water of the silvery Rio Grande,' visited the hide-outs of murderers, examined the petrified rock of Castleton, peered deep into Santa Elena Canyon with its two thousand foot cliffs, held court at the home of 'Judge' Roy Bean; and abandoned camp for home vowing to return and run the rapids of Long and Santa Elena Canyons which, since the days of Cabeza de Vaca had regularly taken the lives of those who dared to venture there in boats."[12]

By 1932, the Witte was trying to survive the Depression and was no longer able to pay Ben a living wage. He and Maida packed up and returned to Amarillo. Ben taught art courses at Amarillo Junior College, and on the second floor of a downtown building, Ben opened what he later referred to as "my little art school." Students took lessons at a dollar a session. Ben did some commercial art work for the radio station in exchange for some radio spots advertising his art school.

Maida's family owned some ranch property a few miles south of town, and Ben—with one helper—built a small house in the

<109>

country. The art students would come out on weekends to sketch and paint along the creek. Then they would all share a picnic lunch.

On one occasion a social worker in Amarillo asked Ben to provide room, board, and tobacco for a young Indian who had been hurt in a rodeo accident. In return, the Indian would pose for Ben and his students. Ben agreed. The man wanted to build a tepee in Ben's back yard. He found saplings along the creek and cut the lodge poles. There was no way to get enough hides of any kind—let alone buffalo hides—to make the tepee, so they went to town and Ben bought dozens of yards of ducking to cover the poles. The Indian lived in the tepee even during the winter, building a small fire in the center. Ben said the tepee made a beautiful sight on early frosty mornings, with a wisp of smoke curling out the top, the sides pearly translucent from the light of the fire, and the pattern of frost remaining on the covering just where the lodge poles insulated it. Ben, of course, captured it all in a painting. After a few months the Indian recuperated and went back on the rodeo circuit.[13]

Work was hard to come by during those years of the Depression. Mead was invited to paint a mural at the Hall of State in Dallas in preparation for the Texas Centennial, but he didn't feel that he could afford to donate the several weeks of work when he needed the income. In 1935, Ben was called to Syracuse, New York, to spend several months doing illustrations for the L.W. Singer Company, which was later to become part of Random House. He worked under poor conditions for two months before that job was canceled.

While he was in New York, Ben decided to make some contacts with agents and publishers. Ben renewed contact with Colonel Crimmins, who helped Ben gain entrance to the museums of the city.

One day in late August, Colonel Crimmins invited Ben to be his guest to a party in Greenwich Village at the studio of sculptress Bonnie MacLeary. Besides MacLeary and Crimmins, there was Edward Larocque ("Ned") Tinker, a wealthy world traveler and writer who had fought in the Mexican revolution; Jack Abernathy of Texas, who had developed a knack for catching wolves with his bare hands; and writer Margaret Bell Houston, granddaughter of Sam Houston.

The Colonel knew Tinker well and asked him to make some phone calls to help Ben meet agents and publishers. As a result, Ben

<110>

met Mary Squire Abbott, who was a leading agent working for the McIntosh & Otis agency, and historical editor Constance L. Skinner. Abbott agreed to represent Mead, and Skinner was planning a series of books on American rivers and asked Ben to illustrate some of them.

During this time Ben also visited the Laidlaw Brothers publishing firm. The brother who ran the New York office suggested that Mead visit their Chicago office on his way back to Texas. The Laidlaw firm gave him enough freelance work to allow him to close his Amarillo studio and work in Chicago. His family joined him before Christmas. They lived in Chicago for two years, before moving back to Amarillo.[14]

*

* *

The Meads moved to Dallas in 1941, where Ben went to work for the largest commercial art studio in the city. In 1945, Mead designed a war bond poster that was displayed in 17,000 theaters across the country.

In 1952, he was hired as art director for Tracy-Locke Advertising Agency in Dallas. In 1962, Ben directed the construction of the waterfall sign on Dallas's Stemmons Freeway. He stood across the highway for perspective and gave the workmen instructions on a two-way radio.

Ben had not attended a Texas Folklore Society meeting since the early 1930s, but in 1973 Secretary-Editor Francis Abernethy encouraged Ben to again become active with the group. Ben came to that year's meeting in Laredo, and his stylized roadrunner drawing from 1932 graced the cover of the printed program. After that meeting, Ben was back in the fold and attended meetings for several years thereafter.

A couple of weeks after the Laredo meeting, Mead was in Tucson to play a small part in one of the CBS television episodes of James Arness's "Gunsmoke."[15]

In July 1974, Ben and Maida celebrated their golden wedding anniversary. In September, Ben completed one of his major works, a magnificent 4x7 foot painting of the Palo Duro Canyon Indian camp, where in 1874, the Comanches were defeated by Mackenzie's Cavalry, bringing an end to the Indian domination of the High

<111>

Plains. The painting was entitled "Battle Site at the Junction of Ceta Blanca and Palo Duro Canyons." When it was finished, just in time for the centennial anniversary of the battle, it went on an exhibition tour of the Panhandle. Within a week it was purchased by the First National Bank of Amarillo.

Maida had survived several heart attacks, but passed away in December 1975.

Mead and history professor David Weber, who had recently moved to Dallas from California to teach at SMU, both had been encouraged to organize a Dallas chapter ("corral") of Westerners International, a group of people who have an interest in the Old West. Weber and Mead talked by phone, then contacted students and friends who shared their interests, and in December 1976, the first meeting was held. Ben gave a talk on his illustrations that evening and was elected the Corral's first Sheriff. The Dallas Corral of the Westerners continues to thrive.

For two or three years Ben was virtually blind in his left eye. Eventually he received a corneal transplant through the eye bank and could once again make headway with his painting.

In February 1979, Ben married Maurice O'Connell, who was a cousin of Maida's; the marriage ended in divorce three years later. Ben moved to Santa Ynez, California, to be near his daughters. In December 1981, he wrote me that he had taken a ride in an airplane glider to celebrate his seventy-ninth birthday. That same day he passed the test for his California driver's license. In 1982, I got a letter from Ben that was brimming with optimism, humor, plans and enthusiasm—as he always was.

In late 1982, Ben had written to the Texas State Historical Association: "I really am still in the saddle, teaching two half-day classes a week, [and] beginning to get students from the little surrounding towns. Trying to start three new canvasses over the holidays . . . [one] of buffalo hunters making a stand with a herd; one of the narrow gauge railway that operated from a port city to this area for many years. Back to the Comanches for [the] third; Quanah Parker, Big Tree and Satante. My students love it when I have something underway."[16]

*
* *

<112>

In his last few years Ben completed three major paintings. One was "The Comanche Horses of Tule Canyon," a 55x40 inch sequel to the Palo Duro battle site painting. It sold to a private collector in California.

In addition to the Texas Folklore Society, Mead had been an active member of the Texas State Historical Association, the Western History Association, the Collector's Institute and the International Society of Artists. He was on the board of directors of the Panhandle-Plains Historical Society and its Museum at Canyon. He was also an honorary life member of the Lubbock Corral of the Westerners.

Ben died on December 8, 1986, at the age of 84. He left behind three children—Jean Ellis, Margaret Mead, and David Mead—and a lot of great art. Three of his murals are on a wall of the Panhandle-Plains Museum at Canyon. Others are in Amarillo at the First National Bank, Pioneer Natural Gas Company, and the Bivins-Childers Estate offices. Ben was "included in that number" in Jeff Dykes's *Fifty Great Western Illustrators*" where Dykes lists seventy-six items illustrated by Mead.[17]

Early in 1979, I received a letter from Ben that closed with, "Bless you all—I love all my friends and relatives. I am completely at peace with the world." That's how I like to remember him.

Notes

1. Esse Forrester-O'Brien, *Art and Artists of Texas* (Dallas: Tardy Publishing Company, 1935), 156.
2. Bill Walraven, "He Might Have Been a Coastal Artist," *The Corpus Christi Caller*, Wednesday, March 8, 1978.
3. Ben Mead, foreword for George Autry, *"Much Obliged!"* (Fort Worth: privately published, 1977), vii-viii.
4. Ben Mead, "About the Drawings," in Paul Green's, *Texas, A Musical Romance of Panhandle History*—souvenir program (Canyon, Texas: Palo Duro State Park, 1970), unpaged.
5. Forrester-O'Brien, 156.
6. Interview with Ben Mead, April 1976.
7. Lon Tinkle, *An American Original* (Boston and Toronto: Little, Brown and Company, 1978), 127.
8. Interview with Ben Mead, April 1976.

<113>

9. *Ibid.* The horse skeleton drawing is in J. Frank Dobie, *Coronado's Children* (Dallas: The Southwest Press, 1930), 203. The apple horn saddle drawing is in J. Frank Dobie, *I'll Tell You a Tale* (Boston and Toronto: Little, Brown and Company, 1960), 92.

10. Bess Carroll Woolford and Ellen Schulz Quillin, *The Story of the Witte Memorial Museum, 1922-1960* (San Antonio: San Antonio Museum Association, 1966), 201, and interview with Ben Mead, March 1977.

11. Interview with Ben Mead, March 8, 1979.

12. Chris Emmett, *In the Path of Events with Colonel Martin Lalor Crimmins* (Waco: Jones and Morrison, 1959), 323-324. Emmett includes Henry B. du Pont in the group. There were several similar trips, and du Pont went on some of them, but Ben did not indicate that he was on this one.

13. Interview with Ben Mead, March 8, 1979. The Indian and tepee are also mentioned in Forrester-O'Brien, 156-157.

14. Interview with Ben Mead, March 1977.

15. Ben Mead, "Ben Mead and Matt Dillon," a letter to the editor, *True West* 21:1 (September-October 1973), 62, 72.

16. A note from Ben Mead quoted in "Southwestern Collection," *Southwestern Historical Quarterly* (Austin: Texas State Historical Association) 87:1 (July 1983), 81.

17. Jeff Dykes, *Fifty Great Western Illustrators: A Bibliographic Checklist* (Flagstaff, Arizona: Northland Press, 1975), 235-239.

<114>

CONNIE RICCI

The Lone Ranger Rides Again

CAN A FOLK hero rise from the dust of abandoned scripts to ride once more across the glittering screen of television, a ghostly reincarnation battling hostile environments and providing frontier justice? In particular, can a character who "thundered across the west upon a silver white stallion, appearing out of nowhere to strike down injustice or outlawry and then vanishing as mysteriously as he came" re-emerge intrinsically intact in the television programming line-up of the 1980s as a modernized folk motif ("The Lone Ranger" Introduction)? Such an occurrence I believe to be the case with "The Lone Ranger."

Created as a radio program by George W. Trendle and Fran Striker, "The Lone Ranger" series debuted on January 30, 1933, on station WXYZ in Detroit, and by the end of the decade aired on over four hundred U.S. radio stations (*Britannica* 7: 462). Then in 1949, at a cost of approximately $1,000,000, General Mills brought "The Lone Ranger" to the ABC network where the series ran until 1957, after which time reruns appeared through 1961 on both CBS and NBC (*New York Times* 3 April 1949, sec. 2: 9; *New York Times* 6 March 1980: D19).

During that time, and throughout later syndications of the program, Clayton Moore, the actor who portrayed the lead character in the television series, brought to life the mysterious "masked hero [who] used simple frontier justice to right wrongs in the old west" (*New York Times* 15 April 1978: 24).

The story that Moore turned into reality for a generation of kids every week was basically a simple one. Wounded seriously, "The Lone Ranger" survived an outlaw ambush which killed five other Texas Rangers, including his older brother, Daniel Reid. Found and nursed back to health by Tonto, the Indian who was to become his

<115>

Clayton Moore as the Lone Ranger with his horse Silver and Jay
Silverheels as Tonto. *Courtesy Universal*

partner and loyal friend, "he then donned a black mask made from
his dead brother's vest, mounted his stallion, Silver, and roamed the
West to aid those in need, to fight evil, and to establish justice"
(*Britannica* 7:462).

These film episodes which reflected this heroic scenario each
week contained certain elements common to most westerns. Mody
Boatright discussed these elements in an essay entitled "The Formula
in Cowboy Fiction and Drama," which was published in *Western
Folklore* in 1969 (XXVIII, 139 ff.). The formula for the action
western was that the emphasis was placed on action; the hero was
introduced in a tense situation early on; the hero solved his problem
"through strength, ingenuity, and true western courage, without

<116>

resort to unmanly conduct;" and the hero was opposed by a villain who was not a weakling.

In addition to these elements, the series primarily followed a common plot structure Boatright classified as Plot II. According to this particular plot, the hero, through the occurrence of some incident, felt morally compelled to act on the behalf of others. Thus upon encountering a situation of distress or oppression, the hero actively participated in actions involving sacrifice and risk on his part to bring about a successful solution to that situation (Boatright, 140).

In essence, consequently, "The Lone Ranger" series varied little from other westerns of the time. Indeed, in a somewhat derogatory review, one critic declared that the television series was "just another western, and not a notably good one at that." In fact, the reviewer even stated that the Lone Ranger himself was "a bit of a panty-waist" when compared to other cowboy heroes of the time (*New York Times* 2 Oct. 1949, sec. 2: 9).

How on earth, one might ask, could I possibly argue then that the Lone Ranger is now, in fact, not only a folk hero, but also a basic motif used in current television programming?

Quite simply, I base my argument on three factors. First, I believe there are certain critical attributes of "The Lone Ranger" series which have manifested themselves, in an updated form, in certain programs aired in the 1980s. Secondly, I believe there is an underlying, universal motif found within that series which lends itself to symbolic permanence, thereby generating its continuation in various genres. And lastly, I believe there is an abstract quality unique to folk heroes which imparts a cultural significance often underestimated or underrated in the higher realms of academia.

When speaking of critical attributes, I am referring to those qualities which make a thing what it is. And as regards "The Lone Ranger," there are several characteristics which set the program and the man apart from other westerns and western heroes. These distinguishing characteristics revolve around four elements embedded within the essence of the primary character and emanate from him as defining qualities in terms of personality, identity, and moral stance.

<117>

Specifically the four attributive elements found within "The Lone Ranger" include the use of an unknown identity, a single-minded determination to battle injustice single-handedly, the intimate bonding of the hero with his horse, and a unique calling card which symbolically connotes the hero's purpose. Simplistically, we see these elements translated into easily recognizable trademarks: the black mask from behind which the Lone Ranger operates because "outlaws . . . fear the mysterious" (*Lone Ranger Movie*); the partnership with Tonto, which aids the Lone Ranger in his one-man fight against outlawry; the Lone Ranger's horse, Silver, whose unique color, intelligence, and loyalty distinguishes both him and his master as superior beings; and the silver bullet, the Lone Ranger's calling card, chosen specifically because it symbolizes the purity of his purpose in battling evil and injustice.

These elements, brought to life by Clayton Moore, distinguish the Lone Ranger. They are what comes readily to mind when one recalls childhood memories of the show and its fanciful hero. In fact, for me, they are so much a part of that particular mystique that their manifestation in current programming was easily recognizable.

Three recent series in particular, "Knight Rider," "The Equalizer," and "Sting-ray," have definitely utilized modifications of these critical attributes belonging to "The Lone Ranger," Each of these shows portrays a hero working just outside the boundaries of the law, yet sanctioned in some form by that system, as was the Lone Ranger. Each show's hero operates from a masked perspective—even to the point of wearing black sunglasses in the shape of the Lone Ranger's mask—in that his identity and background are either unknown or veiled in secrecy much as was the Lone Ranger's. Moreover, each hero has a particular friend who assumes Tonto's role and aids in the hero's one-man fight against injustice: in "Knight Rider" that role is filled by Kit, a computerized, talking car who functions as a combination Silver and Tonto; in "The Equalizer," the role belongs to Mickey, a somewhat out-of-step social misfit; and in "Sting-ray" the role is filled by no character in particular, but by someone different each week. In addition, each hero drives a unique automobile, purposely designed to add depth, dimension, and meaning to the hero's character, as did Silver to his master's. And lastly, each hero has his own distinct calling card with which people identify him in

<118>

his pursuit of justice and fair play: Knight Rider rides the highways in Kit, his wonder car; Equalizer offers to "equalize the odds" in his newspaper advertisement; and Sting-ray always requires a favor in payment of his services.

The use of this Lone Ranger motif, in fact, has not escaped the observance of others, even the story writers themselves. In the 1986 September premier episode of "The Equalizer," a corrupt government agent tells McCall, the Equalizer, that he wants to see if McCall's bullets are really made of silver ("The Equalizer," CBS). And in a review comparing the similarity of style and plot in "Sting-ray" and "The Equalizer," John O'Connor points out that in each episode of "Sting-ray" someone "inevitably asks the equivalent of 'Who was that masked man?'" (O'Connor, *New York Times* 8 April, 1986: C18).

The fact that these programs do indeed appear to be modern manifestations of the Lone Ranger motif leads to my second supposition, the idea of a universal motif found within the Lone Ranger story which achieves symbolic permanence. Max Westbrook discusses in depth the revolt-search motif he finds to be not only a basic American motif but also a basic cowboy motif. "Typically," he states, "the hero rebels against institutional evil and searches for a code or setting that will enable him to express abstract belief." The idea here as Westbrook sees it is "that truth cannot be embodied in an institution or written down in a list of rules . . ." and that it is the hero's "superior insight" and "intuitive . . . understanding of this truth" which distinguishes him from common men. Westbrook goes on to say that this universal motif often translates itself into stories where the heroic sheriff "must go outside the law in order to restore justice" (Westbrook, "The Themes of Western Fiction," *Southwest Review*, 43 [1958], 232-235).

In the case of the Lone Ranger, I believe we see this revolt-search motif come into play when the Lone Ranger abandons traditional channels through which to fight injustice and opts to work from behind his mask. Though never truly in opposition to the law, he operates just outside its bounds in order to accomplish what cannot be accomplished within the system.

Interestingly enough, this same motif crops up in the three programs utilizing the Lone Ranger motif. In each of these programs,

<119>

the hero has left the formal, inefficacious governmental agency for which he worked and is seeking to restore justice to a corrupt society in his own manner. As one critic points out when speaking of "The Equalizer," "the real point (of such shows) is designed for people who feel that the traditional channels of law and justice are failing them" (*New York Times* 18 September, 1985: C26). Certainly such a statement lends credence to the universality of this revolt-search motif and its permeating nature.

The fact that these shows are currently utilizing the Lone Ranger motif and that the revolt-search motif which is basic to the Lone Ranger story is also basic to these updated versions does not necessarily make the Lone Ranger a folk hero. But the truth of the matter is that the Lone Ranger has transcended the boundaries of fiction to become, as Janet Maslin states, a "part of American folklore" (Maslin, *New York Times* 22 May, 1981: C8). And this, I believe, has occurred in part because of Clayton Moore's belief in and devotion to that heroic character and in part because the Lone Ranger embodies those aforementioned elements in such a way as to promote what Marshall Fishwick calls "a simple hero myth for a highly complex culture" (Fishwick, "The Cowboy: America's Contribution to the World's Mythology", *Western Folklore*, II [1952]:86). Succinctly stated, the Lone Ranger is a man with a mission of high purpose, a man easily understood and respected, a man with whom one can easily identify.

In short, the Lone Ranger "represent[s] the dream of order in a complex and difficult world" (*Britannica* 7: 462); and because he does so, he has become for many Americans, as Clayton Moore states, a hero in a country that needs heroes.

<120>

JERI TANNER

Ollie North
Hero, Villain, or Temporary Prince?

ALTHOUGH the Iran-Contra hearings had already involved eight months of investigation, twenty-nine public witnesses, and 250 hours of public testimony, it was not until July 7-13 of '87 that a midsummer madness mesmerized much of America. Fifty million people watched Lieutenant Colonel Oliver North and heard all or part of "the good, the bad, and the ugly."

Called "Two-Gun Ollie" by Larry King, this Texas-born Marine charged up Capitol Hill, "told off Congress right to its teeth," and corralled the masses into believing that the "Wild West syndrome" must manifest itself if we are to master the monsters of this world. And when the "big boys" began to badger him, he stunned them in their tracks. This "Video Olivier" turned the inquisition into a rally and emerged as a hero: "a Moses in uniform," "a modern-day Paul Revere," another Nathan Hale, a reincarnated Patrick Henry, "an embodied Jimmy Stewart, Gary Cooper, and John Wayne," or "a James Bond, fearless agent" who thought it a "neat idea" to apply "Oliver's twist" to the Iranians and send profits to the Contras. North was hailed another Teddy Roosevelt, "the Teflon colonel," "the impresario," and "a man for all seasons," "as comforting and all-American as a Boy Scout" or as baseball and apple pie.

While people of all ages praised and even prayed for the peerless performer, others thought that all was not quite right with "Snow White and the Seven Dwarfs." "The strong North wind" that buffeted Congress cast a chill on many Americans who feared that "the Great Satan got away," and they pointed at the villain who violated the law. Protests were in the press and on television. To some opponents of the hero-image, North acted like "a loose cannon," "a wild man," and a petty "chiseler who dipped into the operational fund . . . ." A woman from Virginia called North "a

<121>

"As far as I'm concerned, anyone who can get Jim and Tammy Bakker off the front page IS a national hero."

<122>

modern-day Savonarola," "an Elmer Gantry in uniform." Molly Ivins from Texas declared on public television that North is "part Klaus Barbi." Others wanted answers, and they wanted facts. Objecting to North's elevated status, Henry Herman of Irving, Texas, asked why North is called a hero when he conspired to overthrow the government. Romeo Guerra of Garland, Texas, noticed the irony of the United States selling arms that might be used against us. Mike Royko believed that if Ollie were Pinnochio, he would have felt his nose extending "halfway to the White House." Johnny Carson commented that Ollie participated in the biggest cover-up since Tammy Bakker's face. John Braun of Lake City, Florida, said that if people take Ollie at his word, he will achieve his "olliegarchy" and be "Lord High Ruler of NORTH America"; and, in July 1987, on *Washington Week in Review*, a reporter asked whether the nation had not instantly turned a toad into a prince.

Nevertheless, though aware of the deceptions, others delighted in North's defense. In *USA Today*, Dan Warrensford wrote, "North's tactics may have been flawed, but his motives were good, and correct." As for shredding documents, William F. Buckley asked, "What's a shredder for?" Then he remarked, "North used his for its only logical purpose." Deborah Thomason of Provo, Utah, said that Ollie merely tried to correct the mistakes of Congress, who fostered the fiasco. Humorist Art Buchwald concluded that "Ollie North altered documents only so they would make sense to Congress." And Ernest Allsop, a retired senior vice-president of Prudential Insurance Company, said: "I think the man's honest. He's told them he lied. That's honest, isn't it?"

During debates over the appellation of hero, villain, or temporary prince, North appeared in homes, offices, doctors' and dentists' offices, stores, on street corners, at roadsides, and on Wall Street, where stocks went up in praise of North. People's emotions were strong, especially toward the interrogators. "Olliemania erupted," and the epidemic spread.

While on Capitol Hill, the Norths received dozens of flowers and "Olliegrams" with messages such as "God Bless You" and "Good Luck Against Those Ill-Bred Hyenas," and banners, billboards, buttons, and bumper stickers were seen from coast to coast. In front of the Smyrna Baptist Church in Pensacola, Florida, church mem-

<123>

bers voiced their support for North. A banner on a front porch in Philmont, New York, read: "God Bless Ollie North." George Mahieu, who placed the sign, said "[Until North] . . . I thought the only good Marine was a submarine, but not anymore." Outside Philmont, N.Y. a board read, "Ollie North, Good Luck! Keep U.S. Free." In El Centro, California, one said, "Elect . . . Lt. Col. Ollie North for President. He'll get the job done." On July 10, 1987, members of Young Americans for Freedom met near the Russell Senate office in Washington, D.C., and held signs of their adulation; and on another street in Washington, D.C., two women held a poster proclaiming North their hero. In Marshall, Arkansas, a citizen kept score of the hearings on a baseball billboard, which one day read: "Inning No. 5: Ollie 3. Congress 2." On a bait and tackle shop on the Maryland shore were the ambiguous words "Go Ollie." And for a few hours in California, the "H" was removed from "Hollywood."

Fans flocked to the fad factories for buttons, caps, and T-shirts, which read "Ollie in '88," "North—American Hero," "I'd follow Ollie into Hell," and "Ollie North for President." Within five days, a company in Tulsa sold 2,500 Ollie North T-shirts. Even Brooks Patterson, George Bush's Michigan campaign co-chairman, "defected" to North one day and wore a T-shirt announcing his vote. With such political sentiment astir for a Uniform in the White House, Pat Robertson, a former presidential candidate, said that he would accept North for his running mate; and many hoped that George Bush would do the same. Catching the spirit of this "wacky" world, cartoonist MacNeil showed the Bush-North alliance in trouble as North began to outshine Bush: "Did you clear this with the colonel's agent, George?"

In July 1987, three bumper stickers caught the attention of Paul Harvey: "Honk if you have contempt for Congress;" "I diverted my political contribution to Ollie;" and a third, seen in Ft. Worth, read, "For the first time, the South loves NORTH."

Not to be outdone, the food and beverage vendors made Oliver North "a symbol for the palates of America." The "Ollieburger" with its beef, baloney, Swiss cheese, and shredded lettuce and "Ollie's Gottem Buffaloed Burger" with its bison meat became honorific foods. At the Hefty Hero Sandwich Shop in Dallas, the "Ollieburger" was flagged with the "stars and stripes" strapped to toothpicks.

<124>

Baskin-Robbins in Greenwich, Connecticut, sold the "Oliver North ice cream cake," decorated with an edible motto: "I don't recall." Not only can a person buy ice cream at the Skinny Dip Ice Cream Shop in Lubbock, Texas, but in 1987 he could also sign a petition to Congress to honor Oliver North. In stores known only to Johnny Carson, there was the "Ollielolly" or the "Olliepop," a four-to-six-day sucker wrapped in khaki green. Pro-Ollie imbibers went to El Greco's in Southgate, Kentucky, and for three dollars enjoyed the "Jolly Ollie"—a strawberry margarita (for the red), a bit of whipped cream (for the white), and Curacao (for the blue).

North has been celebrated in books, videotapes, recordings, and theatrical performances. If Olliephiles want more of the "Leave It to Ollie" show, in Dallas they can buy USA tapes, the full thirty-six hours of North's congressional testimony, or two videotaped versions of North's performance at the hearings. On the stands are books about North, such as *Guts and Glory* and *Taking the Stand—The Testimony of Lt. Col. Oliver North*. It has been rumored that Ollie will write an autobiography, which will turn into a movie. But the question is: Who will play Ollie? Or will Ollie play Ollie and go for the gold? Also cashing in on the Colonel is Rich Little, whose record album, *Ronald Reagan Slept Here* includes Ollie having to take the blame for everything from the explosion of the Hindenburg to the fall of the Joan Rivers show.

The comic strips provided a satiric view of Olliedom. If Ollie should run for President, as "Doonesbury" implies, he'll promise to lie, shred, falsify documents, preserve deniability, and take the Fifth—all for the good of the country. Another Doonesbury cartoon shows a potted plant speaking in North's defense. In "Bloom County," young wooers win their women by emulating Ollie: "[A] . . . Wait, Steve . . . just for me . . . Talk like him again."—"[B] . . . sometimes you need to spill a little Constitutional milk to save the American pie!"—"[A] Oh, Ollie, Shred me . . . !" In the comic strip "Crock," to keep a clean record, men in the military use a shredder to destroy all the "mistakes and goofs" of their careers.

Ollie has also been measured in music. At the Mall in Washington, D.C., an amateur band sang "Ollie B. Good," a parody of Chuck Berry's "Johnny B. Goode," and recorded it for the nation. Others sang "Hooray for Olliewood!" On August 26, 1987, on PBS's "The

<125>

Mark Russell Comedy Special," Mr. Russell parodied Gilbert and
Sullivan's "Modern Major General" with

> He is the very model of a good lieutenant colonel;
> He was serving his commander from the A.M to nocturnal;
> He testified for hours sipping Diet Coca Cola
> With his version of a covert op. to screw the Ayatollah.

> He took the rap for Ronnie, who was in and out of touch again;
> Sometimes he'd lay the blame on William Casey who was dead by
>   then;
> He told of the diversion and how proud he was to do it.
> As the nation watched, he held the hoop and Congress jumped
>   right through it.

> He lashed out at the liberals and assorted Contra wreckers,
> And the only one thing missing was a little dog named Checkers;
> Wives compared him to their husbands whom they thought were
>   not worth keeping—
> 'Why can't you be like Ollie? On the sofa you'll be sleeping.'

> Poindexter had to follow in the wake of North a hero;
> In civilian clothes he puffed his pipe and charisma down to zero.
> He said the Gipper's innocent; the smoking gun is missing;
> That's why for seven months he left his bosses hanging there and
>   twisting.

> So the charismatic colonel filled the nation's needs so vital,
> And the great communicator is relinquishing his title.
> His piece before the Congress surely borders on the rotten.
> The coast is clear 'cause Ollie North is practically forgotten.

A disc jockey in Detroit sang, "If you did what you say, you oughta
know better,/ You and Fawn Hall stickin' stuff in the shredder." In
parts of Florida, the song was "Praise Ollie, from whom all weapons
flow. Ollieluia."

For children of all ages, there were coloring books and dolls. The
whole gang—Ollie, Fawn, Ronnie, and even Nixon—could be

<126>

tinted, but a Lubbock writer warned that "the Ollie Dolly ... [would] remain silent for eight months and then talk only in the presence of the Brendon Sullivan doll."

Olliemania also extended to real estate. In the Lubbock *Avalanche-Journal* of August 16, 1987, a bogus salesman offered supporters of North and Poindexter the opportunity to buy some of his ocean-front property located in Garza County in Northwest Texas. On August 23, an irate reader from Levelland, Texas, responded to the ad: West Texans know for a fact that "there isn't an ocean in Garza County."

Celebrations for Oliver North began soon after his television appearance from the Senate Caucus Room. On August 1, 1987, officials of Ollie, Iowa, a town of 230 people, organized an "Ollie Big Days Parade" and invited North to be the grand marshal. Soon thereafter, Bill Northrop, Ollie's postmaster, said that he was kept busy cancelling letters and postcards since Ollie's postmark had become so popular. On August 12, Philmont, New York, had a parade for Oliver North. Candlelight ceremonies in North's honor were held in Oklahoma, New York, and on the steps of the Utah state capitol. At a bar in Marina del Rey, California, there was a shredding contest, and the winner was allowed to shred sheets marked "Confidential." On July 31, Fawn Hall and Oliver North-look-alike contests were held in New York; and in Dallas, Laird Stuart, a colonel in the Army Reserve, was chosen from hundreds of applicants to play North in a Bright Banc commercial.

In the midst of Ollie folly, the nation's barbers recreated the Ollie look, but their prices varied. Paul Neinast, a Dallas stylist, received seventy-five dollars for the Ollie cut; Isa Saliba of Arlington, Virginia, North's own barber for twelve years, charged six dollars for Ollie and for everyone else; and at Tucker's Barber Shop in Killeen, Texas, Ollie Tucker created an Ollie hairdo for only four dollars. But even though the close-in Ollie sides, the crisp Ollie neckline, and the longer Ollie top were in style, not every male could appear Olliesque, or wanted to.

With Olliemania everywhere, many people were concerned about its effects upon the youth in our society. Mary McCrory wrote:

<127>

It may take schoolteachers several generations to keep their pupils from aping North's lamentable grammar. The objective case is unknown to him. He says, "He told he and I," and "Mr. Nir told he." It may take mothers even longer to cure their children of his one-size-fits-all alibi for lying.

However, on the positive side, North inspired an adult wrongdoer to pay the price for his crimes. After listening to Oliver North's testimony, thirty-four-year-old Mark Lepowsky, a suspect in eight robberies in Jacksonville, Florida, nineteen robberies in the Tampa area, and forty holdups throughout the South, turned himself in to the Jacksonville Police Department on July 18, 1987, because he said that Oliver North gave him "the courage to try to be a good American."

Oliver North's notoriety also gained the attention of analysts, psychics, and soothsayers. Charles Hamilton, the New York writing expert who exposed the forgeries of the *Hitler Diaries*, examined North's handwriting and declared North to be "a cold, methodical 'egomaniac' ready to trample anyone who gets in his way." Anthony Leggett, a psychic and spiritual leader, observed that North has "Celebrity Palms:" "He does what he is told . . . Fate directed him to this role . . . Like most old soldiers he will not fade away." Mark Russell, a self-proclaimed prophet, said, "Because of the influence of Oliver North, Marine Corps enlistments will quadruple. However, many of the recruits will be sent home when it is explained to them that a buck private does not rate a blonde secretary." Mr. Russell has also predicted that "five years from now Ollie North will be the junior senator from New York, who narrowly defeats Bernhard Goetz in a runoff." Peering into the future, the world renowned psychic Sophia Sabak predicts that North will "run for President in 1992 and be elected in a landslide."

Mark Treanor, the head of North's defense fund, has vowed to name his next child after North. Such promises prompted Charles McDowell of the *Richmond Times-Dispatch* to predict that within the next few months many babies will be named Oliver, Ollie, Olive, and Olivia.

However, Fortune is fickle. Three weeks after the hearings, the fanfare began to fade. In the August 2nd edition of the *Dallas*

<128>

Morning News, David McLemore wrote that in the T-shirt race starring Ollie North and the Pope, "Ollie doesn't have a prayer;" and on August 7, the *Wall Street Journal* reported that Ollie North T-shirts were selling at half price. By the end of August 1987, Ollie items had lost their charm; and, so it seemed, had Oliver North.

But honors and dishonors continued. During the summer Johnny Carson designated North as most deserving of the Emmy award for his acting in the Best Daytime Soap Opera of 1987. In late December, North was runner-up for *Time*'s "Man of the Year," and *Life* did not forget him. Nor did *People* or *US News and World Report*, which featured him on their January covers. The Fashion Foundation of America called North one of the Year's Best Dressed Men. Charles Richman, who compiled the fashion list, said, "Even in the colorful Marine uniform, North's individuality comes through." His carriage is every tailor's dream. *Esquire* named him "Dubious Man of the Year." North was one of nine finalists in the *Washington Post Magazine* poll for "Liar of the Year;" however, Gary Hart and evangelist Jim Bakker outranked him by nineteen percent.

Although widespread "sound and fury" has diminished since July 1987, reactions to Ollie North's status continue to be divided. On March 16, 1988, North was indicted on twenty-three counts, which were later reduced to twelve criminal charges. On March 25, President Reagan called North a hero; but, according to Larry Speakes, Mrs. Reagan has a different opinion. When watching North during one of his televised interviews, she reportedly said, "Not funny, sonny." On May 2, 1988, dressed in academic regalia of purple and black, Oliver North "marched to the stage in front of a huge American flag" in the baseball park of Liberty University; and before a crowd of 12,000, he delivered the commencement address, his first speech as a civilian. Accusing his accusers, he said that the charges against him in the Iran-Contra affair are "not a brand" but "a badge of honor." Jerry Falwell, founder of the university, called North a hero, compared his suffering with that of Jesus Christ, and conferred upon him an honorary doctorate in the humanities. While Falwell praised North, an anti-North demonstration took place in downtown Lynchburg.

Since May 1988, North has been on a lecture circuit to earn money for himself and his lawyers, and, before the elections, for 1988

<129>

conservative candidates. Rushing past demonstrators chanting "Jail Ollie, Jail to the Chief" into lecture halls where he is welcomed as a hero, North has made as many appearances as six in a weekend, and he earns about $25,000 for each forty-five-minute speech. In Long Beach, California, when North spoke on behalf of a Republican candidate for Congress, "seventy-five people paid a thousand dollars apiece to have their pictures taken with him." However, Harriet Wieder of Orange County, California, who was a loser in the congressional race, called North a "mercenary" and asked, "What does Oliver North know about issues in this congressional district?"

In August, protesters in El Paso objected to North's visit; and in October, students at Boston College began a campaign to keep him from receiving the $25,000 for his appearance at the college on November 2. North did not attend the Republican National Convention in New Orleans, though it was rumored that he would; however, supporters promoted sales of Bush-North buttons, much to the dismay of Bobby Holt, a Texas delegate, who said that raising money for North at that time and place was an inappropriate move. In July 1989, North's two appearances at a luncheon in Tampa and at a banquet in Orlando, Florida, netted him $108,000. Hundreds in Jacksonville, Florida, paid $100 to have their picture taken with North, and more than two thousand paid $25 to hear him speak.

Because of widespread publicity about the Iran-Contra affair, the selection of a jury for the trial of Oliver North was a laborious effort. In addition to the difficulty in finding jurors who knew nothing of North's previous testimony, Judge Gerhard Gesell became frustrated with TV reporter Tim O'Brien for airing some of North's testimony and, according to Gesell, for obstructing efforts to select a jury. By February 9, the selection was complete; but, because of problems with secret documents, jurors were not sworn in until February 21.

On Thursday, April 20, 1989, nine women and three men began deliberations on North's guilt or innocence. On Thursday, May 4, 1989, after twelve days of "a lot of bickering and arguing" and "a strong prayer," the jurors found North guilty on three counts: changing and destroying documents, accepting a security system for his home, and "aiding and abetting in an obstruction of Congress." He was acquitted on all other charges.

<130>

Although federal prosecutors and North's detractors had hoped that North would be sent to prison, Judge Gesell fined North $150,000, placed him on a two-year probation, barred him from holding federal office, and ordered him to perform 1,200 hours in anti-drug community service during his two-year probation. After lecturing North about his conduct in the Iran-Contra affair, Judge Gesell told him, "I do not think in this area you were a leader at all, but really a low-ranking subordinate working to carry out initiatives of a few cynical superiors." Because of the sentence, the Navy suspended North's yearly pension of $23,000 for his twenty years of service.

During the two years (1987-1989) that Oliver North captured the attention of the American public, honoring or condemning him were epithets, jingles, cartoons, songs, tales, and a four-hour television mini-series, starring David Keith as Oliver North. Is North a hero struggling to overcome the demons of the world? A lying villain grasping for power? A frog who was turned into a prince? Or none of the above? Will Ollie North become the subject of a legend, a tall tale, or a joke? Or, like the fads of Olliemania, will he simply fade away?

[Editor's note: Jeri Tanner's article is definitively documented, 107 footnotes, to be exact. Her references are quite clear, however, and I refuse to interrupt the easy flow of Jeri's writing with footnotes, although WNED-TV in Buffalo, New York as producers of the Mark Russell Comedy Special did give us permission to use the Ollie North song. Other than that, though, if you wish to see footnotes please get in touch with Jeri Tanner, English Department, Texas Tech University, Lubbock, Texas 79409-3091.]

<131>

Paul Patterson
Courtesy Paul Patterson

Ted Baker
Courtesy Paul Patterson

Conway Pickard
Courtesy Paul Patterson

<132>

PAUL PATTERSON

Hallelujah, I'm A Bum

> Hallelujah, I'm a bum
> Hallelujah, bum agin;
> Hallelujah, give us a hand out
> To revive us agin!

FOLLOWING my failure as a country-comedian-commentator disc jockey (Radio KFJZ, Fort Worth, March 1938) I was finding teaching the fifth grade (Sanderson, Latin-American, elementary) a salve to the spirit and a shelter from the Great Depression. At last at home, never no more to roam! I hoped. But when a couple of my fellow grinders-at-the-mill, Ted Baker and Conway Pickard, approached me with a proposition that sounded fail-proof, I snapped it up.

Said proposition was a railroad bumming trip up north. What a relief to lower my sights to the level of my abilities. Instead of hitching my wagon to a star I would be hitching onto something on my level, say like a box car. Or if lured into the lap of luxury, the blinds[1] of a fast passenger.

Though three hearts beat as one, each was making the trip for a different reason. Conway was to pick up a new car in Detroit, Ted was along for the ride, and I was launching another career—hoboing. And just in the nick of time. I was always told that unless one was firmly established in one's career by age thirty, he wouldn't make it at anything. And here I was at twenty-nine. I counted on the fact that nobody had ever heard of anybody failing as a bum. But then, hardly anybody had ever heard of Paul Patterson either, he and his previous career pratfalls.

Favorable planetary aspects! Our landlady's husband, Underwood, depot agent, made reservations for us on a side-door pullman[2] that was destined for San Antonio. Each of us had $45 sewed in the waist bands of his trousers when we nailed a drag:[3] Time: 2 A.M., May 22, 1938, final destination, Detroit by way of the Big Apple, where the World's Fair was in progress.

<133>

By the time we reached Del Rio we had accumulated quite a few fellow knights of the road. I had no idea the brotherhood embraced such a variety. Hence we had stirrings of misgivings, the foremost of these misgivings being Conway's mode of dress. "Make the trip for business as well as pleasure," we said. Fine. But does he have to dress the part? Homberg, tweed trousers, braces, rimless spectacles—the badges of an executive? Jack Newcombe, an old-time 'bo, recalled, "Many were rolled out of a box car just because they were wearing a good pair of shoes or an unpatched coat."[4] Should these gentlemen of the road decide to roll Conway's carcass out the door, could not Ted and our hero be next? There being such a likelihood, I so apprised my comrades and counseled cutting from this crowd. Fast!

In Uvalde our pullman came to a dead stop, forcing us to nail another drag, but not until we had sidled away from our sidekicks. Our first brush with the bulls[5] came when a brakie[6] ordered us into an empty reefer[7] and out of sight.

Adverse planetary aspects! With reefers of sixty-five cars to pick from we selected a car of onions—in 100-plus temperature! Santone, bad bull town, supposedly, gave us a warm welcome—107 degrees in the shade of a box car. Barely time enough to gobble a couple of burgers—"Cut the onions!"—before nailing a drag for Houston, which we did. No sweat worrywise, but plenty otherwise.

Before leaving Santone an unreliable bum gave us a bum steer. "Lay low in that reefer and ride right through Houston," he said. However, no sooner had the drag shuddered to a stop in the Houston freight yard than a barrel-sized gun barrel glinted in the gloom and a bass bull voice bawled, "All right, you bleeps come outta there with yore hands in the air."

Needless to say I came straightaway out of that eight-foot hole before the *bleep* could crook a trigger finger. The mystery of how I did it without the use of hands was cleared up when Conway pointed out my footprints running up his tweed trousers, twixt his suspenders, and ending on top of his Homberg.

A picture being worth a thousand words, picture three budding bums being marched to a nearby highway, the blue-steel glint of a pistol barrel alternating between us and the route we were to take. Result: Marked cooling of burning zeal to become a bum. My

<134>

sentiments! But Conway set the agenda: "Now we sneak back, stretch out in the shade, and lay in wait for another freight."

Around 3:00 A.M. we were roused by the approach of one. From the strum of her drivers she was doing what hobos termed, "Ballin' da goddam jack." On top of this, nailing her would have been by the Braille system. Human eye could not have penetrated an inch of the black that enfolded us. Even so, my intentions were to nail her, for I could not think of a fate more horrible than getting cut off from my buddies in such an alien and hostile land.

My first lunge netted a collision with Ted. Lunge number two terminated in tripping over a switch rail. Lunge number three netted a double handful of empty darkness. Then the leering, fast-disappearing, red eye of the caboose apprised me of the fact that I had missed my train.

Enveloped in a sinking feeling I sank down in the jimsons to await daylight and an increasingly uncertain fate. With my buddies gone, so was my zest for the jolly, carefree life. Now I found myself fighting tooth and nail against an impulse to buy a one-way ticket for home sweet home. But the boys had set so much store by this lark that I felt that I must find them even if I had to push on to New Orleans by myself.

Once I got to studying it, my rustic reasoning made the task seem simple. Happy reunion at the New Orleans depot. Nobody around except Ted, Conway, and possibly the postmaster down to pick up the mail, same as your average depot in every West Texas town. We had agreed beforehand that in case of a split-up, we would reassemble at the next big city station, which at this point was New Orleans.

The reunion turned out even simpler than that, though fate must have worked overtime to arrange it thus. Learning that the next eastbound drag would pull out around ten A.M., I retired into a gondola of gravel to grab a nap. How could it be possible for one to lose so much sleep in a profession, purportedly so free of care.

At 10:00 A.M. a long drag, its couplings groaning and snapping, came snorting out of the Houston yards. In my eagerness to rejoin my pals I latched on just behind the engine. A bull ordered me off. I complied, but nailed on a few cars back. Another bull cowed me so I detrained and moved back from the tracks, but I was contemplating a third try, or however many it took—and at whatever speed.

<135>

"Oh, Lord," I prayed, "deliverest Thou unto me a reefer." But this drag appeared to be boxcars exclusively, all sealed and laden and gaining momentum with the monster's every snort. But hobos can't be choosers. Or can they? Just as I was coiled to nail the front end of a "sealed and laden" the Lord spake unto me as He did unto Job, out of the whirlwind, saying, "Behold, I set before thee an open door and no man can shut it."

No! It could not have been the Lord speaking, for in the door loomed a presence created more on the order of the old Devil himself. In any case, I swung up beside him.

"Jump down; yer buddy cain't nail 'er," he growled, pointing at a panting fat man trying to latch on. Abandoning a buddy was a flagrant violation of the code of the road.

"No buddy of mine," I said. "Besides, anybody slower than I am, better stay home!"

Seemingly satisfied, my new pal retired to the comfort of a corner and was soon wrapped in the sleep of the pure, the innocent, and the just. As for me, that box car floor had to be walked and the prospective reunion with my pals fretted over, interspersed with yearnings for hearth and home.

Some thirty miles on down the road, somewhere between Dayton and Liberty on the SP line, the drag came to a shuddering halt. Now the clatter of running feet along the gravelly right-of-way matched by a set of running ones up on deck. "Another flam damn bull run," I surmised, a prayer to the contrary crossing dry and fevered lips. Reversal of reversals! Ted and Conway were shaking down the rattler in search of me.

"Dr. Livingston, I presume!" Though I uttered it in jest, a more heart-felt utterance never crossed the lips of man. I was beside myself with joy, intermingled with relief.

Happy indeed was the reunion. But back to the train I missed in Houston. Come daylight, it was obvious to Ted and Conway that I had missed the train—but *had the train missed me*? Was pal Paul scattered back and forth and up and down those Tee-and-Pee tracks for fifty yards or so? With this in mind they had stepped off the train—her ballin' the (cuss word) jack notwithstanding—and had called the Houston cops. I couldn't be found either whole or in parts, so they continued their journey.

<136>

As regards my train stopping at the very lonesome spot where theirs stopped—Pure Act of Providence! And a necessary siding. Needless to say we three pals lived happier thereafter. But not much. And not long. We had no idea the jolly, carefree life could be so hard, not to mention hazardous.

After endless hours of unscheduled, unexplained stops, the mist-muffled lights of New OrLEANS or New ORleans (depending upon the pronouncer) hove into view. This was the signal, according to a large, new-found hobo friend, to detrain, fade into the jimsons, and start the long, tiresome trek around the Crescent City's yards. "Why the hell why?" asked Conway. He was of a nature not to take "roundants" on hell itself, were it the shortest route.

"Hell of a lot of sewer work goes on in this damn town" the big 'bo said, "and the way these city dads look at it, no need payin' good money to natives when they can get us vags fer nothin'. So they shake down every drag for hands."

Convinced, we faded with the big 'bo into the shadows. As regards the jimsons I was seized with the shudders. Closing in from all sides, overhead and underfoot was the spookiest jungle God ever let get out of hand.

What is more, from all sides, overhead and underfoot echoed the call and squall of night creatures my west Texas ears could scarce believe.

"Bullfrogs sound big enough to swaller a feller whole; God knows how big the water moccasins and alligators are." I would have sworn I yelled it out loud, but Ted swears that not a whisper crossed my lips.

This awful place! To quote Coleridge—or somebody—"So lonely 'twas that God Himself scarce seemed there to be!" Of course, God scarce seemed there to be! He was either plumb boogered of the place, or He didn't know where the hell it was at!

As if the place was not enough to test a man's valor, what about our guide? How short, sweet, and simple it would be for a co-conspirator lying in wait to help roll us and roll our remains into a friendly alligator's lair.

Here memory picked up a snatch of *Hamlet*: "The undiscovered country from whose bourn no traveler returns!" This instant replay via memory's eye brought me to the brink, not of physical but of emotional disintegration. However, within that fraction of a second

<137>

before psyche explodes, scattering id, ego, and super-ego over a wide area, there appeared a light at the end of the tunnel, the light in this case being a ferry-boat station.

Oh me of little faith! Whilst giving the appearance of a brutish bum, our friendly 'bo was an angel in disguise come to lead us out of the wilderness. Not only so but he gave us fool-proof instructions on how to negotiate the labyrinth of rues, routes, alleys, and avenues that constitute the complicated circulatory system of New Orleans. Then without so much as holding a hand out for a handout he faded quietly into the jimsons from whence no traveler returns. At least, he didn't.

Here a full forty-eight hours were allotted to rest and recreation, at least forty-four of which latter I incorporated into the former. I had no idea how much of the former I found lacking in the jolly, carefree life!

Outward bound from the Crescent City we found ourselves sharing a side-door pullman with six whites, eight blacks, and a smattering of in-betweens. A reasonably reasonable crowd, I surmised. This reassurance I whispered to Ted: "At least we haven't fallen amongst a flock of jungle buzzards. *I hope!*"

"On the other hand, I wouldn't say we find ourselves amongst a communion of saints," Ted said.

Bill Nelson quotes Ben L. Reitman, who tramped a good deal himself, and who wrote that "a hobo works and wanders, a tramp dreams and wanders, and a bum drinks and wanders."[8] In any case I wondered as I wandered, *"What the hell am I doing here?"*

Whether hobo, tramp, or bum any one of these guys could quote you every schedule between Seattle and Miami, Corpus Christi and Great Falls. By merely observing a freight making up in the yards he knew whether she was a manifest or a drag.[9] He could tell you the same by ear, a stethoscopic ear that could determine her speed by the spacing of her breathing when she began to shake out the slack.

On a hundred-car manifest in full momentum a good 'bo could pinpoint a hot box or a flat wheel. He could determine by the way a shack swung his lantern whether he was a man to be reasoned with or reckoned with. And he could—or would—assess not only the mood but the character of the engineer by the way his hand lay upon the throttle. If hung over and out of sorts, everybody at every crossing

<138>

got not a friendly reminder but a wailing, snarling cry of despondency and despair. On the other hand, when Ol' Casey felt high and lifted up, the trackside audience received the equivalent of a Keats ode set to locomotive-whistle music. And if he blew the mating call only to Mama as he roared through home base, he was steadfast and true. Yet blowing the same call—with flourishes—at every jerkwater burg and whistle-stop made him out as a philanderer of the first water.

When it came to handouts and shelter from winter's icy blasts, the traveled hobo was familiar with every hard case and soft touch between Bangor, Maine, and Baja, California.

The consensus among our crowd was that the purest hearts beat within the Cajun bosoms of Lafayette, Louisiana, and the Mormon breasts of all Utah. Jack Newcombe said, "Many of the lines that cut through Utah and friendly Mormon territory were called 'Milk and Honey Routes.'"[10] Consequently, winter among the Cajuns and summer with the Saints was the hobos' equivalent of the rich man's wintering in Florida and summering in the Canadian Rockies.

Women? Tolerated during the Great Depression but "low bridge" (bad luck) in every respect. Bad luck unto others but moreso unto themselves. "Boston Betty got elbowed out of a box car," writes Jack Newcombe, "and climbed onto the cow catcher." Train approached a cow straddling the tracks. Engineer pulled his whistle and Betty let go with a scream but the cow stood fast. A hobo recalled the spectacle for Newcombe: 'The engine was covered with chopped meat—very rare. But you should have seen Betty.'"[11]

Superstition, malnutrition, call it what you will, but riding the rails and romancing were not compatible. Bill Nelson defined it: "Hobo: a man in whom wanderlust is the strongest lust."[12]

Finally, the opposites of Cajuns and Latter Day Saints—Railroad Detectives—bulls. Our crowd could call every bad bull on every trunk line by his Christian name, but didn't. Bad Bill on the Burlington, Old Strikes out of Elkhart, Jeff Carr of Cheyenne, and to the West (and worst) Green River Slim. Bad 'bo bashers notwithstanding, they bothered me not one jot. I was out of their jurisdiction, and expected to remain so.

However, once they began to dwell upon the utter bloodthirstiness of Alabama bulls, their words fell upon attentive ears indeed. Especially blood-clabbering was the 'bo's dossier of a one-armed

<139>

Flomaton, Alabama bull who, allegedly, shot every black 'bo on sight. The fact that this one-armed bull's special meat was dark was no consolation. We were due in Flomaton around midnight—and what with this current coat of cinders, a bull could not distinguish me from the blackest black aboard.

Darkness overtook us in the delta country of Mississippi, and on this stretch we were riding a mixed train—box cars, oilers, gondolas, flats, and an empty passenger coach. Empty of paid fares only. No sooner was this coach hooked on than all our traveling companions, save one, abandoned us for the plush accomodations of the chair car.

It was with considerable sorrow—mixed with envy—that I realized that even the brotherhood was cursed with its share of snobs—passenger stiffs in the parlance of the road, fraternizing openly and lolling luxuriously in direct violation of Jim Crow as well as railroad regulations. And violating southern mores deep in the heart of white supremacy country.

But why did they have to have the lights full on to boot? As if this were a meeting of the executive board. An integrated meeting thirty years before its time! This, on top of our cold and cheerless quarters between cars, was not conducive to our rest and recreation.

Flomaton was as anticipated—terrifying to the Nth. We had detrained and taken long roundants on the town, but just as we nailed our drag a lantern came bobbing along behind us. This lantern, I entertained not the slightest doubt, hung from the stub arm of you know who.

"Giddown offa theah, you sombitches;" heavy southern accent notwithstanding, the message was plain. Nonetheless, I vowed to stick with my buddies even if the next command issued straight from the barrel of that .44!

As if by divine decree a flashback of Tad Lucas trick-riding at the Fort Worth Fat Stock Show filled my screen, prompting—nay urging—me to do likewise. Which I did, swinging down between the critter's cars, hanging from her flanks, leaping the gaps in her spine, whilst all the while she was lurching and snapping like a blacksnake whip.

When the lantern finally bobbed out of sight I felt like Willie Francis back in Louisiana when they threw the switch to electrocute

<140>

him and the charge only tickled!

Here and now it seems ridiculous to think a one-armed bull could hop a moving freight, carry a lantern, and, with a pistol drill a trick-riding target through the pitch darkness of a foggy midnight on the deck of a lurching drag. However, at the time it seemed not only a cinch but a certainty.

From Flomaton on it got progressively worse. A most miserable display of Southern Hospitality in Birmingham. "Shades of the prison house upon the growing boy"—said Wordsworth, probably with Birmingham in mind.

The morning, squinting as best it could through the Birmingham smog, peered disgustedly down upon three sleeping hoboes. And from a distance of ninety-three million miles, half of it through steel-mill smoke, Ol' Sol could plainly perceive them to be the dirtiest, seediest, sorriest trio ever he laid a ray upon.

An 11 1/2 EEE in the ribs of Ted, Conway, and me, respectively, roused us from our sleep of sheer exhaustion.

"Scatter out, you bums, lest they throw yo' asses in jail," said a switchman offering friendly counsel. Conway, all business—with the last vestiges of pleasure gone—was the first to express a unanimous opinion: "I am damn well fed up with this lazy, jolly, carefree life of a bum. What's jolly about inhalin' cinders twenty-four hours a day, huh? What's carefree about dodgin' bulls and sooner or later bullets and 'fo' spots' (forty-four days on a chain gang), huh? What ...?"

So—heartsick, homesick, footsore, and fed up with the jolly life, we were set to nail a drag right in front of the Birmingham round-house when another bum counseled caution. "Few nights ago couple o' 'bos, one an ex-cop, got in a fight on top of a movin' drag. Fell under and were forthwith converted into ground round. Now, them city cops are 'fo' spottin' ever'body caught catchin' out in the yards."

And so for a long walk out of the yards, followed by the daddy of all bull runs in Louisville, where Ted and Conway maintain to this day that I set a track record down that L&N track that was not and will not be equaled at Churchill Downs.

These misadventures plus poop from the brotherhood that Virginia and the Carolinas were low bridge all the way—smokey, chokey tunnels, and worse—caused us to alter our route and bear

<141>

straight for Detroit and the comforts of Conway's new car. In Cincy a bold 'bo graciously offered to share his plush quarters on the blinds of a crack passenger, but we respectfully declined. As Harriet Tubman of underground railroad fame must have felt, we were too close to freedom to muff it.

"DEE-troit," Conway sang out. His enunciation was that of the black 'bos, but the catch in his voice was on the order of Christopher Columbus's when he cried, "Land ho!" five hundred years ago. This was the end of our journey. From here on back to Sanderson we were rolling on our own—or Conway's—wheels.

Re-constructed hobos have been known to throw up everything and sprint for the tracks at the long, lonesome wail of a drag. People like Jack London and Jack Dempsey used to say that the call of the iron trail gets in a man's blood. So does malaria and syphilis, herpes and AIDs. Other ex-bums say that railroad bumming cannot help but leave a terminal after-effect on all who have succumbed to its siren song. In my case it's rheumatism!

Notes

1. Blinds—the enclosed vacant space between the engine tender and the baggage car on old-time passenger trains.
2. Side–door pullman—common boxcar.
3. Nailed a drag—hopped a moving freight train.
4. Jack Newcombe, "The Vanishing Hobo," *Saga Magazine* (September 1960), 40.
5. Bulls—railroad detectives, people with authority to arrest people trying to hitch a free ride on their trains.
6. Brakie (called shack by the brotherhood)—man in charge of everything behind the engine. Also has authority to toss bums off his train.
7. Reefer—ice compartment of a refrigerator car
8. Bill Nelson, "The Vanishing Hobo," *American Legion Magazine* (July 1967), 23.
9. Manifest—non-stop train, either passenger or freight that only stops at the big terminals. A drag was a slow freight.
10. Newcombe, 40.
11. Newcombe, 94.
12. Nelson, 49.

<142>

TOM McCLELLAN

Dogs and Madmen:
Stories from the Sufi Tradition

THE SUFI constitute a mystical tradition affiliated with Islam. Although Sufis claim to be carriers of sacred knowledge originating among the prophet Mohammed's inner circle about 600 A.D., Sufism had its formal beginning two hundred years later. The movement developed as a reaction against growing formalism in the Islamic religion and the luxury and laxity that beset it during the spread of the Islamic Empire. The objective of the Sufi was the perfection of the individual and a union with Allah. These goals were pursued by developing discipline over body and mind and practicing love for one's fellow man.

The knowledge and ways of Sufism were transmitted orally and formally from masters to disciples through direct teachings. Sufism was also transmitted informally and indirectly in parables or stories, such as those below, and in such poems as those found in the quatrains of Omar Khayyám.

Although the traditional folk tales were long existent only in the oral tradition, the publication of Idries Shah's *The Way of the Sufi* (London: Octagon Press, Ltd.,1980) made a number of them available to the public. The stories below are idiomatic recastings of some of the stories from Shah's book.

I

IN A CERTAIN town, some members of the Mosque became concerned about the local madman—he never came to services. So they invited him and, when he consistently ignored them, they came by his hovel and charitably demanded that he go with them that day for prayer. He went, grudgingly.

They glowed with righteous satisfaction at his enforced presence until, at the most solemn moment, the Cantor began to invoke

<143>

Allah—and the madman drowned him out with a chant of his own: "*Ox for sale! Ox for sale! How much am I bid for this ox for sale!*"

Then the madman was silent and the service continued as usual, though the congregation was electrified with outrage. The service over, the madman left amid angry murmurs and hard stares. Some followers of the Compassionate One said they wished him in Hell, and one old acid-tongue said he thought the man's soul dwelt there already and was happy, having grown familiar with the landscape and the populace.

Those unfortunates responsible for the madman's attendance greeted the Cantor with cries of apology; but the holy one raised his hand, lowered his eyes and confessed: "Indeed, my mind was wandering. I am beset with financial problems, and it came to me just before the most solemn invocation, as if inspired by the One High God, that I ought to save myself by selling my ox. At the very moment the madman began to cry out, I was wondering how much it would bring."

So some were mollified and some were mystified, but most said darkness would rule the light before the sun rose on them again in the same Mosque with that madman.

Then he of the acid tongue sought out the madman, who was not in his hovel but in the cemetery, chuckling over the noble sentiments carved upon the grave-markers.

"Fellow student of the Prophet," said the congregationer, "today I cast some angry words in your direction, for which I ask your pardon," and he told the madman what had passed with the Cantor in the mosque after his departure. This is the madman's response:

"It is well that the dung wagon occasionally take on a passenger who will urge the other riders to honesty—especially those most deeply convinced they have boarded the palanquin to Heaven."

II

PERHAPS HE WAS the very same madman who was accosted on the street by an Infidel who had heard the cries of the Muezzin calling the faithful to worship and asked,

"What's that man doing up there?"

"Rattling a nut in an empty shell," said the madman.

One commentator adds:

<144>

Allah the Generous One, the Raiser of the Dead,
the Guardian of All Existence, the Ever Present.

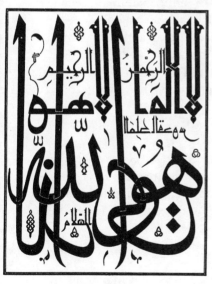

He is Allah

Allah, May His Glory Be Exalted.

<145>

"Some call upon the One, even with ten Names, to fill the void with noise and stifle the cry of the task at hand."

III

A CERTAIN Master was once asked what first inspired him to seek the Way. "It began with a dog," he said.

"One spring of my youth was particularly cheerless. Though lovers walked with one another's love and flowers burst from red-green branches, I found no pleasure, no renewal, only anguish.

"I found a park with a pond and rested, hoping the peace of the calm water would enter my tormented soul. Then a dog arrived, a sorry sight. His hide was scarred by mange; his tongue was thirst-swollen. Every rib announced the extremity of his condition.

"The dog approached the pond but was frightened by his own reflection. He yelped and ran a little way. Then his thirst drew him back just as surely as his reflection frightened him again, so he snarled and whimpered and withdrew, scrawny tail trailing between ankles. Then, again, victim of his need, he approached, and, victim of his fear, snuck away; and so continued approaching and retreating, until only enough energy remained in him to crawl one last time to the brink, gather himself shuddering with terror, and, finally leap with a blood-freezing howl into that which he most feared.

"Of course, he shattered his reflection, and drank and drank and drank and drank, yes, and enjoyed the bath as well.

"Need I say, beloved disciple, that in the plight of that pathetic cur I saw the image of my own unhappy state. Thus, I was inspired to seek salvation, by observing a thirsty dog."

IV

PERHAPS it was this same Master, who was once invited to the home of a rich and powerful man and promised a great feast. The menu listed foods the Master had not tasted since he'd taken up a life of poverty, and some delicacies were so rare he had only heard them praised.

The Master came to the man's mansion at the appointed time. His host met him at the door.

"Get hence!" he roared. "I am expecting a Holy Man tonight. I'll have no rustic bums about the place. Off with you!"

<146>

Without a flicker of countenance or murmer of demur, the Master turned and walked away. When he was nearly out of earshot, his host hailed him back:

"Come, honored sir, I was but jesting. I know who you are."

Showing neither pleasure nor displeasure, the Master again approached the well-lit door, and the odors of the promised feast were borne to his nostrils on the evening breeze.

"By all that's holy!" bellowed the rich man when the Master set foot upon his portico, "Your clothes are as filthy as your feet, and your hair is as ill kempt as your rags! I'll not soil my hearth and table with the likes of you. Be gone!"

Again the Master began to depart, and again, when he neared the gate, the rich man called him back, only to dismiss him yet again with affected anger and still again call him back with feigned repentance. And so the rich man plagued the Master until the rich man realized his folly.

As his guest approached him for the dozenth time, showing neither weariness nor impatience, the rich man spoke with genuine meekness:

"Honored sir, forgive my folly. All I have heard of your perfection must be true and more besides. Your patience and humility declare you the Saint of this Age, for love of whom Allah the Just forbears destruction of our sinful world . . . ."

"Enough," said the Master. "Your praise is as empty as your blame, for you admire no more than a dog's obedience. Any hungry cur would have done the same."

V

THE MASTER ISSA once met a woman near a well beyond the borders of Judea, and she asked him to bless her.

"My people regard yours as Infidels and sand-niggers," the Master said. "Shall a dog eat at the table set for God's children?"

"Even a dog may beg crumbs," she replied.

After a moment Issa responded: "You know me better than my own," he said, and blessed her.

<147>

Kenneth Davis

<148>

KENNETH DAVIS

Bodies and Souls:
Some Partings of the Twain

F E A T U R E stories in supermarket newsheets such as the *Sun* for January 14, 1986, and the *Weekly World News* for April 24, 1984, headlined accounts of sightings of human souls seen leaving the bodies which had been their earthly temples. Although the incidents occurred in widely separated locations—Sweden and Australia—the accounts are quite similar. Both incidents occurred in surgical units; both were witnessed by highly trained physicians and nurses; both contained descriptions of the human soul leaving the body as a flash of light. In one incident, the soul returns to the body and the reinspirited body lives. This phenomenon is referred to in metaphysical circles as the Lazarus Syndrome. The revived person tells about wonderful visions. A striking element in the vision the survivor recounted was his description of smiling, happy faces of long departed loved ones and friends at the end of a tunnel through which a blessed light streamed. A final common element is that the trained professionals who witnesssed such miraculous happenings become convinced of the existence of the soul. Prior to these operating-room soul sightings, some of the doctors and nurses were agnostics, if not out-and-out atheists. The account of the sighting in Sweden supposedly was written up in the prestigious *Swedish Journal of Surgeons*.

Authoritative sheets as the *Sun*, the *Weekly World News*, and that granddaddy of fascinating sensationalism, the *National Enquirer*, appeal to a wide spectrum of the American public. Whether these journals intend to reflect matters long of interest to folklorists or merely wish to sell copies of their papers is hardly an argument. But for the folk, matters pertaining to the soul are probably more important than bodily interests. The folk are a soulful lot. In Texas, where the folk are only mildly corrupted by grocery store checkout-

<149>

stand sensationalism, interesting yarns about body and soul connections and partings live on in the oral tradition. Two yarns about such matters follow.

An informant from San Angelo provided the following brief example recently:

An old man who lived in the county seat believed that when a person died, the direction of a vapor leaving the body indicated where the soul was to spend eternity. He said that if the vapor ascended, the soul had gone to Heaven but if the vapor descended, the soul had gone to Hell. This old man felt very bitter toward his oldest son who attracted his attention just as the vapor left the body of Emma, the old man's wife. The son's calling out to the old man caused him to miss seeing where the dead woman's soul had gone. The old man had kept a long vigil waiting for the vapor to leave the body.

A more extended yarn demonstrates the abiding interest of the folk in the migrations of the soul. I gleaned this one some years ago from my now deceased grandfather, William David Davis, for many years a resident of old Bell County, that repository of much lore— some authentic, and some just interesting.

My grandfather was one of a now vanished breed who were considered qualified to do community service such as "give medicine" and "sit up with the remains." For the benefit of anyone who might not know what "to give medicine" and/or "to sit up with the remains" mean, I will explain. At one time in Texas, literacy was not even somewhat common. Harried physicians in times of epidemics found that far too often, people could not read directions on medicine containers and either did not have timepieces, or could not use them; so in dire cases, someone who could read and tell time would be called in to "give medicine" at the stated hours. My grandfather was literate and had a splendid Waltham watch he probably acquired in a game of chance, so he was often called to "give medicine." He also had the miraculous ability to go without sleep for several days. This trait helped him tend the sick and made him the first man in the community to be called upon to "sit with the remains." Before the days of screened windows, air-conditioned funeral parlors, and houses too small for having the coffin with its contents brought back from the undertakers to await burial after a suitable time to allow

<150>

distant kinfolks to make those melancholy homeward journeys, the custom was to have the remains brought to the family's house where around the clock vigils were held. The custom is rooted in ancient folklore. It probably began for the practical reason of keeping wild animals from consuming the remains. Larry McMurtry, a fair folklorist, gave a grisly account in *Lonesome Dove* of how a varmint took away the leg of one of the deceased protagonists in that long novel. In central Texas the custom of sitting up persisted until the early 1940s.

The incident of a soul-body separation I have to report took place in about 1914, however. At that time in Bell County, there were few undertakers and even fewer establishments where the remains could be kept until time for burial. A lady well up in her eighties "sadly departed these precincts"—as a tattered newspaper clipping described the event. The clipping didn't include what happened the night before her mortal remains were to be buried.

Because of his heroic wakefulness, my grandfather was asked to take the night shifts for both nights prior to the burial. The first night was uneventful. As he usually did, Grandad brought with him some of his domino playing cronies. When the members of the family retired, he and his friends began a cut-throat game. One pious lady in the community called my grandfather and his friends cigar-chomping, whiskey-drinking, evil-smelling old men, long before John L. Lewis maligned the character of the noble John Nance Garner with similar terms. These paragons had played together so long they did not have to speak; they merely gestured. Word got out that Dave Davis and his rowdy friends had played dominoes all night in the presence of the body of the saintly departed, so on the second night, Miss Birdie Pauline McReady, a grandscale prototype of a high-toned woman, was assigned to sit up with my ever wakeful grandfather and his domino playing renegade friends. Miss Birdie was a maiden lady of ample girth whose legendary virtue exceeded that of Edmund Spenser's militant defender of chastity, the lady knight Britomart from Book III of *The Faërie Queene*. She was first among equals at christenings, showers, cemetery cleanings, sheep shearings, confirmations, wakes, weddings, all day singings, hog killings, and the like.

<151>

The only trait she and my grandfather shared was the ability to go for long stretches without sleep. This talent too often brought them reluctantly together in houses of bereavement. So it was on the night before the body of the pious octogenarian was to be buried in the black dirt of Bell County. What happened that night was a folk mini-drama the reporting of which delighted—for years—the spit-and-whittle crews at the Bartlett Gin or under the awnings of Buschland's Cafe and Hamburger Stand and Magazine Rack in Holland.

Promptly at eleven P.M., my grandfather and his three domino partners arrived to be met at the front door by the nearly ninety-year-old widower who had forgotten that his wife had died. He was convinced that anyone who came calling at eleven P.M. deserved to be greeted with a loaded double-barrelled shotgun. His youngest son, a cotton buyer in Taylor, patiently disarmed his father. Grandad and his cronies went to the kitchen table. In just a few minutes, Miss Birdie Pauline arrived in her spotless Model-T touring car with its snap-on curtains. She and my grandfather exchanged menacingly civil greetings, and she hurried to the kitchen where the men began yet another game of dominoes. Miss Birdie sat rigidly upright in an uncomfortable chair. She glared at the evil domino players. Who knows what she was thinking?

Despite her firm intention to remain awake and thus perpetuate the legend, Miss Birdie began to nod sometime after one A.M. She quickly awakened and looked about to see what devilment my grandfather's crew was up to. They were silently intent on their game, so Miss Birdie sought an even more uncomfortable chair than the one she was in. Virtue achieved in comfort is never as meritorous as that wrought in absolute agony. All martyred saints have known this great truth for centuries. But she could not find a more wretched chair, and so she determined to make do with the one she had picked initially.

For another hour, the large kitchen was almost silent. The only sounds which marred the solemn serenity were the muffled clicks of dominoes placed gently on the oak table. Miss Birdie nodded, despite her firm resolve not to do so. Then, at almost exactly two A.M., from the coffin came a shriek of such volume that it caused the dishes in the family's prized china-closet to rattle. Gases in the primitively embalmed corpse had built up and demanded exodus. These gases

<152>

travelled across the vocal cords of the deceased, who for years had a voice which reverberated through all the rooms and even the darkest corners of the basement of Bartlett's First Baptist Church.

Before the epic wail from the coffin subsided, my grandfather yelled: "What in the purple-starred Hell was that?" Miss Birdie, awakened from a sleep deeper than she knew, screamed in utter terror: "My God, Dave Davis, they'll rape us all." Then, in a movement phenomenally quick for one of such heroic girth, Miss Birdie made a dive through the screenless window to the hoped-for safety of the outdoors. In trying to fly through the tall floor to ceiling window, she turned a bit sideways and managed to land derriere first in a cedar washtub, the kind antique buffs today would kill to possess. The tub was mostly dry and had some good-sized splinters, one of which penetrated Miss Birdie's several petticoats and other layerings to come to rest in the left side of her abundantly ample posterior. At that point, she screamed with volume louder than the noise those gases made when they departed the body of the deceased.

The bereaved widower heard all of this commotion, grabbed his formidable shotgun, and charged down the stairs screaming, "Let me at 'em! Let me at 'em! I'll kill ever' one of th' schemin' redskin' bastids!"

Two of my grandfather's friends heard only the part about "schemin' bastids" and reckoned they were sure targets, so they dived beneath the sturdy oak kitchen table. The bereaved had been a famous Indian fighter who had given many a Comanche an early trip to the Great Beyond. The cotton-buyer son hastened to prevent bloodshed and led his outraged father upstairs once more. Momentarily, eerie silence reigned. Then, in tones which commanded total attention and absolute obedience, Miss Birdie ordered my grandfather and the domino players to come to her assistance. By some miracle of leverage too complex to describe, the startled but grandly amused men got Miss Birdie released from the cedar washtub. Peace seemed to be possible again. But the splinter remained in Miss Birdie's backside.

That intruder had to be removed from a region suspected not to have been observed even clinically by any living creature since Miss Birdie turned three years old. Even the militantly virtuous Miss Birdie could not deny the power of a splinter the size of a kitchen

<153>

match. The community's only physician had made yet another of his mysterious departures following the death of the lady whose voice had briefly returned to this world. So, my grandfather had to act. He told Miss Birdie he could remove the splinter with his trusty pocket knife. At first, she was outraged but pain became the mother of diminished inhibitions and she agreed, but there were some provisos. First, only my grandfather and the most nearsighted of the domino players were to be present at the removal of the painfully offending splinter. Second, if my grandfather or any of the others who were sitting up ever told anyone about the incident, she promised them all deaths too horrible to describe. But, why not? She swore she would grind them to death in her McCormick-Deering threshing machine and then feed the scraps to the area's few surviving timber wolves. Miss Birdie was a lady who thought she knew how to prevent leaks to the press. My grandfather and the others agreed to the conditions. Miss Birdie decorously exposed just enough of her bottom to allow the removal of the splinter. Grandad poured a little bourbon whiskey on the wound to disinfect it. Miss Birdie all but strangled to keep from screaming. When she could say just a few words, she repeated her dire threats to those who might be so foolish as to reveal anything about the long night. Then, she left, even if her shift at sitting up did have four hours remaining. Grandad and his friends stood out on the front porch and watched as Miss Birdie, at the wheel of her Model-T, fled across the low hills and valleys with the gas lever set at wide open.

The men were beyond laughter and might not have laughed, anyway, in such a setting. They did have some respect for the dead—even if they saw nothing wrong with a spirited game of dominoes while "sitting up." Instead of laughing, then, the men sat and discussed the event philosophically, which gets us back to the topic of this paper. One said he was sure what they heard was the soul of the deceased leaving the body. He recounted several similar incidents he had heard of in Tennessee, his home state. The two other domino buddies were convinced also that what they heard was the song of the soul leaving this plateau. One domino addict, the near-sighted one who had assisted in the emergency surgery, noted that such happenings were common as could be in Arkansas. My grandfather, a bit the skeptic, said he had never heard anything like the noise which came

<154>

from the coffin. In later years he again broke the promise never to tell about Miss Birdie's splinter. But that time, he had chatted with enough undertakers to know that sometimes, gases do find their way out of the bodies. Grandad was sure he never saw a soul, but despite what the undertakers told him, he still wondered if he and his friends and Miss Birdie heard one begin its way toward those higher realms on wings of shrieking song.

Of course, Grandad and the three domino players had not waited until after the graveside service to spread the story about Miss Birdie's splinter, and all the other details of that night when a cry from the dead brought more liveliness than some of the participants had known in years. Nowadays, only funeral home attendants clad in proper soft-gray suits hear ghastly or ghostly sounds. These professionally somber moderns are not shocked or terrified. I think maybe the world was better off then when Miss Birdie and whiskey-drinking, cigar-chomping domino players could react as they did that fateful night back in 1914 in old Bell County.

<155>

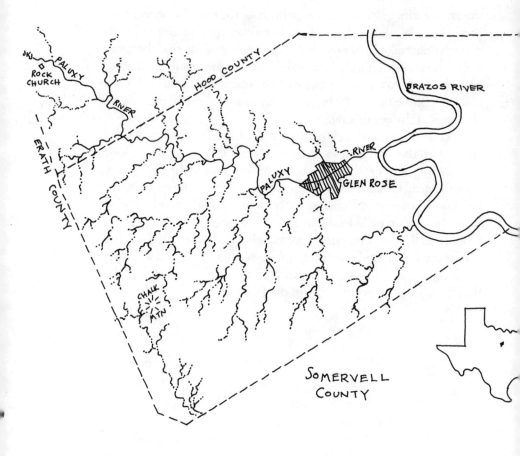

<156>

JANET JEFFERY

Glen Rose 'Shine

CHARLIE MOSS was known for many things in Glen Rose, Texas. He was a veteran of The Great War, a good family man, and he was to go down in the history books as guide to the dinosaur's stone prints left along the banks of Charlie's beloved Paluxy River.

But in the early 1920s Charlie became known as a man who, like many of his neighbors, made up his mind to follow his conscience about the rights and wrongs of the world. And never mind if his sense of right did not exactly jibe with the law. The law, like Lady Justice, was blind and was sometimes made by well-meaning but misguided folks who did not always take the realities of raising a family and the price of corn into account. There was the law on the one hand, and a man's family obligations and traditions on the other, and they didn't always agree. Charlie came from a people who had come to this country to escape government, a people who had settled back in the hills as far as they could get, a people who had happily kept to their own ways. They had brought these ways with them as they moved west across the South and settled in the hills above Glen Rose.

The Glen Rose hills were a sweet, good place to live, with clear water running over and through the purifying white limestone and thick stands of oak and groves of cedar growing along the banks. With the bottom land cleared and planted in corn and wheat, the Glen Rose hills were a good place to raise generations of sons and daughters. And in 1919 when money got scarce, corn plentiful, and legal liquor nonexistent, those hills provided good places to make corn whiskey.

Somervell County is flat in the east for there it is part of the Brazos River Valley. But in the west the county swells and knobs up into

<157>

1 Qt. Sprouted Corn Kernals + 50 lbs. Sugar (Purchased) + 5 gal. Wheat Bran (Purchased) + 50 gal. Water = MASH

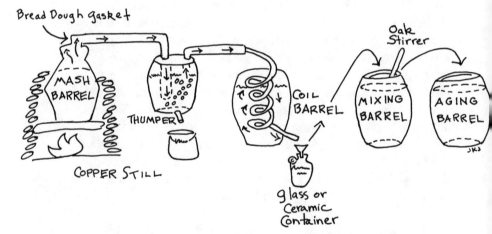

Bread Dough gasket

MASH BARREL

COPPER STILL

THUMPER

COIL BARREL

glass or Ceramic Container

Oak Stirrer

MIXING BARREL   AGING BARREL

Diagram based on illustrations in *Foxfire*, pp. 324-325 and interviews with James Moss, Glen Rose, Texas.

<158>

caliche hills covered with oak and cedar. Green and hilly, white splashes mark limestone outcroppings. And before the population grew and dug deeper and deeper wells, fresh tasting springs produced the best and purest of waters. It was a moonshiner's idea of heaven. He had plenty of cedar to burn hot and fast to get his fire started. Then he had the slower burning oak to feed the fire over long hours. The pure spring water that filtered through the limestone was essential. And oak, now carved into barrels, held the liquid corn as it aged and took on the flavor of the burned wood. Finally the rough terrain with its hills and hollows, its thick trees and thickets was rich in hiding places, especially when the dark of night hid the fire's smoke.

Simple in concept, moonshining relied on natural resources and man's canny use of his environment. Corn made the best whiskey, but bran produced a larger quantity. Originally most moonshine was pure corn, but as time went by bran became more popular for economic reasons. Sometimes some corn was added to the bran for its flavor; even a little corn added a lot of flavor. Barley and rye were also used. In fact, almost anything could be used for distilling, though non-foodstuffs such as corn stalks produced a poison.

One classic recipe given to me by Charlie's son, James, called for a quart of corn kernels soaked in water: ". . . then drop the corn in a tow-sack and bury it in the ground for four or five days, and then take it out and wash it off good. Next grind it in a food chopper and use it for yeast.

"Add the yeast, along with fifty pounds of sugar and four or five gallons of wheat bran, and mix in a fifty gallon barrel. Let this set for five days."

Then the recipe simply stated, ". . . you cook it in a copper still." But this cooking was quite involved. After the mash was added to the mash barrel and until it left the coil and dripped into the waiting glass fruit jar or ceramic jug, it should have touched nothing but copper.

The copper still was made of three parts. Glen Rose moonshiners made their own stills, forming sheets of the orange metal into the shape of a coffin. This was the mash barrel. A copper pipe ran from the mash barrel to the next section, the Thumper, named for its noise during the distilling process. Another pipe, wound into a coil, left the Thumper and entered what was called the coil barrel. The coil barrel

<159>

was made of wood, but the whiskey never touched that wood. This barrel held cooling water as the copper pipe holding the whiskey wound through it.

After the mash was added to the barrel, the fire was started with cedar to get it hot. Then oak logs were fed to slow the fire down and keep it burning steadily. As long as the cooking mash floated to the top and was sweet, it wasn't ready. But once the mash sank and had a bitter taste, it was ready. It was important to get the mash hot enough to make steam, but to never let it boil. Inside the barrel, as the mash heated, steam rose through the pipe, and then fell back into the mash. Raw dough, made of flour and water, was spread to seal the joint between the pipe and the top of the mash barrel. As the pipe got hot, the dough cooked and formed an air-tight gasket. Again and again the steam rose up partway through the pipe, only to fall back again into the barrel. When the temperature was finally hot enough, the pressure forced the steam all the way through the pipe and into the Thumper. The steam followed the tubing through the Thumper and down into the coil barrel. The water in the barrel cooled and condensed the steam into liquid—the whiskey.

The whiskey dripped out of the copper tubing into clear glass or ceramic containers, usually fruit jars.

The liquor would have different proofs, depending at what point in the distilling process it dripped out of the tube into the jar. Some drippings were weak, yet others were so strong they were lethal. It was important to mix the proofs together to even out the strengths and weaknesses and to produce a desirable product. Charlie Moss would taste it just as it came out of the coil barrel to judge its suitability. It was, said James, the only time that Charlie touched whiskey for he was not a drinking man. Fresh from the still, the clear liquid was called White Lightning. This was whiskey for the impatient.

For those who could stand to wait awhile, the whiskey was stored in a large oak barrel. The inside of the barrel was burned out so no fresh wood was exposed. This burned wood was very important. Storing the liquor in green, unburned oak gave the whiskey an undesirable (for some) raw taste of tannin. And the wood had to be oak and not cedar, for cedar would taint the taste. Burned oak mellowed and smoothed out the whiskey flavor and changed the clear liquid to a reddish color. James told me that, for sanitary

<160>

reasons, the law that governs present-day distilleries limits the oak barrels to one use only. This is why we see so many whiskey barrels for sale these days as planters.

Somervell County moonshiners naturally had no such laws governing them so they used the barrels as many times as they wished. Those who had no barrels at all simply stored the liquor in the fruit jars, adding a burned chunk of oak to each jar. This wood mellowed the flavor and reddened the color just as well as whiskey aged in the barrel.

There was, of course, an element of risk in moonshine. There were said to be at least twenty-five stills operating in the dark of night during Prohibition, so it seems to have been a community-wide effort. Nevertheless, it was not done brazenly in the open.

Some citizens were always on the alert for too many men habitually hanging out at a certain farm or for those fellows who routinely bought five hundred pounds of sugar. For the most part, though, affairs went smoothly with the help of friends and family. The little old ladies called the sheriff with their suspicions. The sheriff then called the suspect and told him he was coming out, giving him plenty of time to tidy up his place. Or the shopkeeper, perhaps kin of some sort, would wait around after closing and help the customer load five-hundred pounds of sugar without the interruptions of other, less understanding customers.

The children of Glen Rose learned early not to be too inquisitive, especially about metal contraptions they found buried in the woods. The moonshiner habitually broke the still up into parts and hid each one away from the rest. If children happened on the coil, for example, they knew to let it alone, back off, and forget they had ever seen it.

The most serious danger came from the Texas Rangers, agents of Big Government. Many an operation was interrupted for awhile when the stills were broken up and confiscated and the men were sent to Huntsville. On August 25, 1923, the Rangers started a raid at sunrise. By sundown they had jailed twenty-seven men for violation of the prohibition laws, including the sheriff. The next day the county attorney was arrested, climaxing a raid that swept in forty men, seized three-hundred gallons of whiskey, and destroyed an even greater amount.

<161>

Today a raid would not pull in such a large portion of the male community, nor its most prestigious members. Charlie Moss's still is in the museum in the Glen Rose town square, and his heirs feel no harm in talking about the old days. Nor do lawmen alert for smoke in the woods hang around Somervell County. Even so, there remains a small market for those who prefer the taste of real corn liquor. I heard one story of a moonshiner in East Texas who had carved out a tunnel and a hiding place within a large patch of briars, and did his cooking on a butane stove. For those who wish to hide their activities, the stove with its smokeless steady heat is a wonder of modern technology.

The moonshiner, like Charlie Moss, has now become a folk hero in the tradition of Robin Hood and Jesse James. He bent the law to survive, for his belief in the law of survival was stronger than his belief in the law. He had a family to support and was doing the best he could with what he had. The government became the enemy, for it had no right to interfere. The moonshiner was that typical Texan of folklore with his streak of cussed independence: "No man, no government is going to tell me what to do." This is an attitude that dates back past the 1794 Whiskey Rebellion, further back to the Old World and the kings their forefathers left behind. It is an attitude we continue today everytime we speed past a fifty-five-mile-an-hour highway sign, leave our belts unbuckled on the car seat, or return a creative tax form on April the fifteenth.

<162>

FAYE LEEPER

Storm Cellar Wisdom:
Tall Tales from Down Under

ONE OF THE first structures built in Texas by the white man was the dugout, usually constructed half under ground and half above ground. It was the sole dwelling beyond the covered wagon for many families until money and lumber were available for a frame dwelling. This kind of dugout was still in use as a residence in West Texas as late as 1940.

The residential dugout usually was built into a hill. The farmer cut into a slope on the front side so that the back of the dugout was walled by earth. He then added the walls of the top half of the front out of timber and added a timber door. More often the front wall was made of native stone. A dugout such as this still remains on the W. C. Gilbert ranch near Newport, Texas. Ann Carpenter describes in her article in *Built in Texas* called "Texas Dugouts" how the ones with sod roofs were subject to leaking and how miserable the dwellers were in rainy seasons (*Built in Texas*, PTFS XLII [1979], 53-60).

In some isolated cases, dugouts are still residential habitats. I taught second grade in 1957, the first year after receiving my teaching degree. One of my students told me that his family lived in a dugout, and his personal hygiene seemed to testify to the validity of his statement.

Most country homes, however, both before and after that date, have been equipped with a dugout commonly known as the "storm cellar"—or in shortened form simply "the cellar." Thousands of families produced this structure to more or less common folk dimensions and with comparable materials through the years without ever drawing up a formal set of blue prints or without ever writing down the measurements or specified materials. One needed only to size up one dugout and adapt whatever tools or materials were

<163>

Dugout in the Palo Duro.

accessible to his own building.

Sometimes a man dug his own, and sometimes during slack farming seasons, the neighbors pitched in and helped. A gathering of this sort called for goodies to be cooked by the owner's wife and goodies to be uncovered in the corn crib by the master of the household.

The usual measurements of the rectangular hole used for a storm cellar were six- to eight-feet wide, eight- to ten-feet long, and six-feet deep. The roof was often made by laying cast-off railroad cross ties or tree trunks six to eight inches in diameter across the narrow width. In either case the timbers were usually treated with creosote oil, if creosote were available, to prevent rot and termites. A vent was

<164>

made of an iron pipe or a wooden stack of one by fours to form an air tunnel at the rear of the cellar. A framework for the entire entrance was made of wood. The door was of wood or a wood frame with sheet iron nailed to it. Attached to the door was, usually, a chain which hooked over a large nail driven into the frame of the doorway to hold the door securely closed, even when wind storms tore at it. Many rigged up pulley weights to make the doors more manageable against the winds. Several had filled a bucket with concrete to use as a weight. Others had scrap iron or rocks in them.

The interior generally consisted of wooden benches in a U-shape, about two-and-one-half-feet wide, around the walls of the dugout. Along each side above these benches, and across the back, shelves lined the walls to hold canned goods. A small shelf was near the door on which an oil lamp or a kerosene lantern could be placed when the cellar was used as refuge against a threatening storm. In later years, the more affluent families built a somewhat larger cellar completely enclosed (except for the door) with concrete. Some of these were large enough to house a regular-size bed and various other pieces of furniture.

All these dugouts served many purposes. They not only housed the canned goods that were preserved in summer to last all winter, but farm families stored the potatoes, onions, turnips, pumpkins, and other vegetables under the benches. All these foods were generally safe from freezing. In summer the melons were put there to chill.

Some farmers beat the heat and took their brief after-dinner nap in the coolest place on the farm, the cellar.

Sometimes this extra room underground served as did the hayloft as a bedroom for temporary hired help or for travelers needing respite for the night. It was always a happy time for me when I visited my grandparents, and the cellar became a guest room for the grand-children; it was far removed from the authority of adults. Sometimes we told the most frightening stories we could conjure up. And sometimes the entire cellar was aroused when a sleeping toad came alive under the benches or when we realized we were sharing the hole with a mouse or garden snake.

But obviously not least of its uses was one of life or death consequences; it offered refuge from the imminent storm.

<165>

Secluded in such narrow quarters on such occasions, awaiting the worst that could happen, the cellar offered the ideal setting for the storytellers. They retold stories of their own experiences and those of their neighbors and those of people they never knew but had heard about. Rarely were actual names even offered, but sometimes the teller seemed to remember that it had happened to a familiar name of family acquaintance before he died.

These stories were not without humor. One such story was told by a man who formerly delivered ice. He said that two aging spinsters in our town who were conspicuously active in the temperance movement spent the entire night in the storm cellar where several jars of grape juice from an earlier vintage had popped their lids. Not desiring the juice to go to waste, they had attempted to drink it all. They awoke next morning and resumed their intake of refreshment. The ice man, missing them at the house the next morning, called on them by knocking on the cellar door, as he knew of the storm cloud on the previous night. They came out with wavering footsteps and hailed him generously, offering him some of the rare-flavored grape juice that had such a soothing effect.

A traveler passing our way and sensing a storm to be imminent, once shared our cellar. He told the not-so-humorous tale of a young widow with five small children who were missed by her neighbors the day after a bad tornado. She was discovered slumped forward on the cellar steps with the ax in her back and with the children crying in distress at the gory sight of their mother. The tornado, he said, had lifted the ax from her chopping block, fifty feet from the cellar door, and directed it to its fatal blow. I heard my grandmother retell this story many times with tears in her eyes, suffering, very probably, for a being who never existed.

Another traveler who shared our fearful lot told of a tornado that had swept the water out of a neighboring farmer's cattle tank in a pasture into the air and splashed it down in the middle of another neighbor's cotton patch. It washed the stalks and about two bales of cotton into his own pasture and down his creek bed. The visitor carried a well-worn clipping from Ripley's "Believe It or Not" to lend authority to this story.

Our neighbor told of a tornado that drove an oat straw directly into a four-by-four timber behind his house. Another neighbor,

<166>

hearing the story, said he did not know where it happened, but he had heard a similar story about a storm's driving a straw into a man's skull "just like a nail into a board." Sometimes the entertainment was so electrifying to our brain cells that we hardly noticed when the storm was passed, and our visitors forgot that they were ever in a hurry to get home.

A country doctor and his traveling companion talked with us in this storm-cellar setting late one night. The companion told that his father had had two little brothers who frequently walked across the fields to their grandparents' house for a visit. They would stay a few days and then come home. One day they were going to the grandparents' house, and they were caught in a storm, but there was no telephone to relay any message that they were coming or that they had not arrived safely. Several days later, the two little boys, who had apparently taken shelter under a big tree, were found dead. The big tree had shared their fate in the electrical storm and had been split with lightning.

One night at Grandpa's, as we sat hovered together in the cellar, almost breathless with anticipation of the oncoming storm, we heard a rustle and followed the sound to the rear of the cellar. Grandpa had hung a tin syrup bucket under the vent to catch the drip. He suspected what might be in it, but he was afraid to take the bucket down until we were out of the way. He never took his eye off the bucket until the storm abated and we were out of reach. He then removed it by unhooking it from its nail. We learned that we had been sharing the dugout with a bullsnake. As he told his neighbor about it a couple of days later, the neighbor seemed to remember that the same thing had happened to him when he was a boy, only the snake was a rattler.

Early one evening, Grandpa, Grandma, and I grabbed our coats and started for the storm cellar when we heard a knock at the back door. A man with a long beard, his wife, and nine children had stopped their wagon to get in out of the storm. There was not room enough for all of us in the cellar, so Grandpa, in a quandary about what to do, decided that none of us would go. So we watched out the kitchen window as the wind removed the roof of the chicken house and broke it into splinters as it slammed into the big garden corner post. We were all too stunned as spectators of nature's wrath to seek

<167>

Near Newport, Texas, this more modern home on wheels forms the back drop for the old dugout set in a knoll which forms the lower part of the three walls of the dugout.

This dugout is in North Texas (on which goats frequently take their evening air).

Canned goods lining shelves of a storm cell

Although difficult to see in the picture , the door is weighted with a pulley cable and a cement block for easy opening.

Photos Courtesy Faye Leeper

<168>

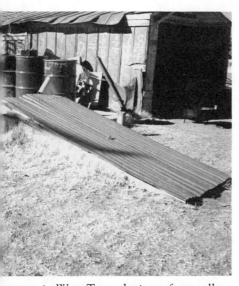

This concrete ceiling of the storm cellar forms the foundation to the storage room on top (Bill and June Russell, Midland, Texas).

s scene in West Texas depicts a farm collec-
of valuables, and the air vent in the storm
ar illustrates an excellent improvisation from
collection.

en this new age, plexiglass, spherical tornado
lter is set in the ground, the floor is flat inside
a continuous bench circles the wall, from one
of the door all around to the other side.

<169>

safety by crawling under the beds or sitting in the hallway. The strong wind sounded, to me, exactly like the big freight trains that used to come through that part of the country. As the turbulent wind lessened, I became conscious that the bearded man was praying aloud to whatever force might be moved by his plight. Grandpa was not too demonstrative, but he quietly bowed his head, and much later, when the storm had passed and the man had ended his praying, Grandpa said, more as a courtesy than not, "Amen."

Years later, I had been listening to the radio announcing a possible storm when suddenly I heard the dreaded sound of a freight train. I took my eighteen-month-old child and attempted to make a game of crawling under the bed so as not to frighten him. I was struck with terror at the sound I recognized, and I dived with such urgency that I received a terrible blow on the head. Shortly, as my vision began to clear, I heard a train whistle. I came out from under the bed much chagrined, and I have not run from a storm since. But I do not promise that I never will again.

The residents of Stoneburg, Texas, tell that a tornado lifted their church clear off the foundation, leaving only the pews and the altar standing. The morning after the storm they found a songbook on the pulpit still open to the last hymn sung in church the Sunday before. Although the storm was climaxed by a torrential rain, the book appeared untouched by any moisture.

In the spring of 1979, one of the most devastating tornadoes that ever hit Texas, left the city of Wichita Falls paralyzed for days. Among the strange stories carried by newspapers around the country was the one that cancelled checks from a family whose house was destroyed in Wichita Falls were found the next day in a resident's yard in Oklahoma City.

One spring day when I was of pre-school age, my father was working his fields; and my older brothers and sisters were in school. My mother, perennially pregnant and with two little children on hand, had put out the family wash. She had a clothes line and some clothes pins. When she used up that space, she hung the rest on the barbed wire fence that bordered our yard. About three in the afternoon, a storm appeared imminent. When the wind became stronger, she ran to fetch in the family clothing and linens, still wet, but too precious to lose in a bad wind. In her fury to retrieve the loose

<170>

garments, she looked up to see a Model A Ford with a man and a woman in it. They asked directions to the Stanfield ranch. My mother told them it was just three miles on down the road but that they'd better come with us to the storm cellar until the wind dissipated. They declined but thanked her generously and quickly departed. By the time she had collected the family wash, a slow rain had started. That was generally her signal that the storm had abated. She came in and watched out the window until it stopped. She sat down at her pedal sewing machine to mend a garment when two policemen on motorcycles pulled up into the yard. When they left, she took the double barreled shot gun off its rack and loaded it. After she put it back on the rack, she sat in her rocker where she could see out the window toward the Stanfield ranch. My brothers and sisters soon got off the school bus. She told them to stay indoors until my father came home. I learned later that the policemen had told her that it was Bonnie Parker and Clyde Barrow that had asked the way to Stanfield ranch. The big gun stayed within easy reach for several days. To the day she died, I doubt that my mother had as much as shot a rabbit, but I do not think her record would have been that good if the Model A had come back.

New tornado shelters, as they are now called, have been invented for modern man because he is still powerless against the earth's windy wrath. One advertised in Odessa, Texas, is an almost complete sphere of plexiglass with a door, of course, and benches inside. It is planted in the earth, and the sides and top are guaranteed never to crumble.

As a child, little happened by way of human affairs to cause any real excitement; but one event I believe even today would set my adrenal glands pulsating is to be awakened in the middle of the night with my grandfather's stock alarm, "Mama, get the coats and quilts and let's get in the cellar as fast as we can." Being too young to be aware of any real danger, I greatly relished the excitement. Although I never wished the house or other building would blow away or that any harm should come to any of us, I certainly wanted to be at the scene to witness it if such mishap should befall us.

<171>

Dinner on the grounds.

<172>

LERA TYLER LICH

Good Providing, Good Eating

THIS ARTICLE is based primarily upon interviews and conversations with two women: Louise Allerkamp Saur, daughter of Friedrich Allerkamp and Auguste Voigt Allerkamp of the Cypress Creek community in Kerr County, who was interviewed by her daughter-in-law, Selina Gewalt Saur, in the mid-1970s; and Kate Wallace Bearden, whom I interviewed in 1979 and who was the daughter of Joe Wallace and Susan Jenkins Wallace of the Patrick community in Rusk County.

Both ladies' grandparents came to Texas in the 1850s. The Allerkamps arrived from the plains of what was then the province of Hanover to settle in the limestone hills of eastern Kerr County. The Wallaces migrated from hills of South Carolina to establish a home in the piney woods of southeastern Rusk County. The first generations held on through the precarious years of frontier existence, through the Civil War, and through Reconstruction. The second generation married and began the third, and by the mid-1880s, the Joe Wallace family of Rusk County and the Friedrich Allerkamp family of Kerr County were what historians call prosperous yeomen farmers. They lived on the kind of homesteads we might imagine in a golden age of rural life. Both families were large (with thirteen children), healthy (twelve of the children survived to be at least seventy-five and many lived past ninety), well-regarded by their community, and well-off but certainly not wealthy. Their neighbors would call them good providers, a high compliment paid by rural Texans and a virtue that was measured largely by a family's ability to spread a good table. Although one family was purely German and the other Scotch-Irish in background, Selina Saur and I discovered that their food ways were remarkably similar. Their practices reveal what

<173>

must have been—and perhaps still is—regarded as the best of good providing and good eating in Texas.

Providing was no easy task. Most of the families' energies were concentrated on getting food on the table three times a day. Forty or fifty plates were filled daily from the home larder. They had to rely mostly on what could be pulled, picked, or killed off their land. They had to be industrious and resourceful to procure, substitute, process, preserve, and prepare food.

They were almost self-sufficient. The Wallaces shopped in Henderson five or six times a year. Although the entire family went to town in spring and again in fall, the father was the primary buyer. Kate Wallace told me that her daddy invariably brought home flour (four fifty-pound sacks), sugar, coffee, salt (one hundred pounds), kerosene (a five-gallon can), soda, baking powder, soap, black pepper, and starch. The Allerkamps also depended upon the father for shopping. Friedrich Allerkamp's monthly market list included flour (a fifty-pound sack to supplement their own wheat which was exchanged at the community mill for freshly ground meal), a big barrel of brown sugar, a ten-pound sack of white sugar, a one-hundred pound bag of coffee beans, several twenty-five pound bags of salt, kerosene (for the lamp, medicinal purposes, and cleaning the house), a big box of soda, a tin of baking powder, castile soap (for the girls), a box of black pepper, starch, rice, shells and ammunition, and tobacco (for Papa).

With the aid of these supplies, the families survived on their resources. The men's fields yielded cash crops—cotton for the Wallaces and grains for the Allerkamps—as well as fodder and food. The Wallace fields also grew corn (yellow for fodder, white for eating), peanuts, oats, sweet potatoes, Irish potatoes, sorghum, maize, and peas of all kinds—California, brown eye, whippoorwill (for late, late fall), black crowder, sugar crowder, speckled crowder. In the bottom lands they grew sugar cane for syrup, brown sugar, and rock candy. Twice a month Joe Wallace carried his corn to the community grist mill. After the miller had taken his toll, the meal was brought home and his wife Susan sifted out the chaff. Although cornmeal spoiled quickly, it was always plentiful and used for cornpone (made from sour milk) and for the most common of all dishes—cornbread, which even the pets ate. Wheat flour purchased

<174>

in town was used for biscuits, cookies, pies, cakes, and on special occasions, for salt-rising light bread (made from homemade yeast, fresh warm milk, a little cornmeal, water, and flour). Kate remembered that it rose in a pitcher and was the only yeast bread her family ate.

The Allerkamp fields were devoted mostly to the cash crops—wheat, corn, oats, rye, barley, maize, and some cotton—but the family consumed much of the wheat since wheat, not corn, was the staple grain that produced ground wheat for breakfast cereal and milled flour for baking four loaves of yeast bread daily and for occasional hot cakes and hot biscuits. Auguste Allerkamp made her own sour-dough yeast, as well as yeast cakes created from potato water, a starter of yeast, sugar, and cornmeal. According to daughter Louise, this flour and yeast also produced apple-cakes, coffee rings filled with raisins and nuts, and puffy doughnuts filled with dried fruit, browned in an old black kettle of fresh lard.

The men plowed and harrowed garden plots and spread them with barnyard fertilizer, but in both families, the gardens, located near the house, were the wives' domains. Susan Wallace allowed her children in the garden only to harvest. From March until frost, as long as the earth was moist, the women planted, tended, and harvested row after row of vegetables. They grew many of the same plants: before spring, they had onions, cabbage, and shallots; as the year progressed they planted sweet corn, okra, sweet potatoes, peppers (sweet and hot), kohlrabi, lettuce, radishes, beets, carrots, tomatoes, green beans, pinto beans, and English peas. Kate Wallace also mentioned her family had mustards, turnips, cucumbers, squash, watermelons, and cantaloupes. An herb section included garlic, sage, and mint. The children grew up distinguishing one kind of seed from another. Some seeds were ordered annually from seed companies. (The Wallaces received theirs from Hastings in Atlanta, Georgia.) Others were carefully saved from year to year, generation to generation. The Wallaces produced annually a special "Fat Horse Bean" whose seed had been brought from South Carolina in the 1850s.

Meat varied as much as the vegetables. Both families enjoyed some wild game like rabbit (six made a tasty meal), squirrel, fish, quail, and dove. The Allerkamps had venison which was brined or made into jerky if not eaten immediately. Neither family depended

<175>

The providers

on game, however, since their own livestock supplied them through-out the year. Flocks of chickens and a few blue-gray guineas, ducks, and turkeys guaranteed the availability of fried chicken, apple-stuffed duck or guinea hen, or roasted turkey as well as eggs. Calves and hogs were butchered. A butchered calf was traditionally shared with neighbors since beef could not be preserved. Pork could be cured, so hogs were butchered in the late fall and winter. From them came hickory smoked ham, sausage mixed with sage and garlic, and bacon—as well as brined backbone, head cheese, pickled pigs feet, and blood and liverwurst for the Allerkamps. The families had several milk cows whose milk was turned into buttermilk, clabbered milk, cream, butter, cottage cheese, and cooked cheese.

The girls in both households tended the chickens, gathering their eggs and giving them left-over milk, corn, maize, or even the skinned body of a coon or possum. They also milked and fed the milk cows. The menfolk tended to other animals—hogs, donkeys, horses,

<176>

Good eating at a dinner on the grounds at Sunnydell Church, Tyler County

mules, dry cows—and fed them oats, corn, peanuts, cotton seed, sweet potatoes. Along with fodder from the fields, the pigs received most of the table scraps—even the dishwater was mixed with mashed grain for their nourishment.

Fruit trees were carefully selected so that each variety produced at a different time from early June through frost. They grew peaches (crimson, white, yellow), apples, pears, apricots, and plums. The Wallaces had carried a special "Jones" apple sprout across the southern United States in the wagon caravan and carefully nourished it in their orchard. Supplementing this produce were native fruits— dewberries, blackberries, muscadine and mustang grapes, walnuts, hickory nuts, pecans, wild plums, crab apples, wild black cherries, persimmons, and in south Texas, agaritas. The Allerkamps used a number of these wild fruits in making wines, but the temperate Wallaces fermented only the mustang grape and that only for medicinal purposes.

<177>

Along with the tasks of growing and harvesting, raising and killing, came the job of keeping these products from spoiling and of making certain that the family was supplied twelve months of the year, even when because of drought or cold weather the gardens and fields were not producing. Glass jars were only beginning to be an option for preserving foods and were used for jellies, preserves, or applesauce. Pork was packed in salt, cured, or smoked. Onions and potatoes were stored in dark, dry areas for winter use. Cucumbers were crocked in differently seasoned brines, corn dried and preserved in the husk, cabbage chopped and stored as kraut in churns or large wooden casks. Peas, beans, and okra were dried, then thrashed and hung in sacks in the smokehouse. Fruit was dried between layers of cheesecloth on the roof or in another sunny spot and later stored in tins or crocks for winter use in pies, custards, cakes, and cookies and as a boiled fruit dessert.

From the smokehouse, cellar, barnyard, and pantry the women brought food for the families' meals into their kitchens. These large rooms were simply furnished. Each kitchen had a wood stove and fireplace. It did not have running water, electricity, or built-in cabinets. A homemade safe stored dishes and leftovers. Shelves lining the wall displayed canned or store-bought supplies. Several small tables held other items. Benches and chairs were tucked under the Wallaces' ten-foot long table, which was covered for everyday use with an oilcloth.

Three times each day the Wallace and Allerkamp tables were filled for the families which had labored so hard for their bounty. For breakfast, the women served hot bread (usually biscuits for the Wallaces and fresh white bread for the Allerkamps), sausage, brown gravy, eggs, syrup, jellies and preserves, butter, and hot coffee. The Wallaces also enjoyed hominy. (A strong homemade lye took the kernels off corn, which was then washed and cooked with bacon drippings.) The noon dinner was the heartiest. Kate Wallace mentioned that her family often counted eight to ten different vegetables, seasoned with ham, at a single, summer meal. Bread was served again. Dessert might be pies (potato, fruit, egg custard, or buttermilk), cake, cookies (from bags hanging in the pantry), ambrosia, or pudding. Supper was simple and apparently almost universal throughout the South and Southwest: hot cornbread filled with butter along with

<178>

buttermilk or clabbered milk. Drinks and dishes were sweetened with molasses or honey. The Wallaces used their sugar cane to make syrup, which could be made into brown sugar for pies, preserves, and puddings. Leftovers from the noon dinner occasionally were placed on the supper table, but usually these were fed to the farmyard animals. One filled plate was often saved in the kitchen safe, just in case some unexpected traveler arrived at the house after dark.

Special occasions called for special preparations. A guest for dinner, a church picnic, a box supper were opportunities for the family to show the wealth of their labors. Louise Allerkamp remembered her family's traditional Sunday afternoon coffee. "Sunday afternoon was open house, so on Saturday, there was much baking of cookies and cake or pie and doughnuts, fresh bread, and coffee cakes," she told her daughter-in-law. The girls had to scrub the cedar pail that held the family drinking water and polish the copper bands that held it together. "Tables were covered with snowy white cloths and good dishes. There were flowers and a few crystal dishes filled with the jewelled color of jellies made of wild plum or mustang grape. Butter was carefully molded in a wooden press that printed a flower design on top. Bread was sliced in even slices and served in a white napkined basket." Oatmeal, buttermilk, brown sugar, and pecan cookies were also served along with cooked cheese, "yellow and rich with cream," and coffee, freshly roasted and ground.

The Wallaces and the Allerkamps may not have been typical turn-of-the-century families, but their productive, comfortable ways are what many of us idealized as rural Texas traditions. The kitchen table—its bounty the product of family cooperation, self-sufficiency, and hard work—is deeply rooted in that tradition both for what it shows and for what it means. As they spoke, Louise Allerkamp and Kate Wallace told of hard-earned, wholesome foods. They also implied the belief that providing well was the outward and visible sign of hardworking, wholesome living.

<179>

Early Volkfestes. *Courtesy W.M. Von-Maszewski*

<180>

W.M. VON-MASZEWSKI
The German Volksfest in Brenham

ACH YEAR in May a colorful spectacle unfolds in the town of Brenham in Washington County, Texas. The event is the Brenham Maifest, which is part of the community's heritage. On two successive mornings fire-engine sirens announce the commencement of a grand civic procession of color guard, parade marshal, dignitaries, school bands, and young people dressed in colorful costumes riding decorated floats. Business stops as the townspeople and visitors watch the parade. The high point of the festivities is the elaborate coronation ceremonies. In a pageantry attended by hundreds of costumed children and young people, the Junior and the Senior May Royalties are crowned on successive evenings. Except for the years of the two World Wars the Brenham Maifest has been observed for close to one hundred years. Its history traces back to the Volksfest (a celebration by the people) organized by the German-Texans of Brenham in the 1870s.[1]

Historically the town of Brenham developed on the periphery of German rural communities that were settled on the land between the lower Brazos and Colorado Rivers as early as 1831 in what are present-day Austin, Fayette, and Colorado counties. By the 1870s in adjoining Washington County, the city of Brenham had grown in importance as a county seat and as a railroad point, which made it an economic center for the surrounding counties. This rail connection to the coast, combined with the improved trans-Atlantic transportation, brought an increasing number of German immigrants to the county in the 1870s and 1880s.[2]

As was the case in other areas where large groups of Europeans settled, the Germans as a minority in a predominantly Anglo-American culture at first made little effort to assimilate. They attempted to live as they had in their native home and socialized among themselves, sharing in common the experience of emigration

<181>

and the adjustment to a new way of life. In the 1870s the German population in Brenham had grown large enough to support social societies which were patterned after fraternal organizations such as they had known in Europe. These societies were an oasis in a country of a different language and different customs. The societies fostered a strong German consciousness. Within their walls members conversed in their native tongue and observed the culture and values of their homeland. The local Germania Verein was the leading society with a large membership and its own facilities. It offered activities for the entire family in the form of dances, musicals, theatrical productions, and lectures.[3]

With such a family-centered activity in mind, another local German society, allegedly the Harugari Lodge,[4] made plans for a "May picnic" in 1874. Held on May 2nd, the day's program centered on entertaining the children with amusements such as sack races, walking a soaped log, and climbing a greased pole.[5] The adults watched the children, visited with each other, and listened to the music of the band. The merrymaking lasted throughout the day with a break at noon for a picnic lunch. In the evening the adults enjoyed a dance that lasted past midnight. Apparently the day's activity was well received by the community since the Anglo-Texans complimented their neighbors for the harmony in which the sexes and the age-groups interacted. The Germans, encouraged by the success, talked of repeating the event the next year but on a larger scale. They would have a Volksfest.[6]

The tradition of the Volksfest accompanied the German emigrants to this country. The term Volksfest is generic and did not come into usage in Germany until the early 1800s.[7] Before that time festivals in Germany were the prerogatives of the nobility in which their subjects had no part. Church festivals likewise were mostly self-serving. They were organized by the clergy to benefit the church, and they followed a prescribed pattern. Entertainment for the peasant was not encouraged because of the "three excesses:" a waste of time, labor, and money, which robbed the peasant of productivity.[8]

The Volksfest emerged in Germany in direct response to the social and political conditions of the country in the early 1800s. The reverberation of the French Revolution (1788) with its call for personal freedom and social equality was felt throughout Europe. In

<182>

Germany the French occupation during the Napoleonic Wars (1795-1815) awakened also a national pride. Interest in the national culture flourished. Folk customs were revived or newly introduced. By the mid-1800s the Volksfest was a popular entertainment attracting large crowds. For a moment it brought together all classes of people and played a large role in the growth of a national identity.[9] The parades, amusements, patriotic songs, and the fireworks only accentuated this feeling. Nationalism and liberalism became the twin slogans championed by the new and expanding middle-class. The liberal elements who advocated unification of the sovereign German states into one nation used the Volksfest as a rallying point for passionate political speeches to the masses.[10] They called for a constitutional parliamentary government to replace the absolute monarchy with the privileges accorded the nobility. The authorities responded with repressive measures which caused many intellectuals, despairing over the conditions, to leave the country.

From these roots German emigrants transplanted the tradition of the Volksfest to their new homeland. The earliest reference to a Volksfest in Texas is in 1853. At New Wied (Comal County) a Volksfest was announced for the Fourth of July. In October of that year a Volksfest developed spontaneously in New Braunfels in the aftermath of the first Staat-Sangerfest (state singers' festival).[11] The next reference is a Maifest in San Antonio in 1868. Also in San Antonio in September of 1869, a festival parade proceeded from Alamo Plaza to San Pedro Springs where a Volksfest took place that included a musical production and a speech by a distinguished guest.[12]

In that same year, 1869, Houston saw its first Volksfest. This may have come by happenstance. Prominent German citizens organized a *Schützenverein* (shooting club) on May 18, 1869. Following the ceremonial presentation of the club's flag, the members, resplendent in their gala uniforms, marched in a body to Schulte's Garden on White Oak Bayou. There they partook of a picnic lunch with their families, and the afternoon was spent at marksmanship shooting. In the evening a dance was attended in town. Local newspapers hailed the day's event as "the inauguration of a new style of outdoor amusement that ought to and we hope will become popular among all classes here."[13] Two weeks later the announcement appeared that

<183>

a German Volksfest "was being planned for the public enjoyment."[14] The timing of this announcement may have been a coincidence, or it may have resulted from the publicity given the *Schützenverein's* outing. Reporting on this first Houston Volksfest the English-language paper praised the event for its democratic character. It marveled that no distinctions were made at the grounds as to nationality and social standing.[15] After this auspicious beginning, the Volksfest was repeated annually for many years, becoming a high point of the Houston social scene.[16]

The town of Columbus followed Houston's example and had a Volksfest in 1872. German societies from other towns participated in the event. On this occasion Galvestons' Turnverein (athletic club), on its return home, revealed plans for a fest of their own, a Maifest, on May 1.[17] In Brenham a successful May picnic in 1874 elicited the promise by the Germans to repeat the event on a larger scale the following year. In April of 1875 representatives from Brenham's German societies formed the Volksfest Association and announced a "Maifest" for May 15.[18] On the morning of the appointed day a procession assembled by the courthouse square. It moved through the principal streets of town for the benefit of the spectators and proceeded to the Fair Grounds.[19] In the lead were the parade marshal and color guard followed by a marching band, a coach with the city fathers, thirteen decorated horsedrawn wagons, a second band, members of the Germania Verein, school boys on foot, and the members of the Hook and Ladder Fire Company. The color guard carried the American, Texas, and German flags. The public display of the German tri-colors was a common practice among German emigrants especially after Germany's unification into a new and modern nation in 1871.

At the Fair Grounds the president of the Volksfest Association opened the festivity with a welcoming speech. He was followed by the principal speakers ("orators") who addressed the crowd in German and in English. The speaker in German exhorted the listeners not to forget their German heritage but at the same time to show allegiance to the republic that gave them a new home and future. The speaker in English lauded the Germans for their industry and their contributions to their new home. After a leisurely picnic lunch the afternoon was given over to the children's amusements

<184>

while the adults, if they did not watch the antics of the little ones, visited with friends on the grounds and enjoyed the choral and instrumental entertainment. The evening closed with a ball.

The Maifest succeeded as an entertainment, and it showed a profit as well. With all bills settled, a sum of about $250 was realized. The suggestion was accepted that the money be set aside for the start-up of next year's Maifest.[20] This recommendation is significant. It showed that the festival became quickly accepted as a local feature.

Over the next years the Volksfest continued to grow in scale. On opening day a gun salute was fired at sunrise. The parades were comprised of more wagons with elaborate displays of the local crafts and trade and with motifs from German mythology and history. Representations of Germania and Columbia, through whom the Germans symbolically gave homage to their former and present homes, were popular. Another figure appearing in the processions and hoisting a stein of beer was King Gambrinus, the mythical god of beer—the German Bacchus.[21]

One feature introduced to the Volksfest, which endeared itself to the public over the years, was the crowning of a May Queen. The first queen was selected by the Volksfest Association in 1877.[22] She and her maids-of-honor rode in the procession to the Fair Grounds where she was crowned by the president of the Association.

On the grounds numerous entertainments awaited the children while the adults were attracted to shooting competitions of the Schutzenvereins and drill competitions by militia companies.[23] The variety of offerings allowed the Volksfest Association to boast annually that "this year's event will be better than ever before." The local paper observed that so many new amusements were appearing which were unknown before that it required special attractions to keep the public's interest and to ensure good attendance.[24]

The Volksfest was successful as an entertainment and it paid its own way. At the same time it was vulnerable. As an outdoor activity its success depended on the cooperation of the weather. The weather determined the attendance and the attendance determined financial gain or loss. Under good conditions an estimated two thousand people attended the Volksfest in Brenham.[25] In 1878 rains kept people away. The income from all sources barely covered expenses.[26]

<185>

It had become the practice to use the profit from the previous year for start-up money for the next Volksfest. Some bills had to be paid in advance of the event: the Fair Grounds leased, the grounds improved, lumber purchased for the construction of a dance platform, medals ordered for the contests and money set aside for cash awards.[27] Income was derived from the auction of food and refreshment privileges on the grounds during the Volksfest, from contributions solicited among the German merchants, and from the gate receipts. No contingencies existed, however, for the loss of revenues due to inclement weather.[28] Bad weather occurred in 1878, and when the financial picture did not improve in 1879 the Association began losing heart.

In June of 1879 the Association asked the local Germania Verein to take over the management of the Volksfest. The Germania owned property suitable for a Volksfest. So far the Volksfest Association had leased the Fair Grounds and incurred expenses for temporary improvements which were a drain on its profits that could be ill afforded.[29] The thinking was that the Germania Verein could build permanent structures on its property, but the Verein showed no interest in the proposal. In 1880 the Association again managed the Volksfest and its problems increased. Low attendance due to another season of unfavorable weather created a deficit.[30] The offer to the Germania Verein was repeated, but again it showed no interest. The members of the Volksfest Association, seeing no other alternative and not willing to continue under the cloud of financial liability, dissolved the organization.[31]

An editorial in the local English-language paper chided the community for taking no steps to stop the dissolution of the Volksfest Association. It pointed out that the burden of organizing the festival had rested entirely on the shoulders of their German fellow citizens. The American businessmen had shown a lack of involvement in the event, and this attitude had contributed to the financial difficulties and the demise of the Volksfest.[32]

The eventual acceptance of the Volksfest in Brenham as a general public event can be attributed to several factors. By the mid-1870s about one-third of the town's population was German,[33] who were commercially integrated with many of their businesses located around the courthouse square. They were politically active in

<186>

national and state elections, and from their midst ran candidates for local offices.[34] They had their own social clubs and societies and a German-language newspaper began publishing there in 1874.[35] The hardships of settling and adjusting in their adopted country were matters of the past. A more relaxed period was at hand. It allowed for reflection on the present and the future, but also the past. Bitter memories of the condition that forced them to leave their homes for new shores had mellowed and were replaced by nostalgia.[36] They were proud of their German heritage (*Deutschtum*) as well as their accomplishment in the new country. Seeing themselves part of the community, they organized a Volksfest. It was an opportunity to show publicly their German identity.

What gave the Volksfest its appeal in Brenham also held true for the popularity of the Volksfest and the Maifest in other parts of the state. A contemporary observer remarked that the state was in the throes of a Volksfest and Maifest mania. On any Sunday in May, he went on to say, one could find a German community, no matter how small, holding a celebration. The main attractions with each were the same: music, song, children's games, crowning of a May Queen— and plenty of beer.[37] The German Volksfest and Maifest made their appearance in Texas in the 1850s as small and private affairs. In the 1870s they burst forth as community affairs. With its popularity it also became an easy victim to assimilation into the American culture. As it lost its German character, it became an American institution. Some expressed regret; others praised the change.[38]

In Brenham the Fire Department assumed management of the festivity in 1881 and called it a Maifest.[39] In retrospect this development was fortunate because a Brenham Volksfest under German hands would not have survived the political situation of World War I, when anything that bespoke of Germany was expunged in the United States. The Brenham firemen managed the Maifest for over half a century, until the eve of the Second World War when it was suspended. When peace returned to the country, popular interest revived in the Maifest. However, the growth of the community over the years placed greater demands on the Fire Department, and the firemen no longer had the time to devote to the Maifest. But in recognition to the Department's stewardship in the past, today it takes the place of honor and leads off the Maifest processions.

<187>

<188>

<189>

The revival of the Maifest after World War II is a reflection of its deep-seated tradition in the community. Presently it is managed by the Brenham Maifest Association, a non-profit organization. As in years past "Maifest time" today sees many an expatriate take a nostalgic trip home to attend the Maifest, visit with other expatriates and reminisce over past Maifests. Rooted in the Volksfest, today's Maifest is robust, and community spirit keeps it that way. With an almost continuous history the Brenham Maifest observed its one-hundredth anniversary in 1990.

NOTES

1. Information is scarce on the Volksfest in Texas. Local histories offer little on these Germans and even less on their Volksfest or its impact on the community:

R. E. Pennington. *The History of Brenham and Washington County, Texas.* Houston: Standard Printing & Lithographic Company, 1915. (Reprint of 1915 edition.)

Charles F. Schmidt. *History of Washington County, Texas.* San Antonio, Texas: The Naylor Company, 1949.

Robert A. Hasskarl. *Brenham, Texas, 1844-1958.* Brenham: Banner-Press Publishing Company, 1958.

O. W. Dietrich. *The Blazing Story of Washington County.* Quanah, Texas: Nortex, 1973. Revised edition.

Sources consulted for this paper are contemporary German-Texas newspapers: *Wöchentliche Texas Post* (Galveston), *Texas Deutsche Zeitung* (Houston) and especially the *Texas Volksbote* (Brenham).

2. Between 1860 and 1880 the German population increased from 1,190 to 4,217 vs. 6,084 to 8,617 for the Anglo-Texans, or an increase by 354% vs. 142%, respectively; for the same period the population in the town of Brenham rose from 48 to 625 Germans, or 1,300%, against an increase from 552 to 1,687 for the Anglo-Texans, or 300% (Handcount of U.S. Census Records for Washington County, Texas, for the years 1860, 1870 and 1880.)

3. Dieter Kramer. "Diskussionsbeitrag zum Fest." In *Hessische Blätter für Volks- und Kulturforschung.* Giessen, Germany (1977), Vol. 4, 51.

The social aspect of a German-Texan society can be followed in: *Century of Agricultural Progress, 1856-1956: Minutes of the Cat Spring Agricultural Society.* Cat Spring, Austin County, Texas, 1956.

4. This allegation comes from a secondary source. Pennington (p. 47) was one of the first writers to make this statement. Later writers of the history of Brenham and Washington County quote her blindly without attempting to substantiate this point. So far primary sources have not been located to corroborate this point. Information on the Harugari Lodge in Texas is almost non-existant. Inquiries in Brenham and in academia have yielded no information at all. This research brought

<190>

to light four scant references to the Lodge, three for Brenham and one for Giddings, but nothing more.

5. *Brenham Banner*, April 30, 1874, p. 3:1&2. The Fair Grounds were located east off Market Street along Hog Branch Creek.

6. Ibid. May 7, 1874, 3:2.

7. Alfred Höck. "Volksfeste in Hessen." In *Hessische Blätter*, Vol. 4, 10. The term "Germany" used in this paper refers to a cultural Germany that transcended the numerous sovereign states. In 1871 the unification of these states created the political Germany.

8. Ina-Maria Greverus. "Brauchen wir Feste?" In *Hessische Blätter*, Vol. 4, 3. Susan G. Davis. *Parade and Power*. Philadelphia: Temple University Press (1986), 35.

9. Heidemarie Gruppe-Kelpanides. "Das Frankfurter Bundesschiessen von 1862 ein 'nationales Verbrüderungsfest'." In *Hessische Blätter*, Vol. 4, 20.

10. William Carr. *A History of Germany, 1815-1945*. New York: St. Martin's Press (1969), 34, 82.

11. Rudolph L. Biesele. *The History of the German Settlements in Texas, 1844-1860*. Austin: Von Boeckmann-Jones (1930), 223.

12. Theodore J. Albrecht. "German Singing Societies in Texas." Ph.D. dissertation, North Texas State University (May 1975), 138, 139.

13. *Houston Daily Times*, May 16, 1869, 3:2; May 18, 1869, 3:2; May 20, 1869, 3:1; May 21, 1869, 3:3.

The German-Americans took to task the English translation of *Schützenverein* as rifle association, rifle club or shooting club. They pointed out that their purpose was to hone their skill to protect and not to kill, the word Schützen having the meaning of protector. Historically, before the creation of an army in Germany, the Schützen protected home and kin. When their services were no longer needed they practiced as a pastime at clubs (*Houstoner Volksfestzeitung* zum 22sten Volksfest. Herausgegeben von der *Texas Deutsche Zeitung*, Houston, 12. und 13. Mai 1892, 3).

The Brenham Schützenverein, organized on March 17, 1876 practiced at the Schützenplatz, west of the city cemetery (*Texas Volksbote*, March 22, 1877, 5:3; *Daily Banner*, May 9, 1878; and April 1, 1879, 2: *Brenham Weekly Banner*, March 21, 1879, 3:5).

After a rash of livestock thefts in Washington County several Schützenverein were organized by the German-Texans in the late 1870s to protect their property. In addition to providing for marksmanship practices these clubs offered an opportunity for social gatherings (*Texas Volksbote*, July 26, 1877, 5:2; Nov. 29, 1877, 5:1; March 28, 1878, 5:1; June 26, 1879, 5:3).

14. *Houston Daily Times*, May 30, 1869, 3:2; June 3, 1869, 3:2.

15. Ibid., June 8, 1869, 3:1; June 9, 1869, 3:2.

16. B. H. Carroll. *Standard History of Houston, Texas*. Knoxville, Tennessee: H.W. Crew (1912), 266.

17. *Galveston Tri-Weekly News*, April 29, 1872, 3:3.

18. The Brenham newspapers for the period of 1875-1880 record that the Volksfest Committee ("das Central Comite") consisted of representatives from the German societies. The advertisements for the Maifest of 1875, 1876 and 1879 are signed off

<191>

by "die Central Comite." At no time is the Harugari Lodge singled out for arranging any of the events or is the lodge mentioned (*Texas Volksbote*, March 2, 1876, p. 4:3; *Brenham Weekly Banner*, March 7, 1879, p. 3:2; and March 12, 1880, p. 3:4). The three German societies represented at the founding of the Volksfest Association were in 1875 (*Texas Volksbote*, April 22, 1875, 5:2; April 29, 1875, 5:4 and 5:5).

GERMANIA VEREIN: organized on December 4, 1870; chartered by the State of Texas on October 28, 1871; merged with the B.P.O.E., Lodge No. 979 in 1929 (Gammel, *Laws of Texas*, Vol. VII, 158; Hasskarl, *Brenham*, p. 70).

HARUGARI LODGE ("Deutscher Order der Harugari" or D.O.H.), Texas Lodge No. 306; organized ca. 1872-73 (*Brenham Banner*, Dec. 11, 1873, 3:1; and April 9, 1874, 3:3; *Texas Volksbote*, Dec. 24, 1874, 5:4). Another lodge existed in Giddings, Texas (*Texas Volksbote*, May 11, 1876, 5:4). Otherwise information on the Harugari in Texas is nonexistant though it had a wide following among the Germans in the northeast of the U.S. (Charles W. Heckethorn. *The Secret Societies*. New Hyde Park, New York: University Books (1965), 297; Alvin J. Schmidt. *Fraternal Organizations*. Westport, Connecticut (1980), 153).

DEUTSCHAMERIKANISCHER SCHULVEREIN: formally organized in 1869 and chartered in 1881 (*Texas Volksbote*, Dec. 1, 1881, 4:6). It functioned in the capacity of a private school board, serving the German community at a time when public or "free" schools were not yet mandated by law. A lot for the future "Deutschamerikanische Schule" had been purchased on the corner of Market and Pecan Streets on June 4, 1867. The instructions to the fee-paying students were with an emphasis on the German language. The student body participated in the Maifest of 1875 (*Brenham Banner*, May 7, 1875, 2:1). Over the years the school operated under different names, depending on the name of the headmaster. A new building was erected on the lot in 1884 (*Texas Volksbote*, Oct. 18, 1883; 5:2-3; Dec. 20, 1883, 5:2; Jan. 10, 1884, 5:3; *Brenham Daily Banner*, Feb. 12, 1884, 3:1). When public schools were opened in Brenham after 1875, they provided instruction of the German language which caused a drop in the fee-paying students in the "Deutschamerikanischen Schule." In 1891 the facility was leased to the Evangelical Lutheran Synod of Texas on a long-term contract. The Synod established the Evangelical Lutheran College that later moved to Seguin, Texas, and became Texas Lutheran College (H.C. Ziehe. *The Lutheran Church in Texas*. Section Two. Private printing, 1954, 240).

19. Parade route: Main to Park Street, formerly Preston or North Street; on this corner J. J. Mullins took a picture of the procession; Park to Commerce, formerly Quitman, to St. Charles to Alamo, formerly Sandy; to Market Street, formerly Goat Row, and on to the Fair Grounds (*Texas Volksbote*, April 29, 1875, 4:2).

Hasskarl (p. 71) shows a picture of a Maifest procession allegedly dating to 1874. This identification is incorrect. The newspapers make no mention of a parade that year (*Brenham Banner*, April 30, 1874, 3:1; May 7, 1874, 3:2). In the background of the picture is the hardware store of M.A. Healy. The sign is faintly legible. Until 1886 the business was located on Main Street when it relocated to the corner of Park (North) and Commerce (Quitman) Streets (*Texas Volksbote*, Dec. 18, 1884, 5:1; Sept. 9, 1886, 5:6). Finally, the advertisement for the Volksfest of 1875 announced

<192>

that a camera would be positioned at the corner of Main and Park Streets facing northeast (*Texas Volksbote*, April 29, 1875, 5:4-5). The composition of the picture agrees also with the description of the parties in the parade: the tri-colors of Germany, boys and girls of the schools and the members of the Germania Verein with their ceremonial sashes (*Texas Volksbote*, May 20, 1875, 2:2).

20. *Texas Volksbote*, May 20, 1875, 5:2.

21. Ibid., May 4, 1876, 4:1; *Brenham Banner*, May 5, 1876, 1:3. The figure of Gambrinus made its appearance also in celebrations in Galveston, Houston, and Waco (*Houston Daily Telegraph*, June 14, 1872, 5:1; *Waco Daily Examiner*, May 11, 1877, 1).

22. *Brenham Banner*, May 4, 1877, 1:2; *Brenham Evening Press*, May 26, 1910, 1: *Brenham Daily Banner Press*, May 26, 1914, 1:3.

23. *Galveston Daily News*, May 11, 1878, 1:4; *Brenham Daily Banner*, May 9, 1878, 3:1; April 11, 1879, 3:2; May 9, 1879, 3:1.

24. *Brenham Daily Banner*, May 10, 1879, 1:3.

25. *Galveston Daily News*, May 16, 1875, 1:7; *Brenham Daily Banner*, May 10, 1879, 5:1.

26. *Texas Volksbote*, May 30, 1878, 5:3.

27. *Brenham Banner*, May 5, 1876, 1:3; *Galveston Daily News*, May 11, 1878, 1:4; *Brenham Daily Banner*, April 1, 1879, 2.

28. *Texas Volksbote*, March 23, 1876, 4:2; April 13, 1876, 5:1; March 22, 1877, 5:2; *Brenham Daily Banner*, April 6, 1879, 2.

29. *Texas Volksbote*, June 12, 1879, 5:2.

30. *Brenham Daily Banner*, May 8, 1880, 3:1; *Texas Volksbote*, May 13, 1880, 4:1.

31. *Texas Volksbote*, May 20, 1880, 5:2.

32. *Brenham Daily Banner*, May 23, 1880, 4:1.

33. *Texas Volksbote*, July 1, 1875, 4:1; see also footnote (2) for handcount of U.S. Census Records for Washington County, Texas, for the years 1860, 1870, and 1880.

34. *Texas Volksbote*, March 25, 1875, 5:1; Aug. 29, 1878, 5:3.

35. Karl J.R. Arndt and M.E. Olsen. *German-American Newspapers and Periodicals, 1732-1955; History and Bibliography*. Heidelberg, Germany: Quelle & Meyer Publishers (1961), 618. *Texas Volksbote*, June 25, 1874, 4:1; Sept. 13, 1895, 4:1.

36. Caesar (Dutch) Hohn in his book *Dutchman on the Brazos* (Austin: University of Texas Press, 1963, 9) relates about his father who prior to World War I listened in on a conversation between German-Texans. They spoke in glowing terms of the Kaiser until Hohn's father could no longer hold his temper. He admonished them to remember that they all left Germany because they were starving there and that the United States had been good to them. If they were so fond of the Kaiser they should go back to Germany.

37. Anton Siemering. "Deutsche Feste in Texas." In *Deutsche Pioneer*, Vol. 12, No. 12 (Cincinnati, May 1882), 79.

38. *Brenham Daily Banner*, May 8, 1880, 3:2; *Galveston News*, May 3, 1878, 4:2.

39. *Texas Volksbote*, March 24, 1881, 5:3; *Brenham Daily Banner*, March 17, 1881, 3:2; April 7, 1881, 2:4.

<193>

Convicts using mule teams plow corn on one of the prison farms. (1930s)
Courtesy Texas Prison Archives

<194>

CHARLES SHAFER

Catheads, Coalburners, and Cho-Cho Sticks
Folk Speech in Texas Prisons

DESPITE the obscurity of their origins or the informality with which we use them, folk sayings are an essential part of our conversational speech. These expressions may be single words or entire phrases, and they vary from region to region. Variety is also reflected among different groups within the same geographical region. Age groups, ethnic groups, and occupational groups contribute a multitude of colorful expressions which, if examined individually and closely, may appear incomprehensible. However, if each phrase is returned to its natural context, then the listener usually understands easily. Sometimes, a particular group invents a language all its own and through time perpetuates this speech. For example, Texas prison inmates possess an argot that is somewhat unique. This language is at once direct, descriptive and, at times, ambiguous; it is also often offensive to a free-world ear.

In September of 1971 (the precise moment of the infamous Attica riots in New York in which numerous convicts and hostages were killed), I made my first trip to the Texas Department of Corrections in Huntsville, Texas. Having spent the three previous years as an assistant principal in a Houston-area junior high school, I jumped at the opportunity to teach English again. Besides, I figured that my experiences at the junior-high level had prepared me for just about anything. Lee College, a community college in Baytown, hired me to teach English to convict students enrolled in college classes at four different units: Eastham, Ferguson, Wynne, and the rather imposing Walls unit in downtown Huntsville.

My apprehension was probably evident that first morning as I passed through barbed wire, several pickets, and a series of heavy steel doors which slammed shut behind me. As my students finally

<195>

filed into the classroom, we eyed each other warily, each trying to assess the prospects of a satisfactory semester. After I called the names on the class roster, a student approached my desk and asked the question which began my journey into the recesses of another language. "Kin I go pour it out?" he asked. I nodded affirmatively without fully understanding what I was allowing. As one might guess, he was asking to be excused to go to the toilet down the hall. Intrigued by the curious question, I began listening intently to prison speech and even eavesdropped on conversations during the class breaks. What I discovered was another language, the language of men serving time in the Texas prison system. In the months which followed, I solicited help from convicts and guards alike. With a notepad and pen always ready, I listened. Students became actively involved in my project and contributed enthusiastically to my growing collection of words and phrases. My *Lexicon of Prison Slang*, as I called it, grew daily until it had hundreds of entries. This lexicon is by no means complete since it reflects the help of only two hundred inmates who were enrolled in my classes. In fact, the use of prison argot seems to be declining as education becomes more a part of Texas' rehabilitative process.

The words and phrases that I collected came from men serving from two to 198-year sentences. Their ages ranged from nineteen to sixty-five. Some of the entries can be traced to the 1930s, while others are more contemporary, born of the drug culture of the past twenty years. Many terms are graphically descriptive of the prison's homosexual population.

One must keep in mind that the prison language can be as relentless as its users. Many words have multiple meanings, depending on circumstance, and may reflect varying degrees of respect or disdain. I learned, for example, that *convict* was a more desirable term than *inmate* since inmate suggested weakness.

I owe a debt of gratitude to the convicts without whom this project would never have been possible. It is their wish (as well as mine) that this argot be viewed as a unique language, conceived in rather unique circumstances, and not as a further indictment of them as individuals.

<196>

A

ace, n.—a dependable friend, a brother; n.—a one-year prison sentence

ace-deuce, n.—a wide-brimmed field hat, not of regular issue

aggie, n.—a hoe used on the various farming units

air in his jaws, n.—extreme anger: "He's got *air in his jaws*."

A-Jones, n.—a drug addict (1940s and 50s)

all day, n.—a life sentence

"Alley!" v.—a command to move over or to get out of the way; n.—space: "Give me some *alley*."

"Alley diesel/Alley gasoline!" v.—a command to get out of the way because a vehicle is coming

alligator, n.—a task that is particularly difficult or unpleasant: "Chopping cotton is an *alligator*."

all of it, n.—a life sentence

anchor, v.—to wait: "*Anchor* it!"

apple, n.—a derisive name; anything bad or not highly regarded; a dimwit, dupe, or goose

arrested, v.—to be caught breaking a rule in prison

asa, n.—a hoe; also see *aggie*

B

badeye, v.—to stare ; n.—one who stares menacingly

bad rap, v.—to say something untrue about someone: to *bad rap* someone; n.—unfair treatment: "He got a *bad rap*."

bag, n.—a small portion of heroin

ball, v.—to have sexual intercourse; balling, n.—sexual intercourse

barbecue, v.—to kill by electrocution; also to beat severely

Beartracks, n.—Warden C. L. McAdams, a warden whose exploits resulted in near legendary status (1950-1972)

beat the ground with a stick, v.—to use a hoe in the fields

beating the man, n.—sleeping; lax time

Belt-buckle Bob, n.—someone who peeks around in another's cell with a mirror

bench warrant, n.—a warrant which requires the convict to go back to court to testify or to face new charges

Bible salesman, n.—a Protestant preacher

Betty, n.—a prison bus; see also *Black Betty*

<197>

big bitch, *n.*—a life sentence

big house, *n.*—the penitentiary

big-six talk, *n.*—talk which is accompanied by little action

big timer, *n.*—someone doing a long sentence

big yard, *n.*—central recreation area in some penitentiaries

bipe, *v.*—to enter motels, apartments, and homes at night while people sleep, mainly stealing cash and jewelry: to *bipe* a home

bitch, *n.*—life as an habitual criminal; an inmate who has been turned into a homosexual

Black Annie, *n.*—prison transfer truck (1940s)

Black Betty, *n.*—the bus bringing inmates to the penitentiary

black box, *n.*—solitary confinement

"Black that eye, Hannah!" *v.*—request for the hot sun to be shaded while working out in the field

blade, *n.*—knife or weapon

blades, *n.*—teeth (1950s)

blanks, *n.*—aspirin tablets (1950s)

blimp, *n.*—a bus (1950s)

block, *n.*—a cheap watch (1950s)

Blood, *n.*—a Negro

"Blow it off!" *v.*—"Forget about it!"

"Blow it out!" *v.*—a phrase used when a person gets loud, telling him to be quiet

blowing smoke, *v.*—buttering someone up; blow smoke, *v.*—to inflate one's ego

bluegill, *n.*—penis

bluegum, *n.*—a Negro

blue John, *n.*—skimmed milk

blue slip, *n.*—a piece of paper used to purchase items that cannot be bought in the commissary with the script book (mid-1960s)

bo'guard, *v.*—to bully your way into something: to *bo'guard* one's way

bomb, *n.*—toilet paper rolled in such a manner that it will burn for several minutes; used to heat water or food

bones, *n.*—the usual Sunday dinner, spare ribs

bonnaroos, *n.*—well-pressed clothes and shined shoes

book, *n.*—a wager; a small coupon book containing different tickets for nickels, dimes, quarters, etc. (to be used in the commissary)

booster, *n.*—a shoplifter

<198>

booty, *n.*—rectum

boss, *n.*—an officer; *adj.*—something that is good

boss con, *n.*—a lifer who runs almost free in the pen

bounce up, *v.*—to prepare to fight; answer a challenge

box, *n.*—a radio; a carton of cigarettes; a form of punishment requiring a man to stand on a wooden coke case for a period of time

box-man, *n.*—a safe cracker

boy-gal, *n.*—a homosexual

breather, *n.*—the nose

bricks, *n.*—the outside or free world: to be on the *bricks*

bring or bring around, *v.*—to break a convict's spirit by hard work, harrassment, or punishment

broad, *n.*—a woman; a homosexual

broad squad, *n.*—homosexuals that work together

broges, *n.*—short for brogans; work shoes

brother, *n.*—a close friend

brought, *v.*—If an inmate claims that he is *brought,* he is claiming to be convinced or rehabilitated; see *bring around.*

brown bombs, *n.*—laxatives

brown eye, *n.*—rectum

brush, *n.*—a mustache

B.T., *n.*—building tender; the inmate in charge of a wing or tank

buck, *v.*—to quit work; to refuse to work; to quit without permission

bug, *n.*—a burglar alarm

bull, *n.*—a guy who can withstand punishment

bull dagger/bull dyke, *n.*—female who plays the male role in a lesbian relationship

bull dog, *n.*—a bully; tough guy

Bull Durham, *n.*—generally, a smoking tobacco

bull pen, *n.*—usually a hold-over tank in city or county jail

burglarize a conversation, *v.*—to butt in on a conversation

burn Bull Durham/burn cornbread, *v.*—to put a curse on something or someone

burn coal, *v.*—to have sexual relations with a Black

bush parole, *n.*—escaping; leaving without permission: "He left on *bush parole.*"

bust a grape, *v.*—to commit an irrational act out of desperation

<199>

busted, *v.*—arrested; *adj.*—written up on a report for disciplinary reasons; out of money

busting a cap, *v.*—shooting guns, usually pistols; to open a soda

C

Cadillac drivers, *n.*—would-be lavish spenders; pretentious convicts

cage, *n.*—a cell

calendar, *n.*—a full 365 days of prison sentence: "He will do the whole *calendar*."

cane, *n.*—sugar

canteen, *n.*—the commissary store in a penitentiary

"Carry your ass!" *v.*—"Go away!"

catch, *n.*—an individual's portion of work; ie: a row of cotton is his *catch*

"Catch a dummy!" *v.*—refuse to talk

catcher, *n.*—one of the two males involved in a homosexual act; the female role in the relationship

catch in, *v.*—to fall into a formation

catch out, *v.*—to go to work; to be beaten and forced out of a cell: "He felt too bad to *catch out*."

catch the back gate, *v.*—to remain at the back gate of the farm when the day is over; results in solitary if caught

catch the chain, *v.*—to leave on the bus; see *pull chain*

catch the grass, *v.*—to wait at the back gate for disciplinary action

cathead, *n.*—yeast roll or biscuit

cat walker, *n.*—nighttime burglar

CC, *n.*—concurrent sentences; also refers to anything mixed together. ie: peaches CC with cream

celly, *n.*—cell partner

certify, *v.*—to pretend to work: "If you don't plan to work, at least *certify* it."

character, *n.*—someone who makes his living dishonestly; hijacker, thief, hot-check writer; also can refer to a criminal in a complimentary manner, depending on the context

cherry wagon, *n.*—school bus

chin-chin man, *n.*—a homosexual

chipping, *n.*—two-timing; going out with someone you do not belong to: *chipping* around on somebody

<200>

cho-choes, *n.*—candies and snacks purchased from a prison commissary

cho-cho book, *n.*—convicts' commissary or script book

cho-cho sticks, *n.*—ice-cream bars on sticks

choc, *n.*—homemade beer

chunkin' it , *v.*—fist fighting

clean up, *n.*—a story used to get out of a good or a bad situation: "You need a good *clean up* for an alibi."

clods, *n.*—shoes for working in the field

C-note, *n.*—a hundred-year sentence

coalburner, *n.*—a homosexual who prefers Blacks

coasting, *v.*—doing easy time; no difficulties

coke box, *n.*—a form of punishment similar to the wall: standing on the edge of a *coke box*

cold buster, *n.*—two aspirin and a cold capsule

cold dude, *n.*—one who has no feeling; one who treats others harshly

cold shot, *n.*—inmates' comment when one is rebuffed or punished: "He took a *cold shot.*"

come on, *v.*—to ask someone to engage in sexual relations by saying such things as "*Come on,* Sweetie." (often in jest)

commissary runner, *n.*—appointed convict who goes to the prison store for others

cop, *v.*—to steal or obtain something

cop a deuce, trey, or ace, *v.*—to be sentenced to two, three, or one years

cop a feel, *v.*—to feel a homosexual

cop a joint, *v.*—to smoke a cigarette

cop out, *v.*—to plead guilty

cop a sneak, *v.*—to hit someone unexpectedly

counting bricks, *v.*—after a prison arrest, a person stands against the brick wall for several hours: other inmates kid him about *counting bricks.*

count time, *n.*—the time to stand still because the officer is counting

court, *n.*—going to court, disciplinary action, usually in the warden's office

Cowboys & Indians, *n.*—a ninety-nine year sentence: playing *Cowboys and Indians*

"Crank one up, boss?" *v.*—asking permission to roll a cigarette

<201>

creep on, *v.*—to sneak up on someone with mayhem in mind

crib, *n.*—a cell

crumb snatchers, *n.*—little kids

cull, *n.*—a convict given a soft job because he could not handle a hard job to which he was previously assigned

curtain pullers, *n.*—little kids

cut, *n.*—a squad's portion of the field work; *v.*—to self-mutilate

cut it up, *v.*—to rap or converse

"Cut me a break!" *v.*—"Leave me alone." "Quit pulling my leg."

cut someone loose, *v.*—to stop bothering someone

cut heads, *v.*—to fight

D

dab-dab, *v.*—to engage in homosexual relations

Daddy, *n.*—the term that a homosexual has for his prison husband

dagging, *v.*—two homosexuals trading out orally

Darby Hicks, *n.*—in TDC a legendary, fictitious character; reputed to be the biggest, baddest, meanest, ugliest man ever to go to prison

day for day, *adv.*—a prison sentence without time off for good behavior: serving time, *day for day*

deck, *n.*—a pack of cigarettes

deuce, *n.*—a two-year sentence

deuce-burger, *n.*—a two-year sentence

"Deuce it up!" *v.*—an order given to get in pairs; pair up

dime, *n.*—a ten-year sentence

ding, dinglame, *n.*—one of little mentality

dinosaur bones, *n.*—oversized spare ribs; any meat that is extremely bony

dirty leg, *n.*—a lady of below average morals and appearance

dis, ditch, *v.*—to discharge; to be released

dobies, doughbies, *n.*—yeast rolls or biscuits served in the chow hall

dog, *n.*—a harshly cruel inmate or correctional employee

dog boy, *n.*—convict who cares for tracking dogs

dog sergeant, *n.*—sergeant who works with tracking dogs

doing time, *v.*—a passive mood: just *doing time*

dooby, *n.*—a cigarette butt

doodle-gaze, *v.*—to look at a female, illegal in prison

<202>

dope, *n.*—syrup

double rough, *n.*—a fifty-year sentence

double saw, *n.*—a twenty-five-year sentence

down and out, *adv.*—an expression used in the Dallas County jail to let one know he is going to court and will get a hard sentence

down only, *adj.*—an expression used in the Dallas County jail to let one know he is to be finger-printed or is going before a lineup

downtown stud, *n.*—a sharp, well-dressed man

"Do your own time!" *v.*—"Mind your own business!"

drag it back, *v.*—to leave an area clean after chopping and cutting grass or weeds: the materials are then *drug back* and the area left clean

drive up, *n.*—a new arrival at a unit

drove, *adj.*—tired; exhausted

drove-up, *adj.*—scared; frightened

DP, *n.*—Dr. Pepper

D-town, *n.*—Dallas, Texas

duck, *n.*—a two-year sentence; also one easily fooled

dug-out, *n.*—a very heavy eater

dump it out, *v.*—defecate

Durham or Derm, *n.*—any low grade of cigarette tobacco

dust, *n.*—a cheap cigarette tobacco given free to prisoners; *v.*—to kill

dyke, *n.*—a lesbian

E

early month, *n.*—the month prior to a convict's scheduled parole review date

easy, *adj.*—cool or careful

eye, *n.*—rectum

eyeballing, *n.*—looking at something or someone

F

fall, *n.*—a conviction or sentence: to take a *fall*

fall partner, *n.*—an accomplice arrested with another

farm, *n.*—a prison unit

fay, *n.*—a white man

felony, *n.*—a major offense against rules and regulations in a prison

<203>

fence rowing, *v.*—clearing an area two-feet wide on each side of the fence

fileboy, *n.*—one who files and stores all the work tools within his squad

finger-snapper/finger-popper, *n.*—usually a younger man who is always playing games; sometimes called a *jiveass*

finger-tips, *n.*—someone good at giving a handjig

fire, *v.*—to hit someone or to get hit: "The BT will *fire* you (hit you)."

fish, *n.*—a new or recently received inmate

five-finger Mary, *n.*—masturbation

"Flake off!" *v.*—a rude way of asking someone to leave

flam, *v.*—to trick, deceive, or double-cross

flat dog, *n.*—bologna

flat time, *n.*—time in which a convict is not receiving any extra days on his sentence

flat weed, *v.*—to cut tall weeds with a hoe

flip-flop, *n.*—a homosexual who plays both male and female roles

floor boy, *n.*—appointed convict who cleans up the tank or wing

fluff, *n.*—the female who plays the female role in a lesbian relationship

fly a kite, *v.*—to send a letter

folk, *n.*—a Black

four bits, *n.*—a fifty-year sentence

frap, *v.*—to whip someone

free world, *n.*—someplace other than prison

free-world gal, *n.*—homosexual inmate who was gay before entering prison

freeze-out, *v.*—to stop associating with someone

fresh meat, *n.*—a new homosexual in a penitentiary

fried, *v.*—to be executed by electrocution

fried ice cream, *n.*—a task for a gullible inmate: To go for *fried ice cream* is to be a fool.

front, *n.*—a man's suit (1950s)

G

gal-boy, *n.*—a homosexual

gasoline, *n.*—any vehicle powered by gasoline

gather it in, *v.*—to work with vigor

<204>

gather real estate, *n.*—to add dirt to the cotton so it will weigh more, a deed that is against prison rules

G.E., *n.*—a name for the electric chair

george, *v.*—to have sexual relations; *n.*—anybody who is willing

"Get in deuces!" *v.*—get in a double line

get on the job, *v.*—to defecate

get off in a wreck, *v.*—to do something that will get you in trouble

gettin' short, *v* —getting ready to leave for the free-world

gibbs, *n.*—a person's lips

girl, *n.*—a homosexual

glom, *v.*—to eat fast

go-backs, *n.*—field work shoes

good people, *n.*—non-informers

good time, *n.*—credit time; accumulated time for good behavior

goody locker, *n.*—commissary store

goon squad, *n.*—a group of the toughest officers who instruct an inmate in the finer points of good behavior by the methods the name implies

goose, *n.*—a person who believes anything he hears

gopher, *n.*—one lacking in intelligence

go to the house, *v.*—to go to your living quarters

"Got that stuff!"—usually refers to a homosexual; often used in a joking manner among friends

go yonder way, *v.*—to try hard; to go speedily or swiftly toward any goal; to make a definite effort

grab a dab, *v.*—to rape

grape, *n.*—news or rumors; gossip: to hear some *grape*

grease out, *v.*—to be lucky

grind, *v.*—to work hard

groceries, *n.*—commissary goods

green dragon, *n.*—heroin

gunsel, *n.*—one who carries a gun; a man of low mentality (1950s)

H

hack, *n.*—prison guard; less complimentary than *boss*

half-a-man, *n.*—half gallon of ice cream

half dollar, *n.*—a man who is doing a fifty-year sentence

<205>

hall, *n.*—a form of punishment: To *catch the hall* means that you have been arrested, you will miss your shower and chow, and you must wait in the hall until you are called for disciplinary action.

handjig, *n.*—masturbation

hang paper, *v.*—to pass bad checks

hang it up, *v.*—to escape; not to get into trouble anymore

Hannah, *n.*—the sun

hardass, *n.*—one who is always in trouble with prison officials

hard-line, *adj.*—a convict is one who follows the old traditions of confinement

hard timer, *n.*—one who breaks many rules and takes much punishment; also someone who is homesick

Harry James, *n.*—Bugler smoking tobacco (1940s)

hat time, *n.*—quitting time in the field; when the captain takes off his hat and waves it

head artist, *n.*—a homosexual

head cutter, *n.*—someone who beats up or jumps on another

head job, *n.*—oral sex practiced by homosexuals

head hunter, *n.*—a homosexual

head running, *n.*—term used to describe excessive talk

heat, *n.*—trouble

heavy, *adj.*—having a great deal of influence; important: "Jailhouse lawyers are *heavy* convicts."

heelstring, *v.*—to cut the Achilles tendon in order to avoid work

"He's going through the change!"—said of someone who is acting strange or different

"Hey, Jim!" interjection—friendly greeting

high capping, *n.*—a bull session

high rider, *n.*—a special guard in the field, armed with a high-powered rifle, two-way radio, binoculars, and rides a horse

hitch hike, *v.*—to read other inmates' mail when one did not receive any of his own

hit the bricks, *v.*—to return to the free-world

"Hit the turn row!" *v.*—order given by the guard to start chopping weeds from a field crop

hoe squad, *n.*—a group working in the field

hog, *v.*—to take something from someone by force

hold, *v.*—to carry a gun: to *hold* a gun

<206>

Convicts return from a day in the field. Workers are riding the mules used to work in the fields. (1930s) *Courtesy Texas Prison Archives*

holding jiggers, *v.*—to act as a lookout
hold your nuts, *v.*—to wish bad luck for someone
hole, *n.*—solitary confinement
homie, *n.*—a homosexual; also someone from one's home town
"Honk, honk!"—used to denote that someone has been a goose (a
    gullible person)
hooked up, v.—to be deeply engrossed in something; to be ostracized
hot buns, *n.*—homosexual
hot head, *n.*—a homosexual
house boys, *n.*—building or inside workers
H-town, *n.*—Houston, Texas
hummer, *n.*—a rib or joke; going to elaborate lengths to play a joke;
    also in North Carolina prisons *hummer* means a bum rap
hustle, *v.*—to live by prostitution
hype, *n.*—a con-man (1950s)

I

ice, *n.*—isolation; solitary confinement
idiot stick, *n.*—a hoe
ig, *v.*—to ignore; pay no attention
in and out, *n.*—a break to go to the cells to use the lavatory and then
    come out again
inmate, *n.*—derogatory name for a convict; denotes a model pris-
    oner, very passive
in the air, *n.*—quitting time; also see *hat time*

<207>

J

jacket, *n.*—a file of accusations against someone

jack pictures, jack flicks, jack books, *n.*—photos or movies of nude women for sexual stimulation

jack rabbit, *n.*—a prisoner with a reputation for taking advantage of escape opportunities

jack ready, *adj.*—ready and waiting for sexual relations (1950s)

Jake, *n.*—Jesus Christ or God; also thunder and rain

Jake or Jack, *n.*—a drunk or alcoholic (1950s)

jaw jacking (jawing), *n.*—talking, usually harshly

jazz, *n.*—sexual intercourse (1950s)

jigger, *n.*—a lookout to warn others by relay; see also *holding jiggers*

jitterbug, *n.*—someone who is trying to impress others

jive ass, *n.*—someone always talking trash or nonsense

jo, *n.*—coffee

job, *n.*—any type of burglary

jocker, *n.*—a pederast; the male partner in sex relations

John Henry or Johnny, *n.*—a sandwich; a sack lunch eaten in the field

joint, *n.*—prison; a penis; a marijuana cigarette

jump ins, *n.*—clothes worn in visiting rooms with draw-string waist; one size fits all

"Jump Judy!" *interj.*—an exclamation used when the whistle blows at five o'clock

jungle juice, *n.*—big and bad conversation

jungle weed, *n.*—a cigarette

K

"Keep it tight!" *v.*—order given to keep men in a line

kicks, *n.*—shoes

kid, *n.*—a young prison inmate who is protected by an older convict in return for sexual favors

kiester, *n.*—ass; also the name of a circular type safe

kill big six, *v.*—to play dominoes

kimp, *n.*—a car (1950s)

kite, *v.*—to send out a letter illegally; *n.*—also a note or letter sent or received

knock, *v.*—to fight

<208>

knock-in, *v.*—to request to play in the next game of dominoes, checkers, chess, etc.

knocked, *v.*—arrested; written up for disciplinary action by an officer

L

lame, *n.*—one who is physically or mentally handicapped; also a foolish person, like *dinglame*

lamp, *v.*—to look over; to examine

lawyer, *n.*—an inmate who files writs

lay in, *v.*—to stay in the cell for official reasons

lay it by, *v.*—to enjoy leisure time, usually a lay in from work

lay it down, *v.*—to quit work; refuse to work

lead row, *n.*—the man who heads a field squad; his is the first row in squad

Lemac, *n.*—a pack of Camel cigarettes

"Let's knock dust!" *v.*—"Let's fight!"

lifer, *n.*—one who is serving a life sentence

line, *n.*—field workers in a penitentiary

line boss, *n.*—the guard outside the gates, usually in the field

little bitch, *n.*—a sentence that is very stiff due to repeated offenses; also a twelve-year sentence

little warden, *n.*—the assistant warden

loggerhead, *n.*—penis

long-haired people, *n.*—one's family or loved ones at home

lope the mule, *v.*—to masturbate

lot boy, *n.*—one who saddles horses and cleans livestock pens

lug, *v.*—to ridicule; to cut someone up with words

M

M, *n.*—morphine

mac man, *n.*—a man who drums up business for a prostitute; pimp

main squeeze, *n.*—the last lover; the one who stands by an inmate during his incarceration

"Make a hole!" *v.*—an order to clear the way; see also *alley*

make it up, *v.*—to fix a cup of coffee

mama, *n.*—name given to a female impersonator

man, *n.*—policeman, major, warden; anyone with authority

<209>

man in red, *n.*—the devil

mark, *n.*—a fool or sucker: an easy *mark*

Maytag, *n.*—an inmate who is forced to hand wash another inmate's clothes

mechanic, *n.*—an expert on gambling devices, dice, etc.

meditation, *n.*—the guards' name for solitary confinement

monkey, *n.*—female sex organ

mouthpiece, *n.*—a lawyer

muff job, *n.*—oral sex act with a woman

mullet, *n.*—someone who is easily deceived

mulligan, *n.*—a disrespectful designation for prison guard or officer; applies more to field and picket guards

my kid, *n.*—a prison wife; a homosexual

my woman, *n.*—a wife in the free world

N

nickel, *n.*—a five-year sentence

nickel snacks, *n.*—oatmeal cookies from the commissary

nineteen (19), *n.*—On a form from the parole board there are nineteen entries. Only one of them (#19) states that a man is still considered for parole. If a man says that he has a *nineteen*, he is saying that he is going home.

nobs, *n.*—shoes (1950s)

O

old head, *n.*—an old convict; a convict that has been in prison for a long time

old lady, *n.*—a name for a homosexual wife or a common-law wife in the outside world

old timer, *n.*—a long-time convict; see also *old head*

"ole thang," *n.*—name used by an officer when he is addressing an inmate, often derogatory in connotation

on the job, *n.*—defecation

on the wall, *adv.*—facing a brick wall as a means of punishment; may last for several hours: "He is *on the wall*." See *wall*.

on the street, *n.*—home or one's hometown

outfit, *n.*—a syringe used by drug addicts

<210>

P

panties, *n.*—men's brief underwear

paper hanger, *n.*—a bad check writer

parole dust, *n.*—fog which aids in escapes

parole man, *n.*—the interviewer of a prospective parolee

part rabbit, *n.*—having tendencies to escape

pass the post, *v.*—to hit someone when he is not looking: to *pass the post* on him.

payday, *n.*—day on which inmates can draw money sent them by relatives

peck, *v.*—to eat

people, *n.*—parents

petty thief, *n.*—one who steals from others in prison

phone call, *n.* —telling someone he is wanted by another for conversation

pick up, *v.*—to observe or watch something or someone

piddler, *n.*—anyone who works with leather, wood, or other crafts

pill line, *n.*—sick call

pimping, *n.*—getting money from another; playing the female role in unnatural sex acts

pimp stick, *n.*—a cigarette holder

pisser, *n.*—solitary confinement

pitch and catch, *v.*—to engage in unnatural sex acts

pitcher, *n.*—one of the two males in a homosexual act; acts as the male

player, *n.*—a put-on; a conman; a lady's man

playing the dozens, *v.*—talking about others' relatives in an obscene manner; black cultural practice of ritual insults

plucking pods, *n.*—picking cotton

politician, *n.*—one who has a good job or position in prison and may be capable of securing a job for another convict; often held in high regard by officials

pour it out, *v.*—urinate

Promising George, *n.*—Dr. George Beto, director of TDC (1962-1972)

pruno, *n.*—homebrew made from prunes

pull-do (*poule d'eau*, or mudhen), *n.*—someone who is lazy

pull good time, *v.*—to sleep or relax

<211>

pull the covers off, *v.*—to reveal someone's true nature

pull up, *v.*—to give up crime as a way of life

pull chain, *v.*—to leave prison or a unit on a chain bus: "He's due to *pull chain* for Houston."

punch it, *v.*—to escape

punk, *n.*—a homosexual

push leads, *n.*—men working in the lead row

put a blanket on, *v.*—to hand roll a cigarette

put it in the woods, *v.*—to escape

put off, *n.*—parole date set off: "He received a *put off*."

put down a story, *v.*—to tell one's side of a story first

Q

quarter, *n.*—a twenty-five-year sentence

queen, *n.*—the female in any sex act

R

rabbit, *n.*—someone who will run or try to escape if given an opportunity

race horse, *n.*—a woman who makes a lot of money; usually a prostitute

rack up, *v.*—to send convicts to their cells

ragged as a Waxahachie pimp, *adj.*—poor; broke

rail, *n.*—punishment of standing on a board; similar to standing at the wall

"Raise me!" *v.*—"Leave me alone." "Stop bothering me."

rank, *v.*—to lose, or *rank*, one's job in prison

rape-o, *n.*—a person convicted of rape; an unpopular crime in prison

ratchet jaw, *n.*—someone who talks too much

ready roll, *n.*—factory-rolled cigarette; also means to sleep fully clothed

ride the broom, *v.*—to point out the possibility that the undesirable may happen: to say, "You may not make parole," is *riding the broom*; to speak of it may cause it to happen

rig, *n.*—narcotics paraphernalia

river bottom, *n.*—a haircut style in which the wearer has a clean head, bald: to get a *river bottom* haircut

R.J.R. (Run, Johnny, Run), *n.*—a tobacco distributed to prisons to

<212>

be given to the population; donated by R.J. Reynolds Tobacco Co. (Bull Durham)

roach, *n.*—an officer or guard; also the butt of a marijuana cigarette

roll bones, *v.*—to fight

roll it , *v.*—to roll a cigarette

round steak, *n.*—bologna

rum, *n.*—someone who is obtuse or doesn't conduct himself in a conventional manner

run water, *v.*—to carry hot water from cell to cell so the inmates can fix coffee

running your head, *n.*—talking too much

S

sack, *n.*—a bag of Bull Durham tobacco

saddlin', *n.*—lubrication in preparation of sex acts

sand, *n.*—sugar

sawbuck, *n.*—a ten-year sentence

scaley-leg, *n.*—an unclean, low-moraled woman

scally biper, *n.*—a thief who steals from motels and hotels

screw, *n.*—a security officer

'scrip, *n.*—a prescription for medicine

sell a hog, *n.*—to try to scare or bluff someone else

"Shake it, Jake!" *v.*—"Make it rain, Jesus."

shank, *n.*—a knife

she, *n.*—used when referring to a homosexual

shell peanuts, *v.*—to punish; being made to shell a gallon of peanuts

"Shine your eye, Hannah!" *v.*—"Let the sun shine."

shit eaters, *n.*—dogs that chase escapees

shitter, *n.*—solitary confinement

shiv, *n.*—a convict's homemade knife

shoe thief, *n.*—a petty thief

shoot out, *n.*—an extremely violent argument

shoot snipes, *v.*—to pick up cigarettes from ashtrays for smoking purposes

shot, *n.*—a spoonful of coffee; also two teaspoons

short, *adj.*—just a little time left to serve

short-time pains, *n.*—anxiety pains one feels just before being released from prison

<213>

Field workers return to the prison building after chopping cotton. Mounted outriders with rif
always monitor such travel on the farming units. (1970s) *Courtesy of Texas Prison Archives*

Convict cowboys pose for photographs before the Annual Prison Rodeo. (1970s) Prison rodeo h
since been discontinued. *Courtesy of Texas Prison Archives*

<214>

shut down, *v.*—to quit work

short stick, *n.*—axe

sing it, *v.*—to tell the story

sissy, *n.*—a homosexual

sister-in-law, *n.*—a prostitute working for a married man

skids, *n.*—shoes

skin, *n.*—money

skin it back, *v.*—to make the ground free of any kind of growth such as weeds in a field row; same as *drag it back*

slick, *n.*—a teacher who cons his students to do their homework

slick head, *n.*—a person with a new haircut (shaved); usually a new inmate

slowbuck, *v.*—to slow down when it is known you can work faster; when one man is behind another

snap your cap, *v.*—to go insane

snow, *n.*—cocaine

snowbird, *n.*—one who sniffs cocaine

solid, *adj.*—regarded as a good convict

Sparkie, *n.*—the electric chair

spike, *n.*—a needle for injecting drugs

spread, *n.*—a get together with friends for snacks from the commissary

spring, *v.*—to leave prison for home

square, *n.*—a cigarette

square John, *n.*—a non-criminal; not having criminal traits

square up, *v.*—to get straight

stacked, *adj.*—concurrent terms

stallion, *n.*—a tall, good-looking girl (1950s)

State'cy Adams, *n.*—state-issue low-quarter shoes

"Step, high, high, high!" *v.*—an order to walk fast

stir, *n.*—confinement

stoolie, *n.*—an informer

straight, *n.*—a cigarette

stretch, *n.*—a term served in prison

streets, *n.*—the free world

striker, *n.*—one who helps the others work together in a rhythmic manner in the field

strum heads, *v.*—to fight

<215>

stuck out, *n.*—a slow worker

stud up, *n.*—a homosexual who tries to change back to a heterosexual

stuff, *n.*—sexual favors granted by a female or the homosexual that plays the female role in unnatural sex acts

suck it up, *v.*—to eat quickly

swap out, *v*—to alternate the male and female roles in unnatural sex acts

swine, *n.*—the word often used instead of *chow* due to the amount of pork served

swing, *adj.*—any row within the center of a squad in the field, the *swing* row

T

T/A, *n.*—a temporary assignment

tab, *n.*—LSD

tail, *n.*—an informer

tail row, *n.*—last man in a squad in the field

tank, *n.*—dormitory-type living quarters for convicts

tear your ass, *v.*—to leave in a hurry

tear it down, *v.*—to gather one's belongings and move

Tee, *n.*—a Black expression for father

Tee-Jones, *n.*—a Black expression for mother

three-fingered handjig, *n.*—three fingered masturbation

tight laces, *n.*—any store bought cigarettes, cigarettes with filters

top heavy, *adj.*—intelligent; smart in learning

trafficking & trading, *v.*—the term used when an inmate carries something illegal from one part of the prison to another; can get an inmate up to fifteen days in solitary confinement

tragic magic, *n.*—heroin

tree jumper, *n.*—a man convicted of raping or molesting a child

trey, *n.*—a three-year sentence

trick, *n.*—a homosexual; also a fool or sucker

tube steak, *n.*—bologna

tully, *n.*—basketball

tumbleweed wagon, *n.*—a prison transfer bus

turnkey, *n.*—one who opens and closes the gates

turn out, *v.*—to give up one's masculine identity in exchange for that of a female

<216>

twist, n.—a prostitute
twist one up, v.—to roll a cigarette
two-row flat back, n.—a double-barrel shotgun

U
Uncle Bud, n.—the state prison system; similar to Uncle Sam
up, v.—to give something to someone

V
village ruffian, n.—the accepted strong man
vines, n.—clothes

W
wolf, n.—a fifteen-year sentence
Walls, n.—main unit of TDC in downtown Huntsville
"Watch your melon!" v.—"Watch what you're doing!"
watermelon talk, n.—cheap, insignificant conversation
whams, n.—cookies
"Where'd you fall from?"—"Where were you arrested?"
white gold, n.—cotton
wired, adj.—having deviant sexual interest or background: "He was
    wired when he came here."
wired up, adj.—high on drugs
work for the man, n.—to snitch or inform
worlds, n.—ready-rolled cigarettes
wrap-in, v.—to work with another squad
wreck, n.—trouble with guards or other convicts, to have a *wreck*
writ writer, n.—anyone having knowledge of the law
writ room, n.—a room where one can work on legal matters

Y
yard time, n.—time allowed a convict in an outdoor recreation area
yoke, v.—to grab; to apprehend
yo-yo, n.—a weed cutter
youngster, n.—a young convict

Z
zip, n.—a fool; a sucker
zoo-zoos or zuzus, n.—cookies or candies

<217>

CONTRIBUTORS

KENNETH W. DAVIS, Professor of English at Texas Tech University, teaches Folklore and Nineteenth-Century British Literature, presents papers on Texas folklore and literature, and has published more than sixty essays and reviews on a variety of topics. With the late Everett A. Gillis, he edited *Black Cats, Hoot Owls, and Water Witches* (UNT Press, 1989). With Lawrence Clayton, he has done *Horsing Around: Contemporary Cowboy Humor* (Wayne State University Press, 1990). He was Vice President of the Society in 1990 and President in 1991. He is particularly interested in folktales.

BERTHA McKEE DOBIE (1890-1974) was reared in Velasco, Texas, received a B.A. from Southwestern (where she met J. Frank) and M.A. in English from the University of Texas. She taught school and after she was married she frequently taught J. Frank's classes at UT. Bertha was a naturalist and wrote gardening and nature articles for newspapers as well as for popular magazines and academic journals. Dobie said that she was his best critic and his best editor. She worked with him as assistant editor of the PTFS from 1923 to 1935. She helped establish Paisano as a writer's retreat after Dobie died. Bertha is buried alongside J. Frank in the State Cemetery in Austin.

J. FRANK DOBIE (1888-1964) was responsible for the resurrection of the Texas Folklore Society after its demise in World War I and for the establishment of the TFS as a solid and lasting academic society. He was Secretary-Editor from 1923 until 1943, and in addition to the editing that he did for the Society, he published the most popular and longest lasting books on Texas and Southwestern folklore and culture.

ROBERT J. (JACK) DUNCAN is a freelance writer and columnist for DFW newspapers and journals who lives in McKinney. He is a

<219>

long-time member, contributor, and former president of the Society. A classic example of well-scripted oral history is Duncan's book on Ross Estes, *I Remember Things: An Informal History of Tioga, Texas*.

ROBERT FLYNN of Chillicothe is Professor of English and Novelist in Residence at Trinity University in San Antonio. He has recently published *A Personal War in Vietnam* and won the Spur Award for *Wanderer Springs*. These are companions to his award winning *North to Yesterday*. And he is the president of the Texas Institute of Letters.

SYLVIA GRIDER is an Associate Professor of English and holds a joint appointment with the Department of History at Texas A&M University. Her doctorate is in folklore, but she also has extensive training and field experience in classical archaeology, including work at Franchthi Cave in Greece. She teaches undergraduate and graduate courses in folklore and cultural anthropology and has developed a new course, Texas Cultural History.

R. A. HILL (1910-1985) is introduced to his reading public in the editor's introductory remarks.

JANET KAY JEFFERY is a graduate of the University of Texas with a B.S. in Art History. Her career has included working as an Assistant Editor of *TV Guide* in Seattle, Washington, researching Arizona history for Arizona State Parks in Phoenix, Arizona, and designing and helping build an adobe house in Abiquiu, New Mexico. She now resides in Austin and works as a technical writer of computer manuals for a software development firm.

ELMER KELTON of San Angelo, Texas, is the author of thirty novels, published over a period of more than thirty-five years. He is a four-time winner of the Western Writers of America Spur award and three-time winner of the National Cowboy Hall of Fame's Western Heritage award, as well as the Tinkle-McCombs award from the Texas Institute of Letters for his entire body of work. Born near Andrews, Texas, he grew up on the McElroy Ranch near Crane and attended the University of Texas. He has been a livestock and agricultural journalist for more than forty years in addition to his fiction writing.

<220>

FAYE LEEPER has been participating in Texas Folklore Society programs and publications since she won Hermes Nye's college student contest in 1956. She has served both as Counselor and as Director for the Society. She has taught high school and college English for 25 years. She has done graduate work at Texas Technological University, East Texas State University, University of Texas, University of Edinburgh, Scotland, and University of Cambridge, England. She is presently seeing the world as a tour guide.

LERA TYLER LICH, an Instructor of English at McLennan Community College, has enjoyed the bounties of her East Texas relatives for forty years. She has contributed to other volumes of the Texas Folklore Society and has written a book and several articles on Texas writer Larry McMurtry.

TOM McCLELLAN was born in Fort Bragg, North Carolina, about three months before Pearl Harbor. He received a B.A. from Southwestern University and taught school in Sanderson, Texas, for three years. He received a M.A. in English from Texas A&M University and has taught at several colleges and universities in Texas. He is a frequent contributor to *The Texas Observer*.

PAUL PATTERSON was born on the Brennan Ranch in Gaines County, Texas. He received a B.A. from Sul Ross in Alpine, Texas. He has been a member of the Texas Folklore Society since 1963, and served as the Society's President in 1966. His bibliography includes *Sam McGoo and Texas Too, Crazy Women in the Rafters, A Pecos River Pilgrim's Poems I & II*, and numerous PTFS articles, with rhyming or alliterative titles. He worked as a cowboy for four years and seven summers, learning bronc-riding from the ground up. He taught school forty years.

CONNIE RICCI is an adjunct English instructor for Cisco Jr. College. She pursues a full-time career as an educational consultant and is a free-lance writer. Having been reared in a family which appreciated its tradition and heritage, Ricci developed an early interest in folklore and folk traditions.

JOYCE GIBSON ROACH grew up in Jacksboro, Texas, and has never gotten over it, nor does she want to. She holds both B.F.A. and

<221>

M.A. from TCU and is a member and past president of the Texas Folklore Society. Joyce is a two time Spur Award winner for *The Cowgirls*, best book of nonfiction in 1978, (currently being reissued by UNT Press) and "A High Toned Woman," best short nonfiction for 1988. She co-authored *Eats: A Folk History of Texas Foods* with Ernestine Sewell. Her latest hit is a stage musical, *Nancy MacIntyre: A Tale of the Prairies*. She teaches as adjunct instructor in English for TCU, speaks, teaches and writes about Texas, and helps with the family business in Keller, Texas.

CHARLES SHAFER is a graduate of East Texas State University with a B.A. in English and history. He received a M.Ed. from the University of Houston. He has taught English in the Galena Park ISD and served as assistant principal. He has taught freshman and sophomore English courses to convict students at Lee College's Texas Department of Corrections program. He is currently teaching freshman composition, developmental writing, and American folklore at Lee College.

PAUL CLOIS STONE was born in Waco, Texas, and raised in Gatesville. In 1974 he graduated from Harvard with concentrations in English and anthropology. He has worked as a journalist, congressional press secretary, film maker, and cowboy. He has written album liner notes for the Desert Rose Bank, Great Western Orchestra, and Don Edwards. Stone is a University Fellow in History at Yale, working on a dissertation on J. Frank Dobie and the history of folklore studies. He now lives in Guilford, Connecticut.

JERI TANNER, an associate professor of English at Texas Tech University, has been an active member of the Texas Folklore Society for twenty years. She has published articles in *Western Folklore, North Carolina Folklore, Kentucky Folklore Record, American Notes & Queries, Studies in Frank Waters, NAMES: A Journal of the American Names Society, The Journal of the American Society of X-Ray Technicians*, and reviews of Australian fiction in *Antipodes: A North American Journal of Australian Literature*.

W. M. VON-MASZEWSKI was born and raised in Europe. He received his B.A. and M.A. degrees in anthropology from the University of Texas, Austin. He is a life-member of the Texas State

<222>

Historical Association and is past president of the Friends of the Sterling C. Evans Library, Texas A&M University. His avocation in the history of the American West and Texas resulted in the publication of *Index to The Trail Drivers of Texas*. He is the editor of the *Handbook and Registry of German-Texan Heritage*, and he continues gathering material for the second volume. At the same time, he is pursuing his own work, researching and writing on the German-Texan cultural heritage. He is currently with the George Memorial Library in Richmond, Texas.

<223>

INDEX

<227>

<228>

<231>

<232>